Involuntary Associations

Postcolonialism across the Disciplines 15

Postcolonialism across the Disciplines

Series Editors
Graham Huggan, University of Leeds
Andrew Thompson, University of Exeter

Postcolonialism across the Disciplines showcases alternative directions for postcolonial studies. It is in part an attempt to counteract the dominance in colonial and postcolonial studies of one particular discipline – English literary/cultural studies – and to make the case for a combination of disciplinary knowledges as the basis for contemporary postcolonial critique. Edited by leading scholars, the series aims to be a seminal contribution to the field, spanning the traditional range of disciplines represented in postcolonial studies but also those less acknowledged. It will also embrace new critical paradigms and examine the relationship between the transnational/cultural, the global and the postcolonial.

Involuntary Associations

Postcolonial Studies and World Englishes

David Huddart

Liverpool University Press

First published 2014 by
Liverpool University Press
4 Cambridge Street
Liverpool L69 7ZU

British Library Cataloguing-in-Publication data
A British Library CIP record is available

ISBN 978-1-78138-025-3 cased

Typeset in Amerigo by Carnegie Book Production, Lancaster
Printed and bound by BooksFactory.co.uk

I do not underestimate the personal vision in the teeth of a mass-media world. It is through such deeply intuitive insights drawn from hard work and concentration that one may reflect in new ways upon areas of history that are replete with ironies of involuntary association between cultures. Such ironies highlight an addiction to invariance, closed minds, and divided cultures, even as they disclose, I think, the mystery of cross-cultural wholeness steeped in the freedom of diversity to cross boundaries that restrict our vision of therapeutic and evolving reality.

Wilson Harris, *Selected Essays*

Acknowledgements

First, thanks to my students and teaching assistants from over eight years of teaching World Englishes. In particular, thanks to Tara Coleman and Chris Tsang, who helped recast its teaching in essential ways. Meanwhile, the final stages of this book would have been more problematic without the assistance of Emily Chow and Franziscka Cheng. I would also like to thank all my colleagues in Hong Kong for their hard work and challenging conversation. Extra thanks for a random selection of things to Peter Skehan, Julian Lamb, Eddie Tay, Michael O'Sullivan, Grant Hamilton, and Simon Haines. Beyond the Hong Kong context, I would like to thank David Ewick, who a long time ago prompted me to begin thinking about some of the issues addressed in this book in the Japanese context. In addition, thanks to Robert Phillipson for detailed and trenchant comments about the manuscript. Finally, I would like to acknowledge that the work recorded in this book was supported by a grant from the Hong Kong General Research Fund, sponsored by the Research Grants Council of Hong Kong (Reference No. 446611).

Contents

Introduction

So linguistic colonialism continues to flourish and expand, even while its
political counterpart is dying out. Perhaps the phenomenon we observe
in the former colonial lands, particularly in Africa, is only a reflection of a
larger linguistic picture, one that tends inevitably toward a single tongue
for world-wide use, one in which all men, swallowing their national pride,
will be able to communicate directly and practically

Mario Pei, *The Many Hues of English*

[T]he use of English in the world has no immediate connexion with the
economic or political supremacy – past or present – of an English-speaking
country.

Randolph Quirk, *The Use of English*

English and Colonialism – Englishes and Postcolonialism?

Although English has long spread around the world, it is only in recent
years that its diverse speakers have come to appreciate the unexpected
consequences. One consequence is a perceived convergence, as Pei suggests,
and resistance to that convergence derives largely from its identification
with the colonialism that he mentions. Nonetheless, there is more to the
picture of English worldwide than a dominant colonial tongue, and, while
Quirk's suggestion must seem a little wishful, there are also increasing
numbers of researchers, writers, and everyday users who are willing to
entertain the idea that English has at least no *necessary* connection with
any particular country or group of countries. That willingness might be
somewhat less evident among those we usually consider native speakers,

but their control of the situation is significantly weaker than it might have once seemed. The discourse of World Englishes seeks to re-imagine our understanding of the English language. The difference between error and innovation can no longer be decided through assumptions about the 'ownership' of the language. In fact, the language is beginning to be a medium of the expression of identity for more and more people in very different contexts. World English must be pluralized, which is why we think in terms of World Englishes. This book puts examples from these Englishes, in addition to the academic and other discourses that surround them, into dialogue with postcolonial studies, in the belief that while postcolonial studies has obviously had a great deal to say about the English language (and increasingly other colonial languages), much of what it has had to say has either directly concerned or been influenced by literary studies. The dialogue that ensues here extends postcolonial studies beyond literary studies, and brings it into discussions most commonly associated with the study of globalization in particular. In some ways, the dialogue will correct partial misconceptions and misapprehensions in postcolonial studies, with the discourse of World Englishes offering renewal for postcolonial studies. At the same time, the dialogue will also see postcolonial studies' powerful political and philosophical tools brought into contact with World Englishes, resulting in something that could be characterized as 'World Englishes: A Postcolonial Perspective'. While it is *not* entitled 'World Englishes Studies and Postcolonial Studies', the book is certainly intended to be a relatively balanced dialogue, despite frequently focusing on issues emerging from postcolonial studies.

The aspiration is for postcolonial studies to be at least as much receiver as giver. Although the potential insights postcolonial studies may give concerning World Englishes are important, the need for renewal in postcolonial studies itself will appear obvious to many critics. For these critics, postcolonial studies has come to seem, even in a period witnessing the ongoing globalization of universities, a narrow set of discourses increasingly communicating within a restricted professional class, and frequently still communicating in the English language. In restricting itself in these ways, postcolonial studies as a discipline has arguably functioned as an extension of a neo-colonial globalization. Unlike the turbulent and dynamic multilingualism of what Robert J.C. Young (2001) calls 'Tricontinental Marxism', postcolonial studies can seem set in its Anglophone ways, dutifully reading the latest novels from celebrity novelists from a postcolonial perspective, occasionally prone to angst-ridden self-examination and calls for self-renewal. Despite this, postcolonial studies can look 'within' for at least some sources of renewal; central figures from the 'prehistory' of postcolonial studies offer us many resources for such a renewal, even if we continue to focus on Anglophone contexts. Writing in and partly about the French language, Jean-Paul Sartre made striking claims about Frantz Fanon's *Les Damnés de la Terre* (1961) [*The Wretched of the Earth*]. Sartre urges us to move beyond the assumption of predetermined interlocutors, and even to remove ourselves from the equation entirely, if indeed we happen to be metropolitan Francophones. As Sartre writes to his French readers of Fanon, 'he speaks of you often, never to you' (1963, 10). One way of de-centring postcolonial studies, or renewing them, is to challenge their Anglophone basis through a focus on other linguistic contexts, whether other imperial languages like French or, instead, dominated languages. If in our academic work we continue to imply the centrality of the English language, it may not necessarily constitute a form of ongoing imperialism, but it is certainly highly restrictive. Other works in this series, and also other series published by Liverpool University Press and other publishers, continue to develop Francophone postcolonial studies and other comparable fields. It is also necessary to move postcolonial studies beyond the colonial languages, however important they were and continue to be; indigenous cultural production has certainly been neglected in some strands of postcolonial studies. These two possibilities redirect postcolonial studies from its Anglophone focus. This book, by contrast, seeks to move beyond Anglophone postcolonial studies by 'doubling-down' on the English language, putting literary contexts alongside broader contexts of cultural meaning, and transforming English into what linguistics has been for decades now calling 'Englishes'. This is again to challenge our assumptions about, or our predetermined categorization of, users of English. English is frequently used to speak of so-called native English speakers without necessarily speaking to them. Indeed, frequently it is used without any thought whatsoever given to those native speakers. This book seeks to contribute to making postcolonial studies adequate to this increasingly evident context of World Englishes.

The Language Myth and the Heterolingual Address

In his preface to *Les Damnés de la Terre*, Sartre highlights the nature of Fanon's address, as if for its reader this in itself were a key point. Of course, however, and despite what I previously implied, Fanon has no *single* kind of reader, and that is the case in a more far-reaching way than is true of texts in general. Sartre's point is important for another aspect of this book's argument, as when writing *about* the English language, it is all too easy for the so-called native speaker to fall into a particular habit that can derive from the very fact of writing *in* that language. That is to say, it is tempting to invoke a 'we' that experiences the language in superficially varying but fundamentally similar ways. It is tempting, then, to employ what Naoki Sakai calls 'the homolingual address'. It is the case that the fallacy of this address can function in discourse focused on *any* content whatsoever, but evidently the nature of writing in English *about* English, in today's worldwide linguistic context, makes the homolingual address particularly problematic. While it may be argued that speaking rhetorically is inevitable, one must never simply dismiss challenges to rhetorically speaking. Sakai outlines particular desires and assumptions that he acted upon in his writing. He suggests that he communicated as part of a community, 'for whom reciprocal apprehension [and] transparent communication' were not straightforward or guaranteed (1997, 4). The community he was indeed attempting to invoke or in fact call into being, 'did not have to coincide with a linguistic community whose commonness is built around the assumed assurance of immediate and reciprocal apprehension in conversation' (1997, 4). In the end, then, no necessary response could be assumed, with transference at best an achievement, and the address designed to call the community into being needed to be appropriate to these structural uncertainties. For Sakai, 'to address myself to such an audience by saying "we" was to reach out to the addressees without either an assurance of immediate apprehension or an expectation of uniform response from them' (1997, 4). While of course still aiming at communication, his writing assumes an irreducible communicative 'lack'. Sakai's address is to be understood as resistant to the homolingual; the address aims at being heterolingual.

The point Sakai makes operates on assumptions more far-reaching than simply the mixed quality of any readership. In seeking to operate in the heterolingual address, we are trying to avoid rhetorical coercion, and the so-called 'royal we' needs to be understood as at best something achieved, and no doubt also something temporary. In particular, it is surely obvious that the experience of reading English concerning any topic will vary depending on location, perhaps all the more (as will be seen) when that location is an outcome of histories of colonialism, and particularly when the content of the written English is English itself (although that 'itself' is already to assume too much). In short, in attempting to employ the heterolingual address, this book assumes that it cannot in fact assume anything about shared community, assumptions, communication, or anything else that is based on the fact of the reader reading in English. While any reader of any language might always have wildly differing assumptions concerning the topic of an author's book, to the extent that he or she is an individual reader, the state of World Englishes suggests a far broader linguistic community that quite possibly should not be given the name 'community' at all, as well as a greater likelihood of what I will for the moment call *disagreement*. *Telementation* (the 'copying' of thoughts from person A to person B) is a problematic ideal, and English in its current diversity fully emphasizes its problematic nature.

This point ought to be central to studying and writing about World Englishes, and this claim can be explored through reference to discussion of what Roy Harris has termed 'the Language Myth' (1981). Harris argues that the language myth is central in Western culture from Aristotle to Saussure and beyond, but also seems to be a general feature of how we understand the importance of language. The myth is a powerful model of how language is a means of communication, but also how language helps to form community. According to Harris, the language myth 'in its modern form is a cultural product of post-Renaissance Europe', which reflects, he argues, 'the political psychology of nationalism, and an educational system devoted to standardising the linguistic behaviour of pupils' (1981, 9). It coincides with the rise of modern nation states, specifically with attempts to defend such states at a point of crisis, and at least one of its effects is to create communities. One thing that is particularly important for this standardizing effect of languages is the technological ability to print languages; of course, historically, at least in Europe, this technology coincided with the creation of modern nations, as explored by Benedict Anderson (2006). The myth itself works through *pattern transference*, in which a determinate thought is transferred from person A to person B. Language operates to communicate that thought from A to B. B, in sharing a linguistic code with A, is able to decode the thought, however it has been communicated, and the thought has thereby been transferred from the isolated mind of one individual to the isolated mind of the other.

The connection between this transference model and language communities is of course striking, and obviously relevant to the study of English, as we will see. This model is all about the reproduction of essentially identical thoughts, working within a fixed language system: 'Individuals are able to exchange their thoughts by means of words because – and insofar as – they have come to understand and to adhere to a fixed public plan for doing so. The plan is based on recurrent instantiation of invariant items belonging to a set known to all members of the community' (Harris 1981, 10). As Harris continues, it is the invariance that elevates this system above the troublesome unpredictability of contexts, or indeed the intentions of individual language users. Knowing this fixed system, and knowing the thoughts they wish to communicate, speakers participate in an exchange with listeners equally familiar with the invariant structure. Accordingly, it does not matter who you are, as an individual; to be a part of this fixed system is to be in communication with others in the system. While it is true that all languages are given discursive regularity, that regularity obscures a great deal about the communication that happens 'within'. In the context of World Englishes, the most important aspect of Harris's analysis is the role this myth plays in our ideas about cultures and communities. For Harris, the language myth has effects, as is clear from the use of the term 'myth'. We can think of myth as providing a solution to a contradiction in our thinking, as in structuralist anthropology, and myth is thus comparable to Althusserian ideology, being the formal or imaginary resolution of actual contradiction. For Harris, the language myth operates in exactly this way. We have a contradiction that must be overcome: the contradiction that we are isolated individuals but that somehow this isolation is overcome, that we *do* share, and that we can be part of a bigger group. Our isolation is characterized as *somatic particularity*, meaning that we are who we are, absolutely unique individuals whose experience is our own, and whose lives cannot be led by others. At the same time, we know that this is highly simplistic, as people *do* share experiences, and we are not entirely cut off from others; obviously enough, if superficially, this sharing takes place through language. According to the language myth, the transference of thoughts either reduces or even cancels the isolation of each individual. According to this model, Harris argues, 'if only an idea in *A*'s mind can be copied into *B*'s mind, by whatever means, then the limitations of somatic particularity have *pro tanto* been overcome' (1981, 15). Harris summarizes the effect of the myth: 'instead of a lot of isolated individuals we end up with what is (significantly) called a *community*' (1981, 15). This process is one in which speech communities are formed, the speech community being a concept that transforms the idea of *Volk* into an only apparently objective aspect of linguistic science (see Hutton 2002). It is readily imaginable that World Englishes represent a challenge to the integrity of such communities.

Harris's analysis can be extended further, and has been explored and contested in many contexts. For the purposes of this book, his work is relevant in the following ways. First, the language myth leads us to imagine that there must be an ideal or standard version of each language, and that any deviations from this standard language are inferior and unacceptable. This is because such deviations stop us from simply communicating ideas from one individual to another. In other words, deviations and non-standard uses of a language undermine the power of language to make each individual part of a community. This is one idea that we will come back to in relation to English, something that superficially appears irrefutable: if English is being used as a communicative tool by non-native speakers, then it must be used in a standard form, otherwise people using different kinds of English will no longer be able simply to communicate with each other. Second, the language myth also gives this ideal standard form of a language a definite *political* power. It is possible to associate the standard language with a very specific community, such as a national community. It is even possible to associate the standard language with a category such as 'race'. When language is associated with a very definite community, then obviously there are people excluded from that community in various ways. From this perspective, languages are conceived as belonging to a people: speaking proper English, whatever that means, is associated with *owning* English, having English as a form of property. Such an attitude is still evident in ideas about how English is spoken, and who can speak English, and many of these ideas we will encounter later. Third, the language myth implies that the language community has some kind of 'common mind'. All of the ways of seeing and thinking that are carried along by any language make up some kind of world-view (as in the Sapir-Whorf hypothesis; see Sapir and Mandelbaum 1962). However, even if you speak a given language with great fluency, if it is not your 'proper' language, not the language you 'own', then you are excluded from the collective understanding that is shared by the community. From this point of view, 'non-native' speakers of English might be unable to share in the supposed common understanding shared by British, Americans, Australians, etc. Further, it might be argued that non-native speakers should not even *want* to share in that common understanding. They have their own languages, their own communities with their own shared understandings, and should use English at most as a mere 'communicative' tool: they should try to minimize the extent to which the world-view that accompanies English affects their own world-views. These ideas are all challenged by the actual facts of English's spread around the world, and also by the idea of World Englishes. Indeed, a challenge to the idea of language ownership is a key aspect of World Englishes studies.

World Englishes Across the Disciplines

The series for which this book was written, 'Postcolonialism Across the Disciplines', aims to interrupt the postcolonial paradigm, and to foreground alternatives to a perceived literary hegemony in postcolonial studies. The other discipline from which the series is to some extent distanced is cultural studies. I will return to literature in a later chapter, to offer a modest defence of the potential still found in postcolonial literary studies. Here, however, I would like to say something concerning cultural studies, as one strand in the study of World Englishes is clearly influenced by certain traditions in cultural studies. That is unsurprising, just as it is unsurprising to find that influence at work in postcolonial studies. Indeed, one of the assumptions of this book is that postcolonial literary studies are fruitfully extended into postcolonial cultural studies. Of course that gesture is not new, being in fact a key driver of cultural studies in its British form, and being extended to a greater or lesser extent in North American, Australian, Inter-Asian, and other versions of cultural studies. This book assumes that it is worth extending this work into further study of World Englishes, and also that this extension is already under way. Of course, much of the disciplinary impetus for the study of World Englishes comes from different (sometimes very different) strands of linguistics, while cultural studies' borrowings from linguistics might seem haphazard and even cavalier. It is clear, however, that increasing attention is being paid to World Englishes from perspectives informed by cultural studies, for example, in versions of Critical Linguistics (e.g., Pennycook 1994; 1998; 2007a). Putting that fact alongside the fundamental aim of this book series, it is vital to understand the nature of the interdisciplinarity we bring to bear on, and that is demanded by, World Englishes. The first thing to be noted is that World Englishes are bound up with institutions of various kinds, such as universities, schools, NGOs, parliaments large and small, and legal systems. Researchers focusing on World Englishes are likewise restricted by *and* enabled by institutions, which is something that cultural studies insists upon. Institutions are neither simply public nor private, nor in any way simply positive or negative, as Paul Bowman suggests: 'the prime movers – or indeed, often, the prime blockers, limiters, or resisters – of political contexts are "institutions"' (2007, 171). Institution and institutions have no necessary meaning or value, in the same way as interruption. It is not necessarily the case that *more* interruption means better, just as it is not necessarily the case that *less* institution means better. Individual instances are to be taken in context, and that context is never saturated. Importantly, the institutional focus of cultural studies is connected to its interdisciplinary status. In his call for cultural studies to embrace anew its operation across the disciplines, Bowman writes that 'today intervention requires a new interdisciplinarity' (2007, 177). In certain ways, Bowman is demanding that cultural studies become *anti*-disciplinary. Being interdisciplinary is being anti-disciplinary, at least in the sense that interdisciplinary cultural studies would cease to be cultural studies at all, operating strategically through other voices, methods, rhetoric, etc. As Bowman goes on to argue, 'interdisciplinary interventions must necessarily be executed in the language of the other' (2007, 179). We might only be speaking the language of the other for very limited periods of time, but during that time we must not be reproducing the comfortable and recognizable language of cultural studies; instead we must be 'monsters of fidelity'. And, as Jacques Derrida's readings demonstrate, fidelity accompanies transformation, which is the structure of what Derrida calls *iterability*. Cultural studies needs therefore to stop reading culture in a comfortable, predictable, and indeed programmatic fashion, and so Bowman recommends, 'the transgression of one's own familiar style of disciplinary discourse' (2007, 205). More recently, Toby Miller has written that 'if the humanities are primarily concerned with explaining how meaning is made, they must consider the wider political economy, and not simply in terms of culture as a reflective or refractive index of it but as *part of* that economy' (2012, 107). Putting humanities alongside social science discourses is one small step towards interdisciplinarity, and is the minimum necessary for a book hoping to move postcolonialism across the disciplines.

It is, however, important to retain Bowman's emphasis on intervening through *inhabiting* discourses. My discussion of World Englishes covers diverse topics related to the field, and these chapters to some extent inevitably read very differently. However, they also operate in different registers, 'within' very different disciplinary formations. This is necessary, I take it, if postcolonialism is to operate (like Bowman's cultural studies) across, between, and through the disciplines. For example, 'postcolonialism across the disciplines' cannot help but prompt thoughts of 'writing across the disciplines', and one of the chapters concerns the broad field of composition as it relates to World Englishes. Discussion of global citizenship, meanwhile, operates in another series of discourses again, and the idea of cultural translation cannot distance itself from actual developments in translation studies, developments often highly critical of cultural translation as a concept. Finally, thinking about lexicography demands engagement with and understanding of yet another set of different disciplinary protocols. While this series of engagements may not constitute intervention in the language of the other quite in the way Bowman has in mind, it should be remembered that researchers in linguistics and related fields frequently already imagine themselves to be involved in interruption and intervention, so this book is making connections with these interventions as they imagine themselves to be and it is hoped already do exist; it is also a *prescription* for them to exist. Indeed, researchers on

World Englishes are also frequently lexicographers, teachers of English as a second or foreign language, British Council employees, and so on. They are necessarily part of the broader political economy, and do not (or should not be able to) imagine themselves separate from its workings, with culture viewed as a mirror of the workings of that economy. Again, it is not surprising at all that the discourses of World Englishes have begun to put cultural studies to work on their object, from which they are yet not at all separate.

Bowman's comments on cultural studies as a form of *interdiscipline* can be connected with specific ideas in postcolonial studies. Of course it is in some ways inevitable that postcolonial studies tend towards interdisciplinarity. Their objects cover many different fields, and so there must be art history-, anthropology-, philosophy-, and linguistics-oriented forms of postcolonial studies. Yet there is another way in which postcolonial studies has been interdisciplinary, and in fact *must* be interdisciplinary. Homi K. Bhabha argues the following about this necessity of interdisciplinarity:

> To enter into the interdisciplinarity of cultural texts means that we cannot contextualize the emergent cultural form by locating it in terms of some pre-given discursive causality or origin. We must always keep open a supplementary space for the articulation of cultural knowledges that are adjacent and adjunct but not necessarily accumulative, teleological or dialectical. (Bhabha 1994, 163)

As in the work of Edward Said, whose idea of travelling theory Bhabha is developing, this emphasis on interdisciplinarity is not only a question of adequacy to a multifaceted object; interdisciplinarity also in principle resists transcendent critical judgements, judgements that would erase difference in an ever more inclusive total discipline. Disciplines (rather like cultures) may well be effects of efforts at stabilization, but they are no less real for that. Interdisciplinary postcolonialism operates on the assumption that duplicating the procedures of its object is unlikely to prove fruitful. As Bhabha continues to argue, 'Interdisciplinarity is the acknowledgement of the emergent sign of cultural difference produced in the ambivalent movement between the pedagogical and performative address. It is never simply the harmonious addition of contents or contexts that augment the positivity of a pre-given disciplinary or symbolic *presence*' (1994, 163). If there is necessary tension between the apparent pre-given feel (the *presence*) of culture and the necessity of its ongoing production, as Bhabha analyses through the tension between 'pedagogical' and 'performative', then the critical language with which this tension is analysed and further heightened ought to mark this understanding. Marking that tension can be achieved in various ways, for example, through the heterolingual address and the related development of 'autobiographical' critical writing.

What Does it Matter Who is Speaking?

Accordingly, one other element of this book is important here, which is its loosely autobiographical tendency. This tendency is partly one facet of attempts to produce a heterolingual address. It is also one strategy for acknowledging what Pennycook refers to as *worldliness*, a recognition that 'while globalization on the one hand pushes us towards a worldly oneness, on the other hand it obliges an understanding that must draw on the multiple worldly localities of its viewers' (2010, 199). While not a systematic, constant, or necessarily insistent presence, this book's autobiographical element is important. There are many broader arguments concerning the development of this kind of academic life writing, and we can certainly argue that there has been an autobiographical turn in critical writing. This turn has taken place partly as a result of the increased visibility of discussions concerning ethics, with Paul John Eakin arguing that ethics is 'the deep subject of autobio-graphical discourse' (2004, 6). Writing against a privacy-based ethics of life writing, Eakin stresses the *relational* quality of autobiography: 'Because we live our lives in relation to others, our privacies are largely shared, making it hard to demarcate the boundary where one life leaves off and another begins' (2004, 8). We are, then, relational in the broadest terms, evident in the writing that common sense tells us to be the least relational and most specific to ourselves. This combination allows us to compare academic life writing with the keen attention paid to institutions by the best forms of cultural studies. As Bowman suggests, institutions are neither public or private, which is suggestive in relation to Eakin's general point, as critical academic writing certainly takes place in institutional contexts that are both utterly specific and also demanding of generalization. Robert Young suggests that a new emphasis on 'chance' in theory is symptomatic of a legiti-mation crisis brought about by the collapse of the culture/academia split: 'The intimate revelations of the inquiring self stand in as a typical example of the wider social structure' (1996, 14). Young identifies a kind of institutional anxiety about the apparently non-institutional exterior, something that is clearly not external at all. Without the possibility of recourse to ideals of cultural guardianship, the divide between culture and academia has been lost, and one response has been to embrace this loss; academic life writing reminds us that academics have lives too, as it were, lives meaning identities that are comparable to or can stand for various cultural, economic, or other groups. From this perspective, in various ways researchers are other too.

But there is another motivation for writing autobiographical theory. Classificatory systems, small and large, construct their objects, which in terms of certain disciplines leads to misrepresentation. The example most obviously pertinent is orientalism as conceived by Said (1978). Instead of thinking that bias is an unnecessary but very real cause of Western misrepresen-tations of other cultures, Said has been taken to argue that misrepresentation is inevitable. There has been much debate over the extent to which this characterization accurately captures Said's position, but even if we moderate it a little, arguing that misrepresentation was (and is) historically the fact, this position still allows us to justify academic life writing in terms of historical intervention. If we accept that the urge to know the other always morphs into a will to master the other (or at least always *might*), then we should fall back on apparently more modest aims, with theory translating itself into a kind of life writing. This is an extension of the point made by Young when he writes that 'if we cannot ever know the other, then we turn back to the self' (1996, 14). This turning back seems to be a shift back towards the non-relational or, perhaps, marks orientation without reference to the objective; it might appear to mark, then, a kind of academic pessimism. However, even this non-relational self is optimized towards a modest ideal, and it can be argued that much of this newly and explicitly inflected work is structured by certain kinds of ethical orientation. We can think about this ethical orientation deriving from the autobiographical turn in humanities writing in the context of orientation towards certain kinds of 'good'. In discussing such orientation, we would be following the work of Charles Taylor, specifically *Sources of the Self* (1989). Taylor reminds us that I say things about my social, cultural, or ethical identity within a context of questions that orients. Following Taylor, David Parker (2007) adapted this understanding of ethical orientation in order to re-cast the study of life writing in particular. In turn, it is clear that critical writing, in taking on characteristics of life writing, is involved in ethical orientation.

I have addressed these and related issues in a previous book (Huddart 2008), and its assumptions continue to inform this work on World Englishes. Institutionally speaking, the theories concerning (for example) the expanded ownership of English, the death of the native speaker, or the confusion of error and innovation, are subject to daily testing in the classroom. Each classroom fits into its own institutional context (a specific curriculum, a wider university perspective, and educational needs, etc.) and a broader politics of language (how English sits alongside other languages, how so-called native speaker cultures are viewed, etc.). Furthermore, the spread of English implies a world, a globe, or maybe a planet (each term having its implications), although that begins to stretch any ethnographic account, and relies upon a mapping of the node's relation to the network that might remain speculative. Accordingly, in my case some specific reference to experiences of Japanese, British, and Hong Kong university contexts is inevitable and necessary. Partly that is due to the general requirement of refusing to theorize a general condition about what is a very diverse series of phenomena; World Englishes really are very difficult phenomena to discuss at a general level, and, despite the same processes, histories, etc., these Englishes are in certain ways more intractable than English as a global language (or any apparent equivalent). But, as I have suggested, it is necessary to foreground some of the goods to which postcolonial theories generally seem oriented, and check some of the ways that reality resists our demands. The classroom teacher comes in many forms, and works in many contexts, his or her research (if they are fortunate enough to be granted the time and freedom) coming up against the unexpected on a daily basis. I earlier mentioned likely and inevitable persistent bias, and I imagine that will come across as a bias towards (or a greater interest in and knowledge of) postcolonial theory, and that partly derives from my own institutional and educational grounding in literary and cultural studies. However, for eight years I have taught World Englishes to students in Hong Kong, immersing myself in disciplinary conventions and expertise quite foreign to my training, with varying levels of success. The results of this book's dialogue between postcolonial studies and World Englishes cannot avoid being marked by this classroom-based prompt for my research, the more institutional aspects of which are often called 'teaching-led research'. But this context is not simply an excuse, and, anyway, as J.L Austin put it, 'the average excuse, in a poor situation, gets us only out of the fire into the frying pan' (1961, 125). Contextualizing or situating knowledge is (or aims to be) less excuse than justification, however difficult they may be to differentiate. But even if it fails, the making of excuses is hardly worthless; as Austin continued: 'but still, of course, any frying pan in a fire' (1961, 125).

The 'Communication' of English

These comments on *situatedness* are not intended to be merely autobiographical comments. In any discussion of global English and World Englishes it is relevant that the writer is one of the so-called native speakers, even if that category is losing some of its exactness and cachet. This helps to make sense of experiences, assumptions, and assertions, and clarifies those moments when, despite best efforts, the heterolingual address slides unthinkingly into the homolingual address. And, if nothing else, writing in English about English inevitably draws on the norms of so-called Anglo cultures. Indeed, as we will see, one of those norms concerns the desirability of one particular kind of communication. As Martin Kayman (2004) has argued, the teaching of English worldwide tends to emphasize the distance between the language and the cultures with which it is inevitably and necessarily associated. In insisting on this distance, English teaching transforms English into a kind of neutral communicative tool. There are many obvious problems with this apparent transformation. For example, Anna Wierzbicka (2006) provocatively argues that linguistics has not had much to say about communication itself. She suggests that even theories of intercultural communication tend to lack specificity when it comes to the question of what needs to be learned when someone learns how to communicate in a language. Such theories can resist the idea that in learning a language you are learning a culture, particularly because of the assimilationist or coercive implications of that idea for immigrants. Wierzbicka argues that this resistance overlooks the actual experience of immigrants, who really do feel they are experiencing a frequently oppressive Anglo culture. In addition, she thinks it overlooks the immigrants' practical needs: 'To deny the validity of the notion of Anglo cultural patterns or Anglo ways of speaking is to place the values of political correctness above the interests of socially disadvantaged individuals and groups' (2006, 22). Interestingly, in exploring the necessity of creating the appropriate 'vibes', Wierzbicka argues that World Englishes approaches and practices already incorporate this recognition, while global English approaches do not. She suggests that 'it is often assumed that the main (if not sole) goal of English used as a tool of intercultural communication is to convey information, that the "pragmatics" of language use are not relevant in this case; and that Anglo conversational norms and conventions are (or should be) irrelevant in English-based cross-cultural exchanges' (2006, 305). Again, this form of English is imagined to float free of any specific culture; World Englishes, meanwhile, are clearly situated in relation in each case to at least one culture. Given this recognition of necessary relation, at least in the specific context of language learning for immigrants, Wierzbicka pursues a renewed emphasis on native speaker cultural norms, not a relativistic and laissez-faire approach.

Clearly, Wierzbicka's argument applies to academic writing as much as any other form of cross-cultural exchange; it is also obvious that the increasingly general pressure to publish in Anglophone publications can lead to problems for those unwilling or unable to conform to the relevant Anglo norms. This is one justification for attempting the heterolingual address, however superficial that address might appear. Wierzbicka focuses on general aspects of what she terms 'cultural script', many of which contribute to a particular take on communicating in a *reasonable* way, e.g., right/wrong; reasonable; being fair; 'I think'; probable/likely/certainly. Of course, her study is part of a highly systematic take on communication across cultures. Wierzbicka considers the question of English's cultural baggage in terms of how different cultural scripts can be broken down into what she calls Natural Semantic Metalanguage (NSM). NSM provides a form of universal semantic grid, which allows the comparison of different languages in terms of semantic domains. It is, then, a way of translating cultural scripts into something more fundamental (indeed, universal), and accordingly a way of attempting to foster better intercultural communication, even if perfection is beyond its ambition, or even its sense of the possible. Seeking 'good vibes' in intercultural communication can be very difficult, she acknowledges, but she also suggests training in cultural norms is both necessary and possible, and that, 'Given the realities of the world today, it is particularly important for both the insiders and the outsiders that the cultural scripts of Anglo English be identified in an intelligible and readily translatable form' (2006, 308). According to this perspective, Anglo communicational norms most frequently go unremarked by Anglos themselves; however, the issue is far broader than instances of face-to-face communication.

One of the norms we could usefully reconsider is 'communication' itself, and there have been numerous attempts to explore it as a situated value in its own right. It has been suggested that even when English and Englishes are not present, a certain form of Anglo norm concerning communication holds sway. Deborah Cameron (2000) argues that a fundamentally instrumental and 'managerialist' vision of communication has become prevalent around the world, with the study of language increasingly divorced from culture (which *this* time is conceived as a *waste* of time). This idea of communication is 'skills-based', focusing on aspects such as 'listening skills', etc. Such communication views diversity as important, but assumes that it is not something that can encroach on a fundamental level at which sameness is necessary; indeed, this communication neutralizes the apparent threat of diversity through a 'unity in diversity', which dominates discourse on global communication. For Cameron, this idea of communication is based on an ethnocentrism that is distinct from (despite continuities) linguistic imperialism as we usually understand it (and as I will describe it in the next chapter); it is an ideology of communication, 'promoting particular interactional norms, genres and speech-styles *across* languages, on the grounds that they are maximally "effective" for purposes of "communication"' (2002, 69). Importantly, this idea of communication dominates, 'even when no attempt is made to export the English language itself' (2002, 81). Indeed, she goes further and suggests that this situation requires teachers to understand exactly what idea of communication stands behind the questions posed about specific languages and specific practices; they must, Cameron argues, 'engage with questions about what kinds of communication are valuable. Such questions are just as significant, politically speaking, as questions about which actual language(s) should serve as means of communication in a globalizing world' (2002, 81). Cameron's point is clear and immensely important. The 'communication' associated with Anglo norms (Cameron actually argues that they are specifically *North American* norms) has been globalized (potentially) independently of the English language. In the proposals for forms of *English as an International Language* (see Modiano 1999) or *English as a Lingua Franca* (see Jenkins 2007), there might seem to be confirmation of Cameron's argument, and yet these ideas also contain the possibility of resistance to Anglo communication. Perhaps, indeed, World Englishes and World Englishes studies offer a challenge to this dominant sense of communication, as this book will suggest.

Similar arguments have been explored by specifically postcolonial perspectives on communication, for example, in the interventions of Raka Shome and Radha S. Hegde, who argue that 'critical communication scholars need to problematize both communication and globalization by taking into consideration historical contingencies and local specificities' (2002, 186). They argue that the idea of communication has become canonical, and requires rethinking in order to become more adequate to the disjunctive and unpredictable realities of global communication (indeed, 'global communication' is not necessarily a better way of putting it, as we will see later). Shome and Hegde suggest that it is necessary to deconstruct assumptions concerning global exchange, particularly through interrogating Western ideals of communication: 'These changing conditions demonstrate that communication scholars need to engage with the narratives elided by linear and consensual models of communication – the narratives of rupture, displacement, and detour' (2002, 182). The existence of World Englishes already challenges us to rethink linearity and consensus. In fact, the frequent use of a vocabulary of *hegemony* in discussing World Englishes implies less consensus (which is what hegemony seeks to achieve) and more *dissensus*. Dissensus may well be what we want, and what we (can) get through World Englishes, and this book assumes that different senses of communication are key to holding in mind the apparently contradictory qualities of English today.

Indeed, questioning communication underlies each chapter in this book, according to the following broad engagements. In the first chapter, it is possible to see the extent to which one idea of communication informs certain understandings of interdisciplinary work. We might want to rethink that idea, and at the very least engage with diverse senses of communication 'between' seemingly discrete disciplines, in this case postcolonial studies and World Englishes studies. In the second chapter, the connection between World Englishes and cultural translation is considered. It has been argued that cultural translation always might turn into a coercive structure given form by yes/no questions and fixed 'target' identities. Indeed, language policy in specific contexts has frequently imagined the use of English in terms of a certain kind of successful translation. However, it can be argued that World Englishes escape from that kind of model of success, which again is a model of communication. In the third chapter, concerning the connection between English and ideas of global citizenship, it is argued that the gap between literal and metaphorical conceptions of that citizenship derives from very different models of communication. Again, World Englishes themselves undermine a particular understanding of what a global language might be for, and exemplify the evolution of forms of 'globalization from below'. In the fourth chapter, focused on what dictionaries make happen, and deriving its insights from Jacques Derrida's analysis of the act of constitution, there is an emphasis on the idea of the performative and its challenge to ideologies of communication. In the fifth chapter, exploring the extent to which composition has been 'postcolonialized', it is argued that the use of Englishes for cultural expression is, at least in some contexts, resisted to the extent that it implies transparent accessibility on someone else's terms, i.e., a particular understanding of globalized communication. Finally, in reconsidering models of postcolonial and comparative *literary* reading, the sixth chapter argues that a particularly valuable aspect of that reading is its resistance to pre-packaged transparency in cultural meaning. Comparing recent ideas of *distant* reading to a kind of slow postcolonial reading, it suggests the necessity of foregrounding of literature and other cultural signs in the teaching of English language, whether that teaching is exonormative or endonormative. In conclusion, the book indicates the potential fragility of the contemporary state of Englishes, partly because the model of communication in question is not as fundamental as it may seem. The inevitability of English as medium of globalized communication is already overstated, but even its present reach is perhaps vulnerable to clear shifts in economic and cultural balance. Yet again communication in World Englishes is at least as open and uncertain as it is closed off (or 'imperialist'). But it is to the question of how to make World Englishes studies and postcolonial studies communicate that I turn first.

CHAPTER 1

Involuntary Associations: 'Postcolonial Studies' and 'World Englishes'

To develop everywhere, in defiance of a universalizing and reductive humanism, the theory of specifically opaque structures. In the world of cross-cultural relationship, which takes over from the homogeneity of the single culture, to accept this opaqueness – that is, the irreducible density of the other – is to truly accomplish, through diversity, a human objective.

Édouard Glissant, Le Discours Antillais

Introduction

This chapter juxtaposes postcolonial studies and World Englishes studies, considering what the two disciplines share, as well as how they may differ. It also explores what it means to think about them as 'disciplines' in the first place. Accordingly, this chapter is about the act of naming, particularly as it gives shape to or calls into being disciplines, something that Philip Seargeant (2010; 2012) has written about at length in the context of World Englishes. Nonetheless, this chapter does not attempt to fix or freeze these two disciplines, as each is necessarily loosely defined. Furthermore, particularly in the case of postcolonial studies, the process of definition is quite possibly exhausted, with scholars having long ago asked 'when was', 'what is', etc. Indeed, Emma Dawson Varughese (2012) begins her recent study of World Englishes literature by refusing to make any attempt to redefine 'the postcolonial'; this refusal is a prerequisite, she argues, for going 'beyond the postcolonial', as her book's subtitle puts it. In order to avoid offering fixed, simple definitions of either World Englishes or postcolonial studies, this book will look at diverse case studies that frequently suggest very different things about the connections between the two disciplines. That approach begins here, as this chapter outlines some of the phenomena that give rise to the critical approaches, considers how the approaches differ, and explores the ways in which other writers have begun to bring them together. To begin, let us consider the proposition that the extent of English's spread constitutes a form of ongoing domination that is best described in terms of *linguistic imperialism*. This diagnosis of linguistic imperialism is part of what is often called the Critical Linguistics approach, but is also and obviously connected with postcolonial approaches, as we will now see.

English Worldwide: Diagnosis Imperialism

Probably the most influential approach to English worldwide, and certainly an example of a postcolonial perspective in action, is Robert Phillipson's *Linguistic Imperialism* (1992). I will refer to Phillipson throughout this book, and his work remains an indispensable prompt for reflection on World Englishes, even as the phenomenon of World Englishes to some extent demands that we extend and adapt Phillipson's argument for specific contexts and conditions. Of course, in simple terms there are two ways to make the connection between English and imperialism. First, we might make the historical connection and demonstrate that English was an aspect of imperialism, its spread part of colonial settlement and imperial domination. Second, we might make an analogy and argue that the spread of English was like imperialism, which is to say that linguistic imperialism is a form of cultural imperialism. Phillipson famously argues that there is continuity between these two forms of connection; indeed, he suggests that 'The British empire has given way to the empire of English' (1992, 1). In making this argument, Phillipson is suggesting that English language teaching (ELT) has become the driver of a new form of linguistic imperialism that structurally positions both teacher and learner. Furthermore, he suggests that this imperialism is based on a more fundamental attitude of *linguicism*, which he defines in the following way: '*Linguicism* involves representation of the dominant language, to which desirable characteristics are attributed, for purposes of inclusion, and the opposite for dominated language, for purposes of exclusion' (1992, 55). Linguicism accordingly attributes different if not entirely opposed qualities to languages in a given context, with English often represented as 'scientific' and 'rational' while other languages are understood to be 'emotional', 'musical', or possibly simply 'irrational'. In the colonial context, these different attributes are used to justify the colonizer's rule. In the end, the linked structures of linguicism and linguistic imperialism have become so successful that it is difficult to imagine how to challenge them, with Phillipson arguing that, 'English is now entrenched worldwide, as a result of British colonialism, international interdependence, "revolutions" in technology, transport, communications and commerce, and because English is the language of the USA, a major economic, political and military force in the contemporary world' (1992, 23–24). On this view, linguistic imperialism appears far more successful, and perhaps longer lasting, than the actual political, military, and economic institutions of empire.

As one example of ongoing concerns about linguistic imperialism, Qiang and Wolff write the following about the role English was beginning to play in China towards the end of the last century and into the current one:

> [T]he nationwide Chinese [English as a second language] campaign brings with it an immersion in Western concepts, including social, cultural, business and political thought. It is inevitable that a certain amount of traditional Chinese thought will give way to a certain amount of Western thought, which translates into a society developing with confusing input. (Qiang and Wolff 2003, 10)

For Qiang and Wolff, increased engagement with the English language will inevitably undermine aspects of Chinese culture, and will have specific political effects. Over the previous decade, they suggest, the increase in English teaching has been alarming, with the specific question of democracy's desirability highlighted. Qiang and Wolf even ask if English language political culture is compatible with Chinese Communist Party objectives. Some of the specific concerns and language used here may be irrelevant or appear exaggerated to readers elsewhere (and also within China itself), but the general concerns remain familiar from earlier periods and other contemporary contexts. We can readily imagine that an equivalent situation in which Anglophones felt coerced into learning Putonghua would be experienced as politically and culturally threatening (although it might be felt that this situation is *not* readily imaginable to many Anglophones, partly explaining widespread linguistic insensitivity). Qiang and Wolf operate with a 'weak' version of the Sapir-Whorf hypothesis, arguing that English is at least a vehicle of Western thought, and even perhaps is *intended* to be such a vehicle. Elsewhere the same authors argue that English should be understood as a kind of Trojan Horse, with the hospitality of host countries being ripe for abuse in the current globalized regime (Qiang and Wolff 2005). In much the same way as Phillipson, Qiang and Wolff are concerned that English is becoming entrenched in China.

Phillipson's important collaborative work on language rights (see Skutnabb-Kangas and Phillipson 1994) is just one example of how this entrenched English might be challenged, and perhaps with changing political and economic realities there is cause for optimism. However, while much has changed since 1992, Phillipson in fact argues that linguistic imperialism through ELT is even more evident, particularly, for example, in the 'normalization' of English within the global university system (itself a loaded description): 'it is a survival strategy dictated by economic and political pressures, which dovetail with linguistic imperialism' (2009, 207). Of course, while it may be someone's strategy, and possibly even that of many, that word perhaps exaggerates the consistency of what is occurring, even when English is demonstrably a serious problem. Indeed, what we probably need is, rather than a more 'balanced perspective', some capacity for holding together both that which English enables and that which it refuses or denies. Phillipson's position remains invaluable, but as I am sure he would accept it requires adaptation for each context. One way to adapt the position is to put the idea of linguistic imperialism in communication with cultural theory. As one example, Kayman (2004) suggests that although English is taught as 'living speech' rather than 'dead writing', and is supposedly therefore quite distinct from the thickly imperialist cultures that led to its spread, in fact there remains a connection with a culture that has now transcended specific national cultures. Kayman thinks of this as a culture of a specific ideal of communication, one that is associated with a version of globalization that values consensus, transparency, connectedness, and accessibility. He argues that 'To the extent that English is promoted as a global language of communication it is likely to serve as the privileged vehicle for such cultures of communication' (2004, 17). Following the argument of Deborah Cameron, Kayman believes that however much English becomes a global language it will remain in thrall to a particular set of cultural norms.

In thinking about the apparent detachment of 'neutral' 'speech' from 'imperialist' 'writing', Kayman explicitly has the work of Jacques Derrida in mind, and Derrida will be an important influence on this book. As Michael Syrotinski (2007) and Jane Hiddleston (2010) demonstrate, his work remains important for postcolonial studies, and I here extend this importance into thinking about World Englishes. Indeed, it is in Derrida that we find the clearest expression of the difficulties of holding on to both the positive and negative aspects of a communication that goes beyond any individual language, even English (although, again, 'individual' and 'English' are problematic terms, and ones that in their inadequacy direct us towards different ideas of communication). It is arguable that what Phillipson has in mind when discussing linguistic imperialism is what Derrida refers to as a kind of *Anglo-American Hegemony*. In the interview 'Globalization, Peace, and Cosmopolitanism', Derrida associates English with a kind of 'homo-homogenization' that simultaneously offers positive and negative possibilities, the latter being perhaps more notable because they are often obscured by specific ideologies of globalization. He suggests that we must oppose such ideologies while holding on to the positive potential of global structures. Homogenization can obviously have negative consequences, but at the same time we need to insist on achieving the kinds of homogeneity that are announced but basically still withheld; new surfaces hide some of the same old profound inequalities.

Accordingly, it is necessary to understand that which in English puts it on the side of undesirable homogenization, and what can be rescued for its more positive potential. Language, he suggests is the most visible site of ongoing or reconfigured inequalities. The delicate balance needed when considering this hegemony derives from the following:

> These imbalances are all the more difficult to challenge – and this is another contradiction – because, on the one hand, this hegemony is very

useful for universal communication (thus equivocal in its effects); and, on the other, because the linguistic-cultural hegemony (obviously I am alluding to the Anglo-American hegemony), which increasingly asserts itself or imposes itself on all modes of techno-scientific exchange, the Web, the Internet, academic research, etc., promotes powers that are either national and sovereign states, or supranational states, this time in the sense of corporations or new figures of the concentration of capital. (Derrida 2002, 373)

Immediately Derrida moves on, almost dismissively noting that all of the above is extremely familiar – as indeed it is, in one sense. It is what follows that is important when exploring the implications of World Englishes, as Derrida outlines what for his readers must remain a challenging logic. It is necessary to be focused concerning English's role in a hegemonic globalization while at the same time attending to the other possibilities it opens, both those that exist outside the official narratives and also those announced as absolutely central to those narratives. Indeed, one conclusion we might draw is the need to insist on realizing that which narratives of globalization tell us we already have; the latter is something particularly problematic, perhaps, beyond the nation state, as we now apparently are, but often in fact prove not to be. He acknowledges that the Anglo-American hegemony is simultaneously that which enables a desirable globalization in the form of participatory exchange (cultural, political, and economic) in a global community. It is necessary, then, to 'fight this hegemony without compromising the broadening of exchange and distribution' (2002, 374). This 'balance' is not something that can be guaranteed in advance, and indeed is something that needs to be *concretized* endlessly: 'a transaction must be sought at every moment, in every singular set of circumstances' (2002, 374). Such a transaction entails the invention and reinvention of apparently stable norms, in what seems like an impossible demand:

> This inventiveness, this reinvention of the norm, even if it must be inaugural, different, without precedent and without prior guarantee, without available criteria every time, must not for all that yield to relativism, empiricism, pragmatism, or opportunism. It must justify itself by producing its principle of universalisation in a universally convincing way, by validating its principle through its very invention. In this way, I am formulating (and I am perfectly aware of it) a task that appears contradictory and *impossible*. Impossible at least for a response that would be instantaneous, simultaneous, immediately coherent, and identical to itself. But I maintain that only the impossible arrives and that there is no event, and thus no irruptive and singular decision except where one does more than deploy the possible, a possible knowledge – where exception is made to the possible. (Derrida 2002, 374)

What this logic demands is that we not apply rules, but invent them. Derrida illustrates this logic with the very example of 'globalization' as a word bearing a history; as is well known, he retains 'mondialisation'. There are of course competing possibilities within globalization – a diversity of globalizations. But Derrida's retention of the French term is partly a question of situating what he is saying in the context of philosophical thinking from Kant to Heidegger and beyond. Is it possible to imagine global citizenship, even one speaking English, as offering a form of access to an experience of the world unlike that of global entrepreneurship? That entrepreneurial vision of engaging with the globe is, after all, one form of global citizenship, as will be discussed later in this book. Is it possible to imagine World Englishes, at least partly resistant to the smooth transparency of a mutual intelligibility and easy access to 'markets', as languages that enable another form of global citizenship? According to Derrida, that is something we have to work out in each singular instance, but according to a universal intent thereby particularized and concretized. Derrida's logic here is one that has relevance elsewhere in the study of World Englishes, and I will return to it in terms of global citizenship, as well as the postcolonial dictionary in particular, and codification more generally. There are clear tensions between centripetal and centrifugal forces currently acting upon English, and it may be unrealistic if not indeed impossible to imagine that we can hold these forces in balance, as might be supposed by the ideal of dual affiliation in English (i.e., to an international standard and a local variety). There might be inevitable forms of linguistic violence brought to bear on English and its speakers, and it would then be our responsibility to secure the lesser violence.

World Englishes as a Term

The various approaches to World Englishes certainly discern the lesser violence. That seems inevitable given that the very phenomenon under consideration is a challenge to the sense of strategy, directedness, or control that continues to reassert itself in the linguistic imperialism paradigm. But what exactly are World Englishes, and why do they necessitate adaptation of the linguistic imperialism paradigm? Superficially, 'World Englishes' as a term seems clumsy or unwieldy. If we extend the term still further, discussing for example, 'World Englishes literatures' or 'World Englishes studies', it might seem all the more clumsy. And yet there are good reasons for the use of this term. If, as Roy Harris (1989, 39) argues, 'New Englishes' functioned as a euphemism for what had been previously dismissed as 'colonial Englishes' or 'non-native Englishes', then 'World Englishes' appears a far less apologetic or euphemistic term, partly because in principle it ought to refer to the so-called native speaker Englishes as well.

To the extent that postcolonial studies makes cultural translation so central, theorizes travelling theory, and in its literary approaches has tended to favour Anglophone writers, it would seem that postcolonial studies and World Englishes studies are natural allies. Of course, there may well be ways in which postcolonial perspectives could plausibly distance themselves from World Englishes. It can be all too easy to assume, for example, that World Englishes studies constitute in some sense a celebration of the spread or rather diversification of English, and such a celebration is obviously likely to meet with resistance. At least in principle, postcolonialism ought to be multilingual, resistant to any Anglophone bias that might be found in current research agendas and past structures of linguistic hierarchy. Postcolonialism as a discipline might also be wary of the institutional Anglophone emphasis that partly derives from a worldwide bias towards Anglo-American universities and English language research. To that extent, it seems that it ought to be quite distinct from World Englishes studies, which by their nature are immersed in the Anglophone world. However, as Seargeant has recently observed, 'world Englishes studies has developed from a number of discursive traditions, yet at the same time one key motivating factor behind its development as a discipline has been a change in the nature of the ecology of world languages, namely, in the nature of the phenomenon being studied' (2012, 117). The Anglophone world, of course, is far more complex than 'Anglophone' suggests, and far broader in scope, with English responding to changing linguistic and other contexts in unexpected and fascinating ways. That change in the nature of the object ought to be a prompt for reflection on postcolonial studies as well. Of course, Anglophone postcolonial studies might still be mistaking a present globalized condition for a general past hybridity, and should avoid that level of anachronism. Nonetheless, present conditions derived from the histories that most usually constitute postcolonial studies' object, and so there is at least that sense of historical connectedness between the disciplines, even if it is obviously undesirable to view one as somehow the *fulfilment* of the other.

Indeed, some commentators have guarded against the possibility of privileging postcolonial studies, and have made a robust defence of the World Englishes approach. Kingsley Bolton (2003, 7) discusses the following overlapping approaches to World Englishes: English studies; sociolinguistics; applied linguistics; lexicography; 'popularisers'; critical linguistics; and futurologists. He later refines this in defining three distinct approaches to the phenomenon in question: 'approaches whose objectives are largely *linguistic* in orientation (e.g., English studies, and corpus linguistics); approaches that share both *linguistic and sociopolitical* concerns (e.g., most sociolinguistic approaches, and the world Englishes approach), and those approaches that are primarily *sociopolitical* and *political* in orientation (e.g., studies of linguistic imperialism, and other critical approaches)' (2005, 74–75). The first of these approaches, focusing on the linguistic features and changes characterizing the spread of English worldwide, one would take to be a precondition of any serious study of the phenomenon. However, the third, which Bolton calls Critical Linguistics, often appears to jettison concern with these actual descriptions of facts and processes characterizing English worldwide. Whether or not Bolton is being too robust in his attack on this latter perspective, it is certainly the case that his second identified approach, balancing linguistic and sociopolitical research, seems preferable, and ought to be a natural complement to the descriptive work carried out in the first approach. Bolton identifies (and, in doing so, is merely following the self-identification of a writer like Pennycook) Critical Linguistics with postcolonial theory, and for him this can be no compliment. His article tabulates different sub-approaches to World Englishes, and under Critical Linguistics he notes that it is 'Derived from a Marxian political analysis and/or postcolonial theory' (2005, 71). As is often the case when one is immersed in a field, it is external perspectives that help bring a measure of clarity; of course, within postcolonial studies, 'postcolonial theory' would more usually be identified with capital-T theory (familiar names such as Deleuze, Foucault, and Derrida), and would most likely remain opposed by more Marxist approaches. From outside the field, however, the narcissism of minor differences is diagnosed.

Given his later remarks about the potential pathos of academic activist discourse, I imagine that Bolton associates postcolonial studies with a misplaced or exaggerated rhetoric of political intervention; as he notes,

> Engaging in 'resistance' and 'struggle' in London, Stockholm or Sydney risks much less than in Beijing, Islamabad or Jakarta. In first-world universities, the politics of 'resistance' is often merely rhetorical, and the rhetoric has few real-world consequences. In other contexts, activism and resistance all too frequently incur dramatically real consequences, particularly in politically repressive regimes of both the left and right. (Bolton 2005, 78)

Furthermore, the rhetoric of resistance begins to obscure actual disciplinary competence, or even simple attention to the phenomena that are apparently in question. Descriptive attention to the actuality of English worldwide is a particular strength of World Englishes studies, as we might expect, but so is what follows the description, an evaluative or interpretive attention that does not already know what it will say about English. Accordingly, at the very least, postcolonial approaches to English might draw on the second approach identified by Bolton, one most usually associated with Braj Kachru, and to some extent this has already begun, as I will discuss a little later.

Postcolonialism as a Term

The other main discipline covered by and guiding this book presumably needs little introduction, given the series in which this book appears. Other than declaring that it is, or must be, an interdiscipline, I have nothing to add to the definition of 'postcolonialism'. I have no new formulation of 'postcolonialism', no new understanding of 'postcolonial theory', and so no exciting new proposals for 'postcolonial studies'. In much the same way as Dawson Varughese (2012), I see correcting the misconceptions of previous versions of postcolonialism to be characteristic of an approach that many commentators have been attempting to go beyond for some time. Postcolonial studies are constituted by a constellation of related disciplinary approaches, often characterized by cross-disciplinary experimentation, and frequently engaged in vociferous 'internal' disagreement. There are no postcolonial studies, we might say. Likewise, there is no postcolonial theory, given that the approaches most associated with capital-T theory (Bhabha, Said, and Spivak) are hardly uniform in themselves, and the approaches most resistant to them are at least as theoretical (most obviously Marxist approaches). As Robert J. C. Young suggests,

> So many disciplines have been, so to speak, postcolonialized, along with the creation of related subdisciplines such as diaspora and transnational studies, that this remarkable dispersal of intellectual and political influence now makes it difficult to locate any kind of center of postcolonial theory: reaching into almost every domain of contemporary thought, it has become part of the consciousness of our era. (Young 2012, 22)

The rhetoric here is provocatively exaggerated, and yet Young obviously has a point, even if on many occasions postcolonial studies as discipline is only 'brought to consciousness' in order to be dismissed. Accordingly, at best we can say that 'postcolonialism' floats free from authoritative categorization, the institutional moorings of a 'Western' university system being useful but in the end restrictive.

Nonetheless, there have been important interventions made in postcolonial studies that clearly have relevance to work in World Englishes studies. Highly situated readings give many examples of postcolonial studies their strength, and of course for a long time those readings were literary and cultural. Even on a more institutional level, a scholar such as Gauri Viswanathan (1989) considers the role of English *literary* studies in colonial education. In terms of postcolonial approaches to the English language as it is found mainly in literature, Bill Ashcroft's work is exemplary. In *Caliban's Voice*, he suggests that 'The most powerful discovery made by an examination of post-colonial language use is that language is used by people. Although it can be an ontological prison it need not be, for the key to post-colonial resistance is that speakers have agency in the ways they employ language to fashion their identity' (2008, 3). This argument is a clear challenge to some of the assumptions that might be derived from the Sapir-Whorf hypothesis, and presupposes the vitality of forms of cultural translation, adaptation, and transformation. Indeed, in the earlier work, *Post-Colonial Transformation*, Ashcroft gives the clearest expression of this kind of approach, writing that 'The language is a tool which has meaning according to the way in which it is used' (2001, 57). Theories, concepts, cultures, ideologies, and languages all have an inbuilt tendency to fail to reach their 'destinations'. Against notions of oppositional resistance, Ashcroft argues that postcolonial culture more commonly (and, he insists, more productively) tends to utilize colonial culture's materials, transforming them in such a way as to mark the fact of colonialism and its aftermath. Postcolonial culture refracts colonial culture's tendency to present itself as monological; the postcolonial consumer of colonial culture is also the producer of postcolonial culture, and this production is an agency, if not one simply opposed to all that emanates from any metropolitan centre. Indeed, this postcolonial subject recognizes something of the *rhizomatic* nature of cultural power, and that intervention can occur in diverse locations, with unpredictable effects. However, the privileged focus of Ashcroft's book is literature: 'it is still, perhaps, in creative writing that the fullest and most energetic interpolation takes place' (2001, 55). That privilege, while still to an extent understandable, is one thing that marks distance between World Englishes studies and postcolonial studies. Accordingly, if we are going to move postcolonialism across the disciplines, we may have to make the connection between the two in different ways that do not begin by privileging predictably traditional forms of cultural production.

Postcolonialism 'and' World Englishes

Of course, to some extent, to refer to these disciplines as 'two' is already to have made an assumption that in practice is very difficult to justify. In each case, as Seargeant (2012) and Huggan (2008), respectively, argue, these disciplines from the beginning accumulate diverse disciplinary approaches. That World Englishes studies suffers relatively little of the criticism deriving from this fact that postcolonial studies has sustained (if often from 'within', as Huggan notes) is certainly interesting, and perhaps derives from the frequently over-ambitious political claims the latter has long made. That being said, at least some elements in World Englishes studies, for example in Critical Linguistics, are concerned to make comparable claims, and often draw on the same sources; indeed, they have more recently begun to come under attack, again often from other areas within World Englishes studies. Interdisciplinarity, it often appears, is a dangerous game, leading researchers to stray outside their remit, to betray disciplinary incompetence, and perhaps to become masters of no trade at all. Of course, this book cannot accept this diagnosis for either discipline.

In the case of both 'postcolonialism' and 'World Englishes', it seems necessary first to distinguish something like a phenomenon under consideration from a set of approaches to the phenomenon. Of course, the set of approaches in each case also partly calls the phenomenon into being, and so the tools you use inevitably affect the object you are observing. Nonetheless, it is also the case that for both disciplines there is something there that calls them into being in the first place. Accordingly, it is a complex picture, and in this book each instance or example (of a theory, of a place, etc.) needs to be taken on its own terms, to some extent. There is no one postcolonial theory, and no single approach in postcolonial studies or World Englishes studies, just as there was no one colonial framework; obviously enough, there is no single phenomenon, only the phenomena of World Englishes. All of the above makes it difficult to bring postcolonialism and World Englishes together, or even postcolonial studies and World Englishes studies. Yet this book presupposes that some kind of interdisciplinary dialogue ought to begin, however problematic or incomplete. It will often (but not always) be modest in its aims. Huggan suggests that a more Utopian future post-disciplinary context is discernable, one that aims at decolonization and disciplinary interaction (indeed, Huggan cites the example of Wilson Harris, from whose work the present book's title is drawn). However, for the moment some more tentative goals are desirable: 'Postcolonialism's more immediate future surely lies in a patient, mutually transformative dialogue between the disciplines rather than in triumphalist announcements of the imminent end of disciplinarity *tout court*' (Huggan 2008, 13). The dramatic transformative ambitions of postcolonial studies have been clear to see, but a certain disciplinary wariness is also important. There is medium term value to dreams of a post-disciplinary version of World Englishes studies, or postcolonial studies, or both. But, for now, it is necessary to develop a dialogue that intuitively should already be well underway. What kind of patient dialogue has taken place between postcolonial studies and World Englishes studies up to this point?

Selected studies already bring together postcolonial studies and World Englishes approaches. My first example is a wide-ranging and provocative article that presents World Englishes as a 'challenge'. In this article, Pradeep A. Dhillon (2008) identifies relativism as the basic issue around which postcolonial studies and World Englishes studies come into contact, and concerning which they may well disagree. Focusing initially on Said's application of Foucault in *Orientalism* (1978), Dhillon argues that its explanatory power was compromised by the extent to which its polemical force produced reified and opposed identities ('us' and 'them'). It is necessary to move beyond such polarizations, in order 'to work towards finishing the humanistic project of the Enlightenment' (2009, 533). World Englishes studies, unlike postcolonial studies, are well placed to play a part in this unfinished Enlightenment project, for the following reasons. Focusing particularly on Braj Kachru, Dhillon argues that, 'the world Englishes approach recognizes the hegemony that lurks under the spread of language through institutions of power. At the same time, however, it does not deny the creativity that allows for human agency even under the most difficult situations' (2009, 536). World Englishes studies, from this perspective, acknowledges the force of a postcolonial critique, and indeed the critique of linguistic imperialism already outlined. However, it also holds that critique alongside exploration or even celebration of the creative potential that has been produced through the spread of English. Furthermore, the basic concepts of World Englishes concern both that which is shared and that which is different: 'The linguistic phenomena captured by the term world Englishes speak no doubt to the language that is shared, but speak with as much force to the ways in which varieties have developed in response to specific life-worlds' (2009, 536). The latter is something to which postcolonial studies pays a great deal of attention, but it may be argued that the former is something about which it is highly suspicious. Now, it may be the case that both Said and Foucault can be read in other ways, or even that, as Young (2001) suggests, a more strictly Foucauldian version of discourse would be much more useful for postcolonial studies. Nonetheless, Dhillon's intervention is an important contribution and poses World Englishes as a powerful corrective not only to postcolonial understandings of the English language, but also to more general assumptions in postcolonial studies.

Dhillon's comparison, then, is broadly in favour of revising postcolonial studies in light of World Englishes studies. Ian Mai-chi Lok (2012), meanwhile, like Dhillon, compares the work of Kachru and Edward Said, partly in order to discern the points on which they both agree and disagree. It is entirely understandable that Said and Kachru would be able to stand for their respective disciplines, partly in the sense that they could plausibly be viewed as the founders and enablers of much of the work that followed them. In terms of the comparison, Lok writes that 'There is definitely a consensus on the need to insist on one's own geographical position and resist against the sort of Western imperialism abetted by the linguistic purist in language and the Orientalist expert in culture that threatens to suppress and extinguish other linguistic, cultural and geopolitical identities' (2012, 424). That 'defensiveness' has translated itself into a kind of regionalism in Kachru's later work, while by apparent contrast Said argued tirelessly against all forms of essentialism as fundamentally dangerous. In Kachru, Lok suggests, hybridity is explored for the ways in which it operates 'within and between the boundaries' (2012, 426), such as in Indian culture and English. By apparent contrast, hybridity in Said tends towards the transcendence of geopolitical boundaries. While, as Lok argues, these positions are only superficially divergent, when he considers it necessary to compare the two figures *contrapuntally*, the greater emphasis on Said seems obvious, because contrapuntal reading is of course associated with Said's work. Indeed, Lok begins by relating a common teaching experience, in which students respond to examples of World Englishes by asking, 'What about cultural hybridity?' In one way, the students are posing postcolonial studies as something that anticipates and perhaps even comprehends World Englishes studies.

In fact, the contrapuntal becomes the central term in Lok's comparison of the two, again apparently favouring the students' response, and, accordingly, Said's anti-essentialist position; however, Lok argues that Kachru's work contains its own comparable emphasis on a positioning that is not fixed to the extent that it contains within it multiple aspects of equally multiple traditions. In explaining Kachru's position, Lok writes that a contrapuntal approach allows us to understand a user of one variety of English in terms of experience that is, 'accumulative, hybrid, and residual, a mosaic that is constantly being rearranged, recalled and deleted, forgotten, and reconstructed through a web of interaction between different agents and contexts past and present, via the assimilation (bits or whole) of different languages and varieties of languages through interactions' (2012, 230). While there are inequalities built into local, regional, and geopolitical positioning, such positioning is only one aspect of identity. That aspect interacts with more connected, supranational, or universal aspects of experience, without being swallowed by them. For Lok, accordingly, it is possible to articulate Kachru's position with Said's work. Indeed, Lok explicitly seeks to synergize valuable and challenging aspects of World Englishes studies and postcolonial studies. At the same time, he notes that work bringing the two disciplines together is hardly likely to be simple and harmonious; indeed, I would suggest that we can extend Lok's position to argue that bringing the two together cannot be unproblematic sublation or a contrived consensus. Lok's idea of interdisciplinarity, despite the drive of this particular article, is one that places emphasis on the point of conflict, and is likely to result in unexpected and often 'unpleasant' refractions; in short, this interdisciplinarity is one likely to lead to a great deal of dissensus.

Other attempts to bring World Englishes studies and postcolonial studies together have gone beyond comparing their theoretical assumptions, and have begun to put into practice a form of hybrid method to explore an equally hybrid object. For example, one version of interdisciplinarity concerned with both postcolonial studies and World Englishes is found in work in Critical Linguistics, which often involves the application of insights from postcolonial studies alongside other cultural studies approaches (see Pennycook 2007b). A more critical perspective on postcolonial studies is found in the ethnographic studies of World Englishes literatures conducted by Emma Dawson Varughese. Indeed, Dawson Varughese's work is fascinating in its practical application of a kind of interdisciplinary approach that yet focuses its energies on directing postcolonial literary studies into vibrant new forms. She focuses her 2012 book on reimagining postcolonial literature in the context of World Englishes. From the beginning, she makes this focus clear: 'within the field of postcolonial studies, it is postcolonial *literature*, its definitions and its terms of reference that are undergoing significant change' (2012, 1). By change, she means that postcolonial literature itself is a label that is being superseded. Accordingly, any critical approach basing itself on that label or category is likely to be to that extent also superseded: 'the framework of postcolonial literary theory has become limiting because, essentially, the production of "postcolonial literature" per se is waning. [...] In short, contemporary and emerging writing has less in common with postcolonial literature from the second part of the 20th century than one might immediately appreciate' (2012, 2). She outlines many ways in which World Englishes literature explores themes and genres very different from those found in classics of postcolonial literature, for example, discussing *Bildungsroman* in Camroonian literature, crime-horror in Nigerian fiction, or erotica in Singapore (however, it should be remembered that postcolonial writers, following a logic given concise critical expression by Aijaz Ahmad (1992), were often themselves rather insistent that the label was unnecessarily limiting). Dawson Varughese's study has points of overlap with the present book, and is certainly attuned to the same apparent limitations in postcolonial studies. Her work brings together fieldwork and

29

sociology of literature, exemplifying one kind of post-disciplinary approach to literary studies. In her book she focuses on World Englishes literature from former British colonies. In each chapter the book follows this structure: 1. historical overview of Anglophone writing in the country; 2. manuscripts received in response to Dawson Varughese's call; 3. analysis of selected stories according to themes and trends; 4. interview (writer/publisher/academic). This is a very different approach from those that went before, and is very different in turn from the present book. Dawson Varughese's conclusion is that '"World Englishes literature" characterizes emerging literature, highlighting the employment of the English(es) of the place in the literature and the interest in the culture(s), country and peoples from which the literature is being produced' (2012, 228–229). By comparison with Dhillon and Lok, Dawson Varughese's aims are in some ways more modest. However, in terms of the originality of her contribution, and some of the underlying assumptions, her work will be a vital prompt for further reflection on the connections between postcolonialism and World Englishes.

Conclusion

By contrast with Dawson Varughese's movement beyond the postcolonial, which signals a movement beyond postcolonial literature and postcolonial literary studies, but remains a study of literature, the present book seeks to extend discussion of World Englishes and postcolonial studies in contexts beyond literature. On the assumption that the two disciplines come together, or can be made to communicate with one another, this book aims to apply the resulting insights to topics and questions that might seem on occasion only distantly connected, which will certainly lay it open to the charge of over-ambition. Bolton wonders about the dangers of Critical Linguistics producing a generation of linguistics scholars who know relatively little about their own discipline, and it is certainly possible that in exploring lexicography, global citizenship, and translation, this book will prove that its author knows relatively little about many of the disciplines it thereby takes in. That, however, is one obvious risk that is taken when trying to extend postcolonialism across the disciplines. It is arguable that postcolonialism is both too comfortable in its enclosed literary world, and yet at the same time cavalier in its pronouncements about related areas and disciplines. World Englishes studies, particularly insofar as they are identified with the kind of critical attention and knowledge exemplified by Kachru's own work, provide a vital model for the renewal of postcolonial studies.

Finally, while both World Englishes studies and postcolonial studies have been here and are elsewhere referred to as disciplines, it is more accurate to describe them as interdisciplines, as discussed earlier. This book brings them together, with their shared and also divergent emphases on language, globalization, histories of colonialism, etc, to see how they might be most productive in discussing English worldwide, which I take to be fundamentally (indeed, *ideally*, but of course not *entirely*) a discussion of English alongside other languages. The very different case studies come together to exemplify the other way in which the book concerns interdisciplines as defined by Bowman, inhabiting different discursive contexts both temporarily and to some extent strategically. As I discussed at length in the book's introduction, what unites all of these chapters, and directs the book's general argument, is a sense of what we might call postcolonial communication, as distinct from some familiar alternatives more usually assumed to constitute communication. The difficulty of communication is of course to some extent a problem with one idea of interdisciplinarity, which might seek to merge disciplines in pursuit of a kind of post-disciplinary consensus. Such an idea of interdisciplinarity implies that one might translate disciplines, taking discrete and possibly even static forms and putting them into dynamic relation. This idea, essentially one of *cultural* translation, is the focus of the next chapter and, as will be argued, it is an idea that is undermined by World Englishes.

CHAPTER 2

Grammars of Living Break their Tense: World Englishes and Cultural Translation

It is normally supposed that something always gets lost in translation; I cling, obstinately, to the notion that something can also be gained.

Salman Rushdie, 'Imaginary Homelands'

Introduction

When we consider the 'official' cultural translation demanded as part of immigration or naturalization, we can readily gauge the difficulties obscured by certain concepts of cultural translation. Consider the example of Singapore. Recent government projections suggest that Singapore's population will need to expand considerably in order to maintain economic growth. If that argument were to be accepted, the question would then become one of *managing* the necessary immigration, helping to produce the target identity 'Singaporean'. Unsurprisingly, one aspect of debates concerning this immigration has been the possibility of a language requirement, with the proposed language most often being English. For example, Vasu and Phua recall English's importance in the making of Singapore, and argue that it will continue to contribute to an inclusive vision of Singaporean identity. Indeed, they note that 'The argument that citizenship requires English competency is not novel' (2008, 34). Their comparisons are Australia, Canada, and New Zealand. It is no surprise that the UK is not on their list, partly because of colonial history, but also because of the facts of contemporary language policy. For if we switch our attention to UK immigration and naturalization requirements we do indeed find already existing language requirements (knowledge of English, Welsh, or Scottish Gaelic) that are often in the process of being fine-tuned. As part of those requirements, there is an exemption list for majority Anglophone nations, a notable absence from which is Singapore. So, one nation debating the possibility of introducing an English language requirement is pointedly if implicitly not an English-owning nation, according to another. How should we respond to this curious mismatch of perception and self-perception? Tempting as it may be simply to blame the ignorance and racism of those who devised UK language requirements, there are more interesting possibilities here. While I earlier mentioned a target identity, by analogy with target languages, intuitively English cannot work with that kind of model of success, which is both the one presupposed by Singaporean language policy, and something resisted by Singlish. That deliberate and instrumental language policies explicitly aimed for forms of cultural translation both within the apparently separate 'racial' communities of Singapore and within the broader Singaporean community is not in question. That these forms of officially sanctioned cultural translation have also been resisted, to some extent, is also I think not in question. Singlish, in common with other examples of World Englishes, seems to exemplify a very different and more open logic of cultural translation. However, as that latter category can be problematic, this chapter seeks to explore it both in the abstract and through the example of Singapore.

Of course, it is postcolonial studies that places much the greater rhetorical emphasis on cultural translation, particularly in its theories of hybridity, third space, and so on. World Englishes, however, certainly appear to be forms of cultural translation, but to argue this is not necessarily to celebrate it, not least because cultural translation is itself controversial. Objections to this concept are numerous, even when focusing solely on its English language form. For example, it might be argued that its mechanisms are left so vague, or described in such broad terms, that it is not meaningfully a concept at all. In the general and explicitly metaphorical terms employed by Salman Rushdie in the well-worn opening quotation, 'translation' becomes highly suggestive but also problematically open. Even in narrower terms, in the context of a discipline such as anthropology, the idea that the scholar was translating one culture into terms familiar to another was extremely complex and fraught (see Asad 1986). It might further be argued that in 'culture' the term foregrounds a troublesome word, as implied by Raymond Williams (1976), who famously calls it one of the three most complex words in the English language. A further and related objection is that in borrowing 'translation' thinkers of cultural translation arrogate translation's precarious magic without fulfilling any of the latter's responsibilities. These objections will be considered later, and have some justice. Principally, however, this chapter focuses on the ways in which the spread of English has resulted in forms of cultural translation leading to different forms of World Englishes. This chapter argues that there are important ways in which World Englishes exemplify processes of cultural translation, demonstrating the positive potential of those processes as well as possible pitfalls. Following Pennycook, it assumes that, 'English is always a language in translation, a language of translingual use' (2008, 34). However, this chapter also suggests that applying cultural translation to World Englishes forces us to consider both the concept's own potential and its problems. The focus on World Englishes makes them examples of cultural translation, partly as a response to the perception that, as Pratt suggests, when the concept is discussed it is frequently without specific examples (2010, 94). Especially for a concept as expansive as cultural translation it is necessary to ground speculation in actually existing processes and phenomena, and to that end this chapter considers the example of Singaporean English. However, it is also the case that examples of World Englishes might confirm the limitations of cultural translation as a concept, and responding to that possibility is a major focus of this chapter.

Before embarking on that discussion it is necessary to make further specific comments concerning the connection between World Englishes and cultural translation. As we have seen, World Englishes as a term emphasizes that the spread of English should not be described in terms of a monolithic global or world English, however much we might qualify such a term with recognitions of the diversity of English. The spread of English leads to a jarring but also exciting diversity of Englishes due to the different languages with which it is code-switched and mixed, and with which it jostles for attention. World Englishes are not reducible to one phenomenon, although their evident hybridity is a basis for shared discussion. If we discuss them on this shared basis, however, we see problems in the actual phenomenon of cultural translation, not least deriving from the ways in which English can overwhelm the languages with which it is brought into contact. Furthermore, thinking about these processes of contact in terms of cultural translation can itself be problematic, as it is not clear that World Englishes involve translation at all, given that non-Anglophone cultures again seem to be responding to the linguistic demands of economically and politically 'central' cultures. Accordingly, there are two potential issues here: that World Englishes are themselves somewhat problematic, and that cultural translation is a problematic concept in itself. One way of making the connection between World Englishes and cultural translation is to think about World Englishes in relation to bi- and multilingualism. Yet fears about the spread of English focus our attention on that other implicit term, monolingualism. That term is important because the spread of English seems to introduce a kind of monolingual imperialism in different languages and at different speeds (whether local, international, or transnational); cultural translation produces a cultural black hole, even if World Englishes do not overtly coerce monolingualism. Of course, in fact this chapter assumes that there is a certain bi- or multilingualism within English 'itself'. There are multiple versions of standard English, multiple standards within each standard, numerous dialect forms, and so on. Furthermore, World Englishes also introduce new multiplicities. Next, the idea of cultural translation might be an aspect of an outmoded research paradigm; Braj Kachru suggests that discussion of the spread of English has assumed that, 'monolingualism is the normal communicative behavior in which the mother tongue has a crucial function' (1996, 141). Finally, and more narrowly, thinking about monolingualism reminds us of Jacques Derrida, whose work can be fundamental to the understanding of linguistic imperialism; Derrida's enigmatic assertions (1998) on the original 'coloniality' of all culture remind us of the moment of stabilization necessary to the production of cultures. Rey Chow brings together these three emphases concerning monolingualism when discussing Derrida; she writes that in contemporary debates about language 'monolingualism often tends to be invoked pejoratively, with the implication that it can only be a parochial, impoverished, and shameful opposite to a sophisticated, cosmopolitan multilingualism' (2008, 226). This pejorative emphasis is understandable, although we should follow Chow in criticizing smug counting of languages spoken. If cultural translation is an aspect of monolingual stasis, then it is hardly a translation worth the name; as Pratt suggests, critics can be forgiven for seeing discussion of cultural translation as 'another plumed display of intellectual authority by privileged metropolitans who don't know any languages and still want to uphold their monopoly on ideas' (2010, 94). This chapter will consider this possibility by using World Englishes as examples of *another* cultural translation.

The Transparency of Global English

While the global spread of English appears an extension of linguistic imperialism, with both other languages and translation marginalized, World Englishes studies as a discipline is proof of increased interest in studying varieties of Englishes. These varieties show evidence of the complex and transversal movements of globalized culture. Indeed, World Englishes appear another example of the uneven magic of cultural translation. Of course, the promise of that latter term, as Boris Buden and Stefan Nowotny (2009) would suggest, is dangerously celebratory. This dangerously seductive promise should prompt us to pay attention to the uneven quality of the translation, especially when no 'translation proper' takes place, and English is reconfigured to meet the needs of a local population. As Kachru observes, 'the impact of World Englishes is Janus-like' (1996, 138), working on the English language as well as the other languages with which it is in daily contact. Under the influence of other languages, English undergoes processes of localization, acculturation, and sometimes indigenization. Meanwhile, other languages undergo processes of *Englishization*. Each of these processes is an aspect of a more general cultural translation, and in World Englishes such translation regularly occurs when no actual translation takes place.

Of course, the use of 'translation' in this context is problematic, and has been severely criticized. Furthermore, the term's limitations frequently disappear in the celebration of World Englishes that coincides with the basic assumptions of postcolonial theory (a central theoretical site in the discussion of that translation, as will be discussed later). Postcolonial theory has long been questioned for its apparent bias towards old imperial centres that it is theoretically opposing. For example, Graham Huggan highlights a neo-imperialist quality to postcolonialism as a 'critical industry'; he suggests that 'English is, almost exclusively, the language of this critical industry, reinforcing the view that postcolonialism is a discourse of *translation*, rerouting cultural products regarded as emanating from the periphery toward audiences who see themselves as coming from the centre' (2001, 4). Globalization and global English coincide with a consumerism bent on making cultural 'products' accessible to old imperial centres. Cultural translation is unidirectional, in this scenario, with the translation we see fundamentally governed by the demand of global English, and so ultimately by the desires, motivations, and assumptions of native speakers of English. Relatedly, we might argue that cultural translation functions as a kind of demand; as Harish Trivedi suggests, 'cultural translation is not so much the need of the migrant, as [Homi] Bhabha makes it out to be, but rather more a requirement of the society and culture to which he has migrated; it is a hegemonic Western demand and necessity' (2007, 284). This translation is assimilationist, and would most likely be inimical to the creativity of bi- or multilingual reality seen in so many cultures. Kachru is known for his emphasis on the significance of bilingual creativity, particularly in the context of outer circle countries like India or Singapore. It is Kachru's contention that creative vitality in English today is to be most readily found in such contexts; through this argument, he outlines a position familiar from various traditions in postcolonial studies, which tend towards a critical view of monolingualism as connected with imperialism. Comparative literature scholar Michael Holquist writes that 'Monolingualism has at its heart a passion for wholeness, a desire for unity, a lust for order in a world in which variety and contingency seem to rule' (2003, 24–25). From Holquist's position, which is shared by many postcolonial commentators, monolingualism represents a tyranny of the same that must be countered by a philosophy and politics of difference: let variety and contingency rule. Of course, it is not necessarily the case that bi- or multilingual expressiveness simply frees us all from any desire for wholeness, and nor will it necessarily produce a chaotic Babel. As Radhakrishnan suggests, the world is simultaneously 'pure' and 'impure', its languages pulling together and flying apart; he continues that this conflict characterizes, 'a world trying to understand itself through its one own cacophonous, contradictory, and unorchestrated modalities' (2003, 85). English is only one aspect of this cacophony, and in becoming Englishes is perhaps all the more characteristic of a world trying to understand itself.

While difficult to summarize opinion on the controversial issue of global English's investment in cultural translation, it is clear that overall the commentary is divided, and seeks either the (actually) negative or (potentially) positive in the global spread of English. One example of each position will be useful here. To begin with the negative consequences, Michael Cronin has argued that 'The fulsome rhetoric of global communications bringing us all closer together in the global village is in effect a form of bad faith if there is a failure to recognize that connectedness has as a necessary prerequisite the identification and maintenance of separateness' (2006, 121). The difficult question of balancing distinctiveness and connectedness will be discussed later. It is a question that touches upon fundamental philosophical questions about identity and difference, as well as on practical questions of policy and politics. Even in terms of policy, however, the question of balance is frequently raised, as it is difficult to argue that there is an ongoing linguistic conspiracy at work, implying instead that we focus our critical interest on the ways in which English's spread has happened 'naturally' (even if the discourse of the 'natural' is a dubious one that is a central issue). Of course, it could be argued that language policies have simply been too limited in scope to come to terms with the spread of English. In almost all cases, such policies operate on a national scale, when something supplementary and global in scale is now necessary. Proposing such a supplement, Jacques Maurais and Michael A. Morris write the following: 'A global linguistic strategy is needed which balances the ongoing spread of English with maintenance of linguistic diversity' (2003, 9). Interdependence deriving from globalization produces the danger of a creeping monolingualism that will continue to undermine linguistic ecology. Yet, at the same time, this danger partly derives from a lack of adaptation to changed contexts: it is necessary to make decisions on a different scale, and implement global language policy. English might well be an aspect of globalization's negative consequences, but it is also one that needs *managing*.

Alternatively, depending on our investment in the idea of a global citizenship, English as Englishes could instead be entirely appropriate linguistic markers and producers of the simultaneous belonging and non-belonging necessary for such a citizenship to function. For example, Tom McArthur, accepting the relevance of a limited Whorfianism, suggests the following:

> if anything can reduce the Sapir-Whorfian separateness of mind across languages it could be the flowing together of elements and structures from several languages into one language. If this is so, and if the world must have a single medium available to all, then it could be beneficial if that language is itself traditionally a hybrid and open to further hybridi-zation. (McArthur 2002, 15)

One way to approach McArthur's suggestion is to reduce it to two fundamental assumptions: the disadvantages of separateness, and a sense of English as (actually, although not intrinsically or necessarily) *hospitable*. Cronin, then, stresses that separateness should not be cancelled in the name of connect-edness or what postcolonial theory tends to call hybridity, and this stress derives from reasons of politics, policy, philosophy, and pragmatism. McArthur, meanwhile, advances the possibility that connectedness is an important step to more global understanding if not necessarily shared citizenship. McArthur, I would argue, envisages the processes through which World Englishes come about and continue to change to be processes of cultural translation. Of course

37

if we understand cultural translation as a fundamentally Anglophone demand placed on other linguistic cultures, we might then see World Englishes as only further forms of the linguistic imperialism fundamental to the global spread of English. There is simply not a big enough difference between global English and World Englishes, from that perspective. As we will now see, even critics sympathetic to the idea of cultural translation suggest that in practice it often enacts a kind of violence.

The Routine Violence of Linguistic Imperialism

It might be thought that the spread of English around the world, despite beginning with British imperial domination and extending through American power, is a process that can be at least adapted if not accepted. At the same time, however, the apparent 'historical accident' of English's spread clearly has ongoing negative consequences. As perhaps the key thinker on the ongoing domination exerted by the English language, Phillipson analyses different aspects of the spread of English in terms of 'linguistic imperialism', through which he suggests, 'the dominance of English is asserted and maintained by the establishment and continuous reconstitution of structural and cultural inequalities between English and other languages' (1992, 47). As already discussed, for Phillipson, the British empire gave way to the empire of English. Linguistic imperialism serves to support foreign policy objectives, economic domination, and other features of a contemporary globalization that is little more than an extension of earlier international inequalities. While, as I mentioned earlier, it would be possible to counter this argument by citing changes in relative economic and cultural power since 1992, when Phillipson's argument was given its fullest expression (changes relating to apparent American decline, or to the continued rise of the BRIC countries), that would be to miss the point that English's imperialism can function quite independently from the core countries with which it is associated. Beyond any real cultural, economic, or political influence, English is arguably a threat to linguistic ecologies across the world. Its threat is all the more potent for being detached from any directed or intentional manipulation, and has been normalized or naturalized: it is, as we will see, a form of *routine violence* (on that term, see Taussig 1992; Pandey 2006). Communication and the English language appear to go hand in hand in the global context. Accordingly, insofar as it seems to be mandatory to speak English in order to communicate most readily (indeed, *transparently*) in international contexts, we appear to be in a situation in which culturally linguistic violence has been internalized and accepted.

Phillipson is explicit in using hegemony as a concept that holds open the possibility of resistance to this violence: in needing consent, hegemony implies dissent, at least potentially. As he notes, 'Analyzing English linguistic imperialism in a context of hegemony, with its reproduction under continuous contestation and with its own internal contradictions, holds open the possibility of change' (1992, 76). Accordingly, while the brute reality of English domination seems insurmountable, in itself it implies resistance. Indeed, that resistance was evident throughout the colonial period and has been evident through to the globalized present. While much of that resistance is pedagogical or political, some of it is also aesthetic, in, for example, literary or cinematic form. Attempts have been made to theorize how English can be simultaneously used and not used, we might say, and a key term in this effort has been cultural translation. One example is the theorist and filmmaker Mieke Bal; in theorizing a version of cultural translation in terms of the *remainder* and accent, Bal addresses the question of global English's apparent unavoidability. She seeks 'a de-naturalization of translation into English as a world language' (2007, 111). Even advances in machine translation that have become facts of daily life, such as Google Translate, can resort to translation from one language through English into a third language. In that sense, even if people ceased feeling the need to learn English, its utility has found its way into mechanical and impersonal procedures, and so again it has been naturalized. In addressing this apparently unavoidability, Bal utilizes the concept of linguistic imperialism; she begins by asking, 'How can we work with, yet resist, the linguistic imperialism of English in the contemporary world?' (2007, 109). In other words, recognizing that there is indeed a certain necessity to using English, how can people for whom it is not a first language install a sense of difference within it? What Bal desires to retain is 'the precious promise of untranslatability' (2007, 110), something marked by accent, that which is 'the trace, the remainder, of the language the subject cannot speak', and also 'an extra, an unexpected resource' (2007, 110). When someone speaks a language that is apparently not their own, speaking with an accent is usually seen negatively. Bal explores what happens if we reverse this assumption: 'Instead of being a deviation of a smooth self-evident mainstream [...] accents that remind us of the translated quality of the words spoken can also be seen as cultural, specifically linguistic, enrichments' (2007, 111). Of course, the idea of non-accent is a kind of myth, as Lippi-Green (1997) argues; all native speakers speak with accents too, and Bal also seeks to defamiliarize the native voice. In fact, she goes on to discuss some specific examples of her own filmmaking that use editing techniques to lessen the routine violence of English, believing that the moving image is well placed to make the necessary cultural translation to challenge the violence of imposed global English. This kind of translation marks a resistance to the smooth translation (usually into English) expected by a globalization that operates in terms of units of *equivalence*; it is a translation that marks a resistance to reading. In discussing her film *Lost in Space* (2005), Bal emphasizes the ways its aesthetic registers the experience that the film theorizes: 'the dissociative nature of language in the realm of global English' (2007, 113). Here it is the lack of linguistic ownership that is felt most deeply, and it is felt as problem rather than potential.

In theorizing cultural translation, Bal draws on specific work from translation studies. One translator she cites is Lawrence Venuti, specifically for his exploration of the lack of translation in this realm of global English. Venuti is particularly interesting when he describes some of the political motivations underlying his translation practice. Describing his desire to 'shake the regime of English', he analyses his own choice of texts to translate. In a Deleuzian manner, he is interested in literature that will be 'useful in minoritizing the standard dialect and dominant cultural forms in American English'. He explains his preference through the following observation: 'This preference stems partly from a political agenda that is broadly democratic: an opposition to the global hegemony of English. The economic and political ascendancy of the United States has reduced foreign languages and cultures to minorities in relation to its language and culture' (1998, 10). Certain kinds of text offer possibilities for translations that make this apparent monolith foreign to itself; however, of course, Venuti acknowledges that even global English is not monolithic. Venuti's translations accord with Bal's interest in maintaining accent; through retaining or even exaggerating accent one resists being subsumed in the fluency of a monolingual globalization. Again this emphasis accords with her goal of defamiliarizing the native voice, mentioned earlier. Accent operates as a kind of solution to the problem of all cultures appearing instantly accessible to Anglo hegemony; through it Bal insists on actual labour in cultural translation, rather than 'smooth transparency'. Yet this emphasis raises certain questions. In Bal's example, a movie she made in which two non-native speakers (Bal and an asylum seeker fluent in Farsi and Greek) were forced to use English, it is certainly arguable that she 'becomes' the native speaker, in that the category is relative rather than absolute, and mobile rather than fixed (clearly, this mobility is structural, and no *choice* of Bal's). Such a possibility is a logical extension of Kingsley Bolton's (2008) suggestion that by using the category for speakers of, for example, Indian or Philippine English, we may better understand it as applied to speakers of American or British English. As already mentioned, such a shift in emphasis helps remind us that all native speakers have accents anyway, which is something that native speakers themselves can lose sight of, and something that global English underplays. It is also something that the diversity of World Englishes forces on our consciousness, as will now be explored.

The Translation of World Englishes

World Englishes introduce a clear difficulty in categorizing all forms of English as 'imperialist'. While it may be possible to think of the native speaker Englishes as fundamentally equivalent, and then identify these Englishes with a hegemonic global English, it is rather more difficult to equate that linguistically imperialist English with phenomena such as Hinglish or Singlish. Of course, as we will see, in a location such as Singapore there are also people who insist upon the importance of an exonormative standard English, associated once with British English, now perhaps with American English. However, there is something else in process and progress, something irreducible to yet more instances of linguistic imperialism, even if that imperialism remains a constant presence, to be reckoned with and guarded against. It is not just that English is now spoken by so many communities that the association of the language with a distinct community breaks down; it is also that English itself translates and is translated, being both a medium through which cultures are forced and one that is thereby made other to itself. These forms of translation derive from the frequently proclaimed need for a lingua franca to serve globalization. A lingua franca, through its use for exchange beyond native speakers, seems like a language that cannot be owned by any one national community; indeed, Nicholas Ostler sees the history of English as a challenge to the easy association of languages with communities: 'for the world's leading lingua franca, the whole concept of a language community begins to break down' (2005, 24). The reasons why English no longer defines a community are some of the same reasons that globalization is not simply Americanization, or Westernization. While we have been globalized before, we discuss globalization as something relatively recent to the extent that new technologies have introduced a qualitative change in experience.

These changes will be discussed in greater detail later, but are obviously potentially relevant to the study of World Englishes. Sociologist John Urry (2003) isolates five distinct elements of globalization: structure, flow, ideology, performance, and complexity. Structure refers to increasing (largely corporate) global and international interaction. Flows prompt us to understand individuals, corporations, etc. as nodes in the series of *scapes*, along which flow objects, people, images, etc. Ideology refers in particular to neo-liberal assumptions about the natural qualities of global capital's organization. Performance sees globalization as less a state of affairs and more of an enactment or process. Complexity, finally, helps us to understand globalization as system or series of systems, characterized by their overlapping and disjunctive organization. The most pertinent of these elements for the study of World Englishes are *flows*, *performance*, and *complexity*. We can no longer assume that information is all flowing in one direction. The so-called global system was often imagined to be polarized between centres and peripheries, with the centres dominating the peripheries, and the peripheries dependent on the centres; this model operates explicitly in Phillipson's analysis of linguistic imperialism. However, of course there are centres and peripheries within nations, such as the US or China; indeed, there are disproportionately powerful financial centres that function much the same way as countries (as in the case of London). In such a changed situation, it is necessary to rethink our paradigm when it comes to English. The term World Englishes introduces significant new assumptions about the state of the language, and moves us beyond paradigms stressing a stable distinction between native and non-native speakers. In examples from across both formerly colonized countries and locations that have never been formally colonized, it is possible to see new instances of agency and cultural identity in World Englishes. In particular, it could be argued that the study of World Englishes assumes the necessity of the theory of the performative (although such a theory may well be impossible), given that Englishes are not expressions of pre-existing identities, but instead are part of processes that produce new identities characterized by the complex flows of globalization.

While routine linguistic violence can still be a major aspect of these complex flows, it is becoming more difficult to ascribe blame to a centred linguistic power, or to claim (for example) that the spread of English serves the foreign policy aims of Anglophone nations. Increasingly, the diagnosis of linguistic imperialism has been refused by those apparently subject to that imperialism. To take one example, Nigeria, Joseph Bisong responds directly to Phillipson by arguing that, 'Arguments that carry the implication that the users of [English] do not know what is in their interest should not be seen simply as patronizing. They reveal a monolingual failure to grasp the complex nature of a multilingual and multicultural society' (1995, 131). Nigeria cannot be grasped or indeed defended from a rapacious Anglophone monolingualism from a perspective that assumes monolingualism as norm (although it should be noted that Phillipson does not assume that). The Nigerian context is one in which translation happens all the time and which is also *in* cultural translation, to the extent that we might find it difficult to be sure of the bounds of the languages we find in that space. This question of counting languages (for example, in a national space such as Singapore, we might officially count four: English plus Mandarin plus Malay plus Tamil) gets to the heart of the question of cultural translation. Naoki Sakai raises this question when he wonders about differentiating Japanese and English as clearly bounded linguistic entities; he asks, 'Can the multiplicity of languages without which translation seems unnecessary be measured numerically, so that one can assume that languages are countable? What constitutes the unitary unit of a language that is not implicated in another language or other languages?' (1997, 3). In asking these questions, Sakai is again raising the difficult question of connectedness and separateness. In her commentary, Rey Chow writes that '[For Sakai] translation is not simply an act of transfer between units of two self-contained languages which exist regardless of whether translation takes place. Rather, he sees translation as the a priori condition, the very ground that enables linguistic exchange to proceed *as though* languages were autonomous, individuated phenomena' (2012, 133). Such frameworks operate with the same assumptions informing many (but not all) postcolonial theories of hybridity. As we will see, Homi K. Bhabha's understanding of cultures is that they are effects of processes of stabilization, rather as Sakai imagines languages. It is important to grasp this if we are to understand cultural translation as a concept, and how it might relate to discussion of World Englishes. World Englishes globalize and make explicit the contact zone out of which stabilization eventually comes, while raising questions about future stabilizations or codifications, given changed technological conditions.

According to postcolonial theory, perhaps the most important aspect of this contact zone is its agonistic quality. It is not that it is oppositional exactly, more that there is necessary conflict rather than non-political harmonious hybridization. Cultural translation often seems to be a neutral process with broadly positive outcomes. However, it occurs without guarantees, and is anything but neutral. Cronin raises this issue explicitly; referring to a 'tyranny of compliance' (2009, 218), he argues that cultural translation is evidence of a tendency to avoid confrontation: 'the notion of cultural translation highlights an even more fundamental feature of contemporary societies than the oft-repeated lingering hegemony of nation states, namely an intolerance of conflict' (2009, 217). One aspect of this intolerance is found in contemporary media, whose very form implies 'balance', but through which a pithily reduced and reproduced symmetry forms: 'in reality, points of view are irreducible, as speakers are situated very differently, both materially and structurally, but the false symmetrization of the media sphere conceals the very genuine conflict of interests through the irenic fiction of the representative soundbite' (2009, 218). Of course, this symmetrization is *false* in the specific sense that the symmetry is something that has to be achieved rather than being something that pre-exists, but also to the extent that the implied translatability or accessibility is unidirectional, when it would have to be multidirectional to avoid recurrent structures of linguistic and cultural domination. While conflict is fundamental, Cronin argues that translation grants us insights into how to convert conflict into engagement. In this, he is writing against the oppositional theory of translation, insisting as he does that, 'translation is not confrontation; it is conflict as engagement with the multidimensionality of texts, languages and cultures' (2009, 218). Developing his argument in this way, Cronin himself seems to be extending translation into a concept of cultural translation.

Indeed, in the work just cited Cronin is participating in explicit discussion of cultural translation; this work is his response to the discussion of the concept by Boris Buden and Stefan Nowotny in the journal *Translation Studies*. Buden and Nowotny take a balanced view of the concept; indeed, they make the point that cultural translation is a concept that has no *necessary* meaning: 'the concept of cultural translation can be generally understood and applied in the service of both the contradictory paradigms of postmodern theory and postmodern political visions: essentialist multiculturalism and its counterpart, deconstructionism' (2009, 198). They give the example of a citizenship test in which one is translated into being German through demonstrating knowledge of a quite openly arbitrary selection of cultural details (the name of a particular art exhibition, etc.). Cultural translation can operate as a demand to which one must respond and acquiesce in order to be translated. Accordingly, they argue, theorists such as Judith Butler and Bhabha are unable to avoid the possibility that cultural translation is part of a fixing process through which occurs 'the transmutation of translational processes into yes-or-no questions' (2009, 203). One might wonder if this other cultural translation that makes demands is still worthy of the name, and yet it is clear that Buden and Nowotny are raising an important objection in that the idea of translating across cultures implies a steadiness if not fixedness of cultural identity. Responses to Buden and Nowotny, such as that of Robert J.C. Young (see Ha, Lieven, and Young 2010), question their presentation of Derrida and the ideas of cultural translation that derive from his work, for example, in Bhabha. Accordingly, it is now time to discuss Bhabha's work in terms of one specific example, and the theory of hybridity that coalesces around it. Bhabha's understanding of cultural translation raises the issue of how and why cultures are brought to a 'halt', and asks the same questions as Buden and Nowotny, if in a different way.

As we have seen, cultural translation is a contested concept, if it can be considered a coherent concept at all. Critics argue that its metaphorical appropriation of 'translation' serves to undermine actual translation and multilingualism, or at least can serve to undermine them. Furthermore, it appears that the concept derives at least partly from a school of thought, postcolonialism, that ought to be central and unambiguous in its opposition to English linguistic imperialism. In order to think through this apparent paradox it is helpful to consider the very example that Harish Trivedi mentions in his criticism of cultural translation: Bhabha. Buden and Nowotny, as we have already seen, discuss Bhabha as an example of a critic whose theories of cultural translation appear incapable of facing its darker possibilities, and whose personal history implies a particularly narrow framework from which the idea springs. They suggest that, 'cultural translation may not only be a vehicle of progressive development, but also a means of exclusion that finally turns its promise of liberation into oppression' (2009, 201). Like Trivedi, they see the over-emphasis on cultural translation's promise as deriving from a privileged diasporic perspective that is unable to face the truth of its rarefied cosmopolitanism. You can only unreservedly desire the proliferation of hybridity if that proliferation is already part of the cultural and intellectual milieus in which you participate. To some extent, Bhabha, and by extension postcolonialism, is understood to be utopian. If we understand World Englishes as themselves examples of cultural translation, then again we might be responding to an understandable but regrettable utopianism, one that ignores the routine violence of English as the assumed and transparently communicative linguistic norm.

However, there are other ways to understand Bhabha, in particular his arguments concerning the constitution of cultures, and his development of a specific and important notion of cultural translation. In order to understand the important connection between postcolonial theory and World Englishes, it is then necessary to begin with Bhabha's understanding of how cultures come into being. Instead of conceiving them as discrete objects of theoretical contemplation, Bhabha views them as consequent on stabilizing processes that act upon a flux of hybridity. It is well known that he develops many ways of describing this flux, but a particularly striking one is the notion of 'third space': '[T]he importance of hybridity is not to be able to trace two original moments from which the third emerges, rather hybridity to me is the "third space" which enables other positions to emerge. This third space displaces the histories that constitute it, and sets up new structures of authority, new political initiatives, which are inadequately understood through received wisdom' (1994, 211). Such a sense of hybridity is connected to Cronin's attempts to think the combination of separateness and connectedness. Hybridity is fundamental, undermining claims to absolute cultural identities, and yet such identities are real effects enabled by hybridity. Bhabha puts emphasis on how hybridity enables us to imagine different positions, or different cultural identities, distinct from the ones that arose during the colonial period. Flux might be just what exists, linguistically speaking, and it can be difficult to resist attempting to maintain that flux or hybridity (see Pennycook 2008).

Returning to Bhabha's arguments concerning culture, it is arguable that Cronin's position regarding the irreducibility of conflict is suggestively reminiscent of postcolonial theoretical assumptions. For example, in delineating cultural *difference* as opposed to cultural *diversity* (e.g., 1994, 34–36), Bhabha argues that models of multiculturalism follow a logic of cultural translation even when they explicitly resist ideologies of assimilation. That is because they imagine contexts (usually national) accommodating harmonious accumulations of cultural forms. His logic of cultural translation, by contrast, insists on the point of conflict; Bhabha stresses agonism without necessarily imagining resulting progress as we might unthinkingly use that word. Accordingly, what is required is a form of cultural negotiation, without which cultural translation can lapse into coercion or unthinking repetition of cultural coexistence. We can understand Bhabha to be arguing, like Cronin, for translation as something that forces us to rethink our models of multidirectional engagement. Indeed, this engagement is fundamental to the postcolonial paradigm, a paradigm that assumes a fundamental level of difference, hybridity, or cultural translation. Hybridity goes 'all the way down', and cultural translation (e.g., translation of 'the English book' in diverse and unpredictable forms (1994, 161)) is inevitable. Accordingly, Bhabha's position is that we cannot imagine cultures as entities that exist and would then later be translated; instead, cultures are the effect of processes of stabilization. Difference is what there is, and its denial, or rather its resolution into distinct self-same cultural identities, produces colonial authority. That authority, however, must be produced and therefore is never a final achievement (e.g., 1994, 326). It is unsurprising that Bhabha uses the concept of the performative to explain this cultural translation, because of the influence of Derrida's work, some of which concerned J.L. Austin (e.g., Derrida 1988). As already mentioned, studies of World Englishes have also adapted Austin's concept in order to analyse the distinctiveness of World Englishes speech acts (e.g., Nelson 1991; Y. Kachru 1998) or to celebrate the difference-in-adaptation of English (e.g., Pennycook 2008). It should be noted that a writer such as Pennycook is rather more interested in Derrida's sense of the performative than writers such as

Nelson and Kachru, who are more interested in how linguists have taken up the work of Austin as well as Grice and John Searle. The postcolonial sense of the performative, derived by Bhabha from Derrida's work, is illustrated in the many forms of World Englishes, but the next section returns to the famously vibrant example of Singapore, partly because its language policy has been so clearly based on a model that distinguishes *desirable* and *undesirable* forms of cultural translation.

My Neighbour is Another Language: English in Singapore

Writing on shifts in *Chinese* language policy in Singapore, specifically those planned by its government since 2004, Charlene Tan (2006) outlines a fascinating example of the accumulative version and vision of cultural diversity. Recognizing that educational materials were outdated and inadequate in light of China's recent transformation, the Singaporean government developed plans for the creation of a 'bicultural elite' that would be best placed to engage with the reality of China today. This elite would exemplify, exaggerate, and make explicit the logic implied by Mandarin being the mandated language of the Singaporean Chinese community. The education system would translate them for a very specific purpose, and would offer some fairly clear rewards for students who could excel (scholarships, employment, etc.). This example is contrary to Bhabha's understanding of cultures in some clear ways, but its interest lies in what it demonstrates about the official attitude towards language and policy; there is little left to the imagination here, but what Singapore reveals is relevant to broader questions in the study of World Englishes, as this section will explore. Much of this chapter has outlined connections between cultural translation and World Englishes at a theoretical level, running the risk identified by Pratt of continuing to assert dominion over otherness. Accordingly, it is important to stress again the importance of discussing *examples* of cultural translation, and to focus on something other than a theoretical example, however important Bhabha may be. The utility of ideas of third space and hybridity has been questioned, tested, and demonstrated on numerous occasions in diverse postcolonial contexts, and it is intuitively a useful category for understanding World Englishes.

The specific example on which this section focuses is Singlish, recognized for a long time as something that elicits often wildly different reactions (e.g., McCrum Cran, and MacNeil 1986, 370–371). The Singaporean government's Speak Good English Campaign gives a clear sense of what is at stake in its 'translations' of Singlish into a standard English. For example, 'You ask me I ask who' becomes 'I don't know', while 'Off your handphone, lah' is corrected to (the poster switching from cross to tick) 'Please turn off your mobile phone'. The National University of Singapore, meanwhile, urges the Promotion of Standard English (PROSE), with its own set of translations; 'Why you never bring come?' becomes 'Why didn't you bring it?', and 'He take go already' becomes 'He has taken it with him'. The extent to which this prescriptive drive is a public issue is clear from the case of the comedy show *Phua Chu Kang* (1997–2007), whose main character (PCK) became so closely identified with Singlish that people began to refer to 'Phua Chu Kanglish' (as implied by a brief reference in Jack Neo's (2002) movie *I Not Stupid*). As Selvaraj Velayutham notes, government comments on the dangers of the show's influence were followed by actual interventions (2007, 134). Following these interventions, the show developed rather playful storylines incorporating PCK's attempts to rid himself of Singlish ('I haven't said "lah" for three weeks', he wistfully remarks), including the appearance (in season 3 episode 1) of a British Council teacher who seems alarmingly laissez-faire in his attitudes (he corrects the pronunciation of 'Aloysisus' (and is corrected back), and gently informs PCK that 'Arsenal' is not a place, but is rather relaxed about Singlish). Ultimately, PCK comes to the depressing realization (in season 5 episode 9) that he is maybe no longer a 'Beng' (a particular stereotypical identity associated with young Chinese men), which seems to indicate that he has been translated out of his identity, an identity expressed by and also partly produced by speaking Singlish. According to Velayutham, government intervention on this matter, in common with others relating to Singaporean culture and memory, seeks, 'to undermine the sorts of organic "we-ness" that emerges with hybrid cultural products such as Singlish' (2007, 150). The vitality of Singlish indicates the need to balance perspectives with a more descriptive response, through which it might be seen as promoting inter-ethnic exchange, or (more persuasively and fundamentally) as functioning as an insider language.

The linguistic conditions leading to this vital and controversial form of English are complex. Of course, it is certainly arguable that (for good or ill) it is not recognizably a form of English at all. Positively, we might argue that to continue to think of Singlish as a form of English, to judge it by standards that are either 'colonialist' or 'international', is to misunderstand the processes of creative adaptation that have produced it. Negatively, we might argue instead that Singlish has lost its status as a form of English, and now stands as an obstacle between Singaporeans and international intelligibility. That, of course, has been the Singaporean government's position, given clear expression on numerous occasions (see Bruthiaux 2010). This position reminds us just how closely connected are theories of language identity with practices of language policy in Singapore. Lee Kuan Yew, recalling the moment of the split from the Federation of Malaysia, asks, 'How were we to create a nation out of a polyglot collection of migrants from China, India, Malaysia, Indonesia and several other parts of Asia?' (1998, 22). What a collection of translated men and women the inhabitants of Singapore, 1965, must have seemed, cut off from their neighbours and requiring dynamic leadership. That leadership was provided by a somewhat smaller collection of translated men, led by Lee, and a key aspect of their leadership was specifically linguistic. In his memoir, Singapore's first prime minister recalls his linguistic context growing up in the 1920s, reflecting that he spoke English to his parents, pidgin Malay mixed with Chinese to his grandparents, and Malay mixed with Hokkien to his own friends. 'Mandarin was totally alien to me, and unconnected with my life' (1998, 35). In reflections on learning Mandarin, he reminds us of the purpose of this language for Singapore's Chinese community: 'it is very important that we keep Chinese, not just for economic reasons, but for reasons of identity, sense of self, and pride in our own culture and civilization' (2005, 42). These comments give a clear sense of how Lee imagines his story to be *the* Singapore story, and demonstrate exactly why personal linguistic experience was translated into political linguistic policy. Keeping 'his' Mandarin 'alive' is basically a matter of learning it (at the age of 32), and its transformation from the language of 1 per cent of Singapore's Chinese population into the language that 'unites' it is a very clear example of the force of political will Singapore has shown in language policies that both insist on cultural translation (making everyone 'Singaporean') and yet resist it (to the extent that English might become Singlish).

Language policy has evolved from being integral to a 'melting pot' perspective to being an aspect of an idea of Singapore based on 'overlapping circles'. Singaporean 'multiracialism' defines three fundamental identities that are kept distinct and identified with single languages: Mandarin, Malay, and Tamil. Other languages are not encouraged, and are not officially part of these identities. For example, although Hokkien is the home language of around 75 per cent of the Chinese community, it is understood to be a 'dialect'. Mandarin is, as already mentioned, the language that unites the Chinese community, even if the Speak Mandarin Campaign, launched in 1979, continues to give official credibility to the fear that the language is often not spoken well (the campaign's English name is notable in what is omitted when compared with the Speak Good English Campaign). The other 'racial' communities are also united around their languages, which provide what is referred to as cultural 'ballast', helping to maintain 'Asian Values' and guard against the potential corruption that attends English (see Lee 2000; Han 2011). English, the language policy insists, is both essential for giving access to 'new knowledge' (technological and economic power) and dangerously decadent in its threat to 'old knowledge' (traditional cultural values). Singlish, it would seem, is evidence that the dangers of English have blurred the boundaries of the other languages which it is supposed to be only *alongside* in Singapore. While Edgar Schneider, summarizing a common perspective, discusses Singaporean English (including Singlish) as 'the means of expression of [a] newly emerging Asian-cum-Western culture' (2007, 156), other commentators are less positive in their interpretations. Debbie G.E. Ho (2006) argues that Singlish is evidence that Singaporeans are stuck in a form of 'cultural limbo', translated men and women who never quite finished the process of translation. *That* understanding of translation is, of course, the issue. It suggests that there are two or more pre-existing cultures that come together, leading to a form of 'bad' hybridity from which they are then unable to escape. But, as is quite explicitly the case in Singapore, the identity of 'Chinese

Singaporean' as produced through linguistic policy (alongside other policies) is an *effect*. It is obviously then difficult to see that identity as simply being corrupted or undermined through linguistic exposure to English, Hokkien, and so on (indeed, it might seem that Hokkien and other Chinese languages were violently thrust aside in favour of Mandarin).

Objectively, it might seem striking that such a situation arose, and that such linguistic policies were implemented; as Annaliese Kramer-Dahl puts it,

> That cultural decisions of such enormity could be made unilaterally by the minority English-educated Chinese elite of the time and could be so successfully implemented that 20 years later local native languages and cultures have been eradicated attests to the fact that most Singaporeans had willingly accepted the inherent legitimacy of particular languages, as well as the legitimacy of those who had determined which languages count. (Kramer-Dahl 2003, 187)

It might also seem that anxiety concerning the use of Singlish, surely one of the most famous of the World Englishes and a clear example of cultural translation, marks the unnecessarily long-standing influence of that small elite. Nonetheless, the first category of cultural translation (a form of 'either–or', as Buden and Nowotny might put it) was clearly accepted as fundamental, as least for a time. That the debate over Singlish continues to function in terms of that model of cultural translation is more regrettable. Wendy Bokhorst-Heng, indeed, argues that the different discursive constructions of Singlish (a language form that is necessarily impossible to demarcate) demonstrate that 'the debate unfolds within the more general socio-political processes of the imagining of the nation' (2005, 205). This again brings to mind Benedict Anderson's work, but also specifically Bhabha's comments on the ways in which there is a tension between the pedagogical and performative in the work of imagining the nation (e.g., 1994, 145). The extent to which Singaporean language policy attempts to remain on the side of the pedagogical, whilst having been from the beginning explicitly performative, demonstrates the great difficulty involved, but also perhaps the impossibility of such work remaining the sole responsibility of a restricted group of decision-makers.

What kind of cultural translation actually happens as and through Singlish? Cultural translation in Singapore, as embodied in code-mixing and code-switching, has a specific set of functions, it appears. As Alsagoff argues, 'such shifts are more saliently used to establish, represent, negotiate and signal identity, group membership and cultural orientations' (2010a, 336). But these are shifts not between two clearly defined language forms, as in diglossia; instead, they are movements within a zone of cultural translation that is complex and diverse, as Alsagoff suggests: 'In a move towards a more holistic understanding of the indigenization of English in a context such as Singapore, it is imperative that language be seen as a means of identity formation and representation, where local appropriations of global forms by speakers to construct and represent their thought, practices and culture are realized as fluid variations in a multidimensional discursive space' (2010b, 126). Singaporean cultural translation seems to retain this fluidity, at least for now, in terms of what we might call *glocalization-from-below*. While that might sound as though it verges on the tautological, it is clear that glocalization is sometimes imposed by authorities within a local context. Of course, 'from below' stereotypically appears to be something that the Singaporean context discourages. Indeed, government policy first encouraged and then halted this translation. Initially it worked to stabilize so-called racial identities through linguistic and other processes of translation, then it sought to guard against further translations away from 'Asian values'. However, in the development of Singlish, we find a further form of cultural translation away from the fixities of 'Asian' and 'Western' cultures. Only in the most pessimistic of diagnoses could this further cultural translation be understood as loss rather than gain.

Conclusion

It is important to remain cautious in discussing World Englishes as cultural translation, as, by contrast with the dynamism of Singapore, other examples are still both imposed and imperialist. It is also worth remembering that no theory could account for every aspect of all the Englishes that have developed, given the diversity of political, economic, and cultural contexts in which they have gained their different degrees of prominence. Indeed, it might appear that while we can differentiate real translation from cultural translation, it is also necessary to differentiate forms of cultural translation themselves, if we are to find value in the latter concept. The principal ways to differentiate these forms would be, first, to acknowledge that there is a form of cultural translation that implies only translation of cultures and subjects according to the demand of monolingual Anglophone cultures. Such a cultural translation through English would remain an aspect of linguistic imperialism. In other disciplines, such as anthropology, this charge has been levelled at processes of cultural translation that seek to translate one culture into the terms of another, principally because it is so difficult to salvage this translation practice from its evidently unequal power relations. In postmodern ethnography, one of the strategies adopted to foreground the power relations in cultural translation is to open texts to their apparent objects, i.e., to stress the agency of the culture studied, and to allow the observed to become observers. It should then be stressed that cultural translation as an aspect of World Englishes is unavoidably bound up with the agency of speakers of World Englishes. Accordingly, this form of cultural translation needs to be described distinctly.

Second, differentiation of useful forms of cultural translation also requires acknowledgment that Englishes and Englishization (i.e., other languages affecting English and English affecting other languages) are evidence of a bi- or multilingualism within English. Indeed, Tom McArthur refers to a 'bilingualism within world English' (1998, 32), while Edmund Weiner suggests that, 'The English vocabulary is now federated rather than centralized. No one person's English is all English, but each English speaker is to some extent "multilingual" within English. We are competent in varieties of English in which we do not perform' (1980, 501). Weiner is discussing the dictionary, hence the emphasis on vocabulary, but we are implicitly invited to extend the argument. The fact is, however, that while cultural translation can be found in so many examples from World Englishes, and speakers of World Englishes might indeed be both the translated and translators, there is a danger that the study of World Englishes remains an instance of an Anglophone academic imperialism. Indeed, without some exploration of the heterolingual address, as delineated by Sakai and extended by Buden and Nowonty, we (that 'we' already being undermined by Sakai's heterolingualism) risk being the 'monolingual' Anglophone academic subjects studying others in all their gloriously accessible and translatable object-hood. Further, being bilingual within English might seem to imply that no other bilingualism is as important, when of course the stronger versions of bilingualism within English derive from and occur within multilingual contexts such as those in which World Englishes thrive. Moreover, as Ashok Bery reminds us, 'The culturally translated are translating even as they are being translated – they are not just being observed, they are observing' (2009, 215). That applies to researchers as well, who would do well to explore processes by which they might translate and transform their own paradigms. In any case, as has been widely noted, scholarly interest in English and Englishes is now a worldwide phenomenon, which is all the more reason to situate our interventions in cultural translation. If all of us are indeed global citizens, with some kind of access to Englishes, it will become increasingly important to insist upon internal differentiation, as the next chapter will explore.

CHAPTER 3

English in the Conversation of Mankind: World Englishes and Global Citizenship

English allows us to advance toward global exchange and solidarity among the institutions of civil society, extending bonds between citizens far and wide across the globe. For this reason, considering English as an international language can also bring a sense of possibility in terms of strengthening what might be called 'planetary citizenship', i.e. alliances among citizens with a universalist intent.

Telma Gimenez, 'ETS and ELT: Teaching a World Language'

Introduction

Scanning the shelves in one of Shanghai's bookshops reveals that there is not only a clear appetite in China for English language materials but also, and unsurprisingly, a well-developed local industry in textbooks for learning English. Many textbook covers currently bear the charismatic face of Barack Obama, as we are invited to buy selections of his interviews, TV debates, and best speeches ('Wisdom on the tongue', 'Yes, you can!'), and through these examples learn how to speak like Obama himself. A very particular model of communication seems to have made its way to centre stage under globalization, and it is one that, while not necessarily requiring the English language, is certainly associated with English, whether British or more likely American. Obama appears to be the very best example of this model of communication and, if China is any indication, this communicative model is not necessarily felt to be linguistically imperialist. Is it possible, speaking idealistically, for all our diverse voices to conduct our global conversation in English? Michael Oakeshott (1962) famously argued for the role of poetry in 'the conversation of mankind', a conversation that was very much not an argument with a sense of directedness, expected resolution, or feared assimilation of one voice to another. Of course, from the perspective of critics of linguistic imperialism, English is without question an assimilative force, one that has been used to win arguments, arguments that were initially framed in terms beneficial to Anglo-American centres. Indeed, Oakeshott stresses the need for a 'diversity of voices', which in one sense is lost under the sway of English's hegemony. Yet there are other ways of understanding the spread of English, as we have already considered. This chapter will discuss the connection between English and global citizenship through considering shifts in scale brought about by globalization, different models of global citizenship, English's role in global institutions, cosmopolitanism, and alternatives to English. Through all of these sections runs the necessary shift in perspective from English to Englishes, a shift that enables a *potentially* positive connection to be made between English and global citizenship, even as the baleful influence of English's spread must also be acknowledged. There is the possibility or the coexistence of both leap and fall, with hard cultural and economic reality constantly shadowing the more optimistic rhetoric about English as a medium of global communication (with that hard reality invading the optimism through the very term 'communication'). Indeed, the other extreme side of Obama's current popularity in English learning materials in China is someone such as *Crazy English*'s Li Yang, a man for whom English learning is a patriotic duty (see Bolton 2003; Gao 2012). Communication would then be very much a question of winning arguments, a diversity of voices something that should ultimately pay its respects to authority.

In fact, this coexistence of leap and fall can immediately be found in then presidential candidate Obama's invocation of global citizenship in a speech delivered in Berlin in July 2008. This speech is an excellent place to begin this chapter's exploration of connections between English and global citizenship; indeed, Robert McCrum (2010) also uses this speech as part of his discussion of 'globish', although he discusses the speech uncritically. Obama suggests that, despite differences between America and Europe, 'the burdens of global citizenship continue to bind us together. [...] Partnership and cooperation among nations is not a choice; it is the one way, the only way, to protect our common security and advance our common humanity' (2008). Through his appeal to the ideal of global citizenship, and describing himself as a fellow citizen of the world, Obama recalls the shared histories of Europe and the US over the course of the twentieth century. Speaking in English, naturally (but given the speech's venue, not inevitably, and so not in fact naturally at all), Obama implicitly grants that the differences between the two are very much a case of the narcissism of minor differences. That English itself is both a cause for controversy and a part of everyday working life both in Brussels and more generally across Europe (despite the UK's vocal if only apparent problems with the continent), matches the sense that Obama is addressing not 'those left behind in a globalized world' (whether in Burma, Iran, Zimbabwe, or Darfur) but is instead assuming a citizenship shared with those in Europe, one to

53

which others ought to aspire (and indeed many such others do have those aspirations). Later I will return to the question of Europe's relationship with the English language, partly as a way of thinking about regional citizenships, and partly as an example of practical engagement with English in terms of governance. But, of course, subject position frames debates such as these in diverse ways, and it is important to recall that even the English-speaking global elite is not quite as homogeneous as it may seem. That being said, there are surprising aspects to the debates considered in this chapter, and not all the surprises are directly or solely relevant to that elite. Even acting with high-handed indifference to the fate of hundreds of millions, the English-speaking elite is not the only group of English speakers out there, and we would best begin by recalibrating our expectations regarding connections between the language and the world econocultural system (see Brutt-Griffler 2002, 110). That recalibration is partly a question of *scale*, as this chapter now considers.

Re-scaling English

Writing of the challenges facing democratic thought under globalization, David Held (2010) describes today's world as made up of *overlapping communities of fate*. In this situation, sometimes understood as a new state of affairs and sometimes as an extension or intensification of earlier networked cultures, there is a need for new models of governance and citizenship. Much discussion of this need has advanced the case for different versions of global citizenship, usually not as a replacement for but instead as a supplement to national citizenship. Language enters these discussions in various ways, for example in relation to practical governance, or alternatively the imagination necessary for transnational empathy. Language is also, in postcolonial studies, a key aspect of discussion of nationalism, as in the idea of imagined communities. Such communities have been extended if not of course undermined. and the idea of global citizenship is partly one of a transnational imagined community. If English is the language of globalization, this association clearly bears on the nature of the global citizenship we have and the citizenship we might desire to construct. One response to English puts its spread in the context of international documents addressing human rights. It might appear that English will be the language of such documents, even if that does not (indeed *must* not) imply that the legal frameworks thereby put in place are somehow English (British, American, or related) (see Toolan 2003). Of course, it is also possible that English (or indeed any other language) is simply unable to function in this neutral fashion when framing universal human rights. Our unease concerning English could be focused here on the issue of specific *language* rights (see Skutnabb-Kangas and Phillipson 1994). Additionally, as already suggested, we might be concerned about the export of specific ideas of communication, which operate to impose certain cultural norms even when no specific language is necessarily imposed (see Cameron 2002; Kayman 2004). Global citizenship implies at least some of the time the defence of the local, and that defence is obviously necessary in the specific case of local linguistic cultures. But there is an interweaving of practical and metaphorical levels again that sometimes blinds us to the potential of World Englishes precisely as contributions to this defence, and accordingly this chapter will address both practical and more metaphorical dimensions of the connection between English and global citizenship, in the spirit of grasping some of the potential of English as well as the obvious and numerous problems there are in thinking of it as that language.

Returning to the place of English in universities worldwide, we can focus on the responsibility for educating global citizens. In their study of the intersection of universities and global citizenship, Rhoads and Szelényi argue that 'the crises of the twenty-first century increasingly will need to be confronted by individuals consciously thinking and acting as global citizens' (2011, 258). They see a key role for universities in educating 'globally informed collectivist citizens' (2011, 287), which they examine through case studies of institutions in Argentina, China, Hungary, and the US. A key issue for such institutions, although obviously in very different ways, remains language, as part of a group of concerns largely focused on the West. Ennew and Greenaway summarize these concerns in the following way: 'for some [critics] the process of internationalization and globalization gives rise to concerns about the dominance of the western model of the university, the perpetuation of inequality, an over dependence on the English language and the re-invention of a form of colonialism' (2012, 9). While English is in the centre of their list, in fact it provides a focus for the other anxieties, because it perpetuates inequality and functions as an extension of older forms of colonialism. Of course, it is difficult to see how the situation could be otherwise, even if it is desirable that it should be. In a later chapter, on composition, I discuss what I call a *realist* vision of internationalization in the university context, by which I mean a specifically multilingual vision. And yet, as realists, we also know that English is currently the international language of research (pressure being brought to bear on scholars to publish in Anglophone journals), that models for universities have in more recent times tended to be Anglophone (even if overlaid on a German one), and that the centre of the academic world is broadly (at least perceived to be, according to university league tables, etc) North American. This present situation realistically does not match our aspirations, and intuitively it is not clear that English could be anything other than a hindrance to global universities producing global citizens. Returning to the broader issues, Nolan argues that in fact universities can readily function as both guardians of local culture (including language) and as key points of access to global networks:

> It is possible that with regards to knowledge, ideas and cultures, globali-
> zation will serve to highlight and accentuate differences and reveal the

power of cultural differences in stimulating new thinking and innovative ideas. This may provide a basis for universities to reconcile their role as guardians of national or regional cultures and histories with a desire to engage (and have their graduates engage) on a global scale. (Nolan 2012, 114)

We can think about this balance through language yet again, as it is certainly arguable that if we think less of English and more of Englishes, both possibilities are engaged. Yet if we shift our perspective in that way, we are not only in conflict with present realities concerning research, but also losing some of the broader utility deriving from the use of English. The rest of this chapter grapples with some of these difficulties concerning balance.

If we focus on global citizenship as both an abstraction and a very practical matter, clearly universities are addressing the question of such citizenship as part of a broader consciousness that it is desirable (although polling demonstrates that such consciousness is variable, and could well be in decline (see Patel 2011)). One way to think about the global spread of English is to understand motivations for learning it as deriving from emerging global identities, specifically from a growing informal sense of global citizenship. However, any sense of global citizenship that is connected with English seems destined to remain controversial, because the English language remains a contested presence. As already discussed, the worldwide spread of English can be understood as producing the hegemony of English – as Robert Phillipson argues, linguistic imperialism remains powerful. If there were to be a language of global citizenship, it could not be an English that imposes itself and is imposed as an alternative to local languages; rather, we would need to revisit other models, perhaps even an artificial auxiliary language such as Esperanto. At the same time, the localization and indigenization of English have produced a variety of World Englishes, varieties that are arguably irreducible to instances of that linguistic imperialism. These Englishes illustrate the tension between centripetal and centrifugal forces in the present state of the language, but they may also indicate possibilities for conceiving the connection between English and global citizenship in terms beyond rejection or celebration. Accordingly, I will consider the possible connections to be made between ideals of global citizenship and concepts and practices of World Englishes. The rest of this chapter will use ideas of World Englishes that in many cases directly challenge the assumptions behind terms like 'World English', 'Global English', 'Globish', or even (after C.K. Ogden, I.A. Richards. *et al.*) 'Basic English'. Some commentators celebrate the potential for such a centre of gravity; one example is McCrum (2010), who adapts Nerrière's use of the term Globish. Other writers such as Nicholas Ostler (2010) consider English the last lingua franca, soon to be rendered obsolete *as* a lingua franca by technological (alongside political and economic) shifts. These technological shifts would also potentially render all cosmopolitanisms redundant; indeed, Ostler is particularly interested in the increasingly realized potential of machine translation, and suggests that people will soon enough be able to communicate globally in their own languages. The first perspective implicitly (frequently not so implicitly) celebrates English as the language of global citizenship, while the second considers its days severely numbered. Furthermore, each perspective has obvious implications for any argument about English as a (or even *the*) language of global citizenship. However, it is perhaps necessary to emphasize the extent to which English is now Englishes, if we are not to remain again trapped by a choice of either naive celebration or impatient rejection. Indeed, if we direct our attention towards the shifting and diverse range of World Englishes we can imagine a role for Englishes plural as the languages of global citizenship that shadow languages associated with formal citizenship, rather than being the controversial alternative apparently offered by Global English. Accordingly, although World Englishes appear to represent the dangers of centrifugal forces driving English to disintegrate, they could also be understood as offering enough autonomy to fulfill what Richards (1943) called the 'supranational impulse'.

That impulse animates desirable forms of globalization, understood as distinct from *globalism*. Clarifying this distinction, Norman Fairclough makes a point central to critical discussion of globalization: 'Certain aspects of globalization may be inevitable and irreversible, but there is nothing inevitable or irreversible about the strategy of globalism. Globalization can be steered in less damaging, more democratic, and more socially just and equitable directions' (2006, 163). As one aspect of critical discussion of globalization, it is clear that democracy, social justice, and equity can be understood in terms of language. One point that might appear obvious is that the spread of the English language, understood as global or world English, is on the side of globalism. Democracy, social justice, and equity would then, according to Fairclough's argument, require a highly sceptical perspective on that spread; once an aspect of different dispersals deriving from colonialism, slavery, and so on, the English language now appears central to versions of globalization understood as globalism. Accordingly, there seems no obvious way that we could defend the English language as the language of global citizenship; it is simply too historically freighted, not to mention being fundamental to ongoing global imbalances. It would seem very difficult indeed to square the spread of English with the aspirations of human rights discourses and (developing and often inchoate) international systems of democratic governance. As English has spread worldwide, it has come into conflict with provisions such as Article 27 of the Universal Declaration, covering free participation in communal cultural life. It is difficult not to retain sympathy for critical perspectives on the consequences of this spread, even if English is already the language of one dead empire and quite possibly soon of another. However, this chapter attempts to delineate if not limitations in this position then at least a way of understanding how in spite of this globalist world English we can also find evidence of the uneven development of globalized world Englishes. Indeed, Fairclough discusses *re-scaling*, meaning the development of new relations between scales, such as the nation state and the global or the local, as key to the critical linguistic study of globalization. World Englishes can be understood as a series of phenomena that help us understand this re-scaling in everyday action. If global citizenship can be understood to shadow formal national citizenship, then the relationship between these scales, in certain contexts far more than others, can be understood in terms of lingua francas. World Englishes demonstrate the potential of popular linguistic re-scaling, as people switch between numerous regional, national, and local tongues, as well as localized and often indigenized Englishes, and also some form of English as an International Language, beyond the direction of traditional native-speakers. The world does not speak English, but to a great extent it does speak Englishes; in order to understand the connection between these Englishes and global citizenship, we need to consider how, when, and with what values and attitudes.

Models of Global Citizenship

Global citizenship might not be world citizenship, and there might be many fine distinctions to be drawn with other competing and/or complementary ideas such as cosmopolitanism, but, however we come to understand it, it is, as Heater (2002) suggests, just like world citizenship in the important regard that it remains an enigma. Needless to say, there are competing visions of global citizenship that must be taken into account before we can discuss the role of language for global citizens as such. In addition, it is necessary to make at least some distinction between metaphors of global citizenship and its actual practice, even if that distinction cannot be absolute; clearly, the metaphorical level impacts upon the practical level, as, for example, in debates regarding EU citizenship. Clearly, however, some distinction is possible, given that there are issues of governance intertwined with practical global citizenship. Meanwhile, on a metaphorical level there is clear evidence of literary representation and exploration of global citizenship, for example, in the fiction of Hari Kunzru (2005) or Kamila Shamsie (2009), and in many other forms of culture, popular and otherwise. It is impossible to privilege one over the other, particularly because the metaphorical and practical levels are so internally differentiated, but also because they unpredictably touch upon one another throughout global existence, even when it seems least global and most local. Furthermore, it is very difficult to discuss the relationship of these levels in terms of causation. One may provide context that enables or encourages the other, but again this is not predictable. This complex relationship is certainly relevant to our understanding of the place of English as both potential and actual language of global citizenship, as we will see. Practically speaking, it seems an unfortunate 'choice', but metaphorically speaking it may be a choice that we cannot easily make again in the present context; it would certainly be useful to describe what it enables as well as what it precludes.

Before considering how English blocks or enables global citizenship, it is important to recognize that there is a great deal of disagreement concerning that citizenship's desirability, at least in the present neo-liberal context, the orthodoxies of which remain dominant. If we focus our attention to global citizenship on the question of what kind of global governance is in the process of emerging, then it is difficult to ignore the fact that such citizenship is emerging under neo-liberalism in different forms. These conditions of emergence imply that, as April Biccum suggests, the citizens in question would most likely be those best able to take advantage of globalization, and so can be understood as *entrepreneurs*. With regard to who is designated by 'global citizen', the demand that global citizens be global entrepreneurs would apply to citizens from the South, desired to open themselves to the global market. But this demand would also, as Biccum discusses, imply the need for education in the North, where global citizenship nominally already exists. Biccum's principal example is the shift in the discourse of international development initiated by the UK's Labour Party under Tony Blair and Gordon Brown, which apparently required a shift in British citizens' values and attitudes, a shift that can be understood as the education of global citizens. Biccum argues that global citizenship is apparently something from which many are excluded. At the same time, although it seems that global citizenship already resides in a location such as the UK, the DfID (Department for International Development) also suggests that UK citizens need to be educated into understanding development and being global citizens themselves; this education would aim to make the diversity of often critical voices in the citizenry more homogeneous and accepting of neo-liberal orthodoxy. Biccum is arguing that UK (followed by US and EU) subjects are being produced that are appropriate to the new imperialism, and that competing voices are being silenced through a kind of marketing campaign that normalizes that imperialism: 'The current paradoxical climate of border paranoia, global migration, globalization, millennium development and foreign intervention has the potential to heighten awareness of ambivalences in the construction of contemporary metropolitan social life, and this is what the marketing campaign and development education in its neo-liberal variant is trying to quell' (2010, 163). To a large extent, her references to the EU notwithstanding, Biccum's global citizen of the North is likely Anglophone. The place of English in this narrative is then likely to be the unquestioned norm, or even the language of propaganda for this normalizing *narrative of contemporaneity* (as Biccum describes it), that stresses the break between undesirable past empires and a benevolent present and future. Needless to say, English should not be fulfilling this mystificatory function. Alternatively, the association of English with neo-liberalism reminds us of arguments about the commodification of English, a process that perhaps also functions to neutralize the language (which would be quite different from arguing that English is in some way already neutral) through insisting on its instrumental functions. This commodification accompanies discussion of English as a global language in exhibiting the following discursive characteristics: 1. English is easy to learn; 2. English is practical; 3. people's desire to learn English is instrumentally motivated. As Watts argues, 'The commodification of language is closely associated with commercial interests, with a new kind of metaphorical conceptualisation of language as a valuable human resource' (2011, 264). While Watts is concerned to describe this commodifying discourse, his description implies a critical perspective that we can extend here, as this convergence of English, global citizenship, and neo-liberalism inevitably seems culturally, politically, and economically biased.

Of course, there are alternative perspectives on what it means to be a global citizen, and so there are alternative connections we might make between English and that citizenship. Indeed, one such perspective can be drawn from postcolonial studies. If Biccum is correct about more 'official' versions of global citizenship, it becomes important to shift our attention to other potential resources for a *vernacular* cosmopolitanism. A key postcolonial thinker on this question is again Homi K. Bhabha, who theorizes global citizenship alongside minoritarian agents, those who in one way or another are *translated* without choice. One way he approaches this question is to return to earlier thinkers, recalling that we have been globalized before. In an example relevant to this chapter, Bhabha uses W.E.B. DuBois to argue that 'The responsibility of the minoritarian agent lies in creating a world-open forum of communication' (2007b, 191). The sense of communication involved here cannot be reduced to transparency or immediate accessibility, possibilities that would again favour the few at the expense of the many, as will be considered again towards the end of this chapter. Here it is important to understand why, for Bhabha, minoritarian agents are well placed to aid in the creation of such a forum, given that it would seem to be generally desirable. He argues that they are well placed because minoritarian agents have specific understanding of the need for closeness and negotiation as alternatives to oppositional positioning. Placing stress on contiguity (on metonymy rather than metaphor, as in Jakobson, Waugh, and Monville-Burston 1990), Bhabha suggests that, 'solidarity depends on surpassing autonomy or sovereignty in favor of an intercultural articulation of differences' (2007b, 191). However, it is difficult to articulate such differences at the same time as maintaining solidarity. In the terms of this chapter, it could be argued that Englishes provide and represent means of being contiguous, and this possibility derives from their *affiliatory* qualities. Unsurprisingly, Bhabha stresses that the minoritarian perspective tends towards processes of affiliation rather than assumptions concerning filiation: 'This is a dynamic and dialectical concept of the minority as a process of affiliation, an ongoing translation of aims and interests through which minorities emerge to communicate their messages adjacently across communities' (2007b, 191). In terms of human rights, this implies a difficulty in the sense that the concept of minority enshrined by Article 27 seems to assume a pre-existing group identity demanding protection. Bhabha thinks about this kind of minority identity in terms of totality, and a tendency towards some form of realizable national identity. For him, this assumed tendency is a weakness in the discourse of rights: 'Such a strong preference for cultural "holism" prevents Article 27 from envisaging, or providing protection for, new and affiliative forms of minoritarian agents and institutions who do not necessarily choose to signify their lifeworld in the political forms of nationness and nationalisms' (2007b, 192). A minority is a product of filiation, while the minoritarian is the result of affiliation.

Discussion of English and Englishes maps on to the minority and minoritarian distinction, even if World Englishes are not exactly results of choices, except in limited terms in specific cases. In any case, it is clear that Bhabha makes postcolonialism central to his idea of global citizenship; when it comes to the global subject, the postcolonial provides examples of the ongoing experience of transition: 'The territoriality of the global "citizen" is, concurrently, postnational, denational or transnational' (2003, 50). This global citizen is difficult to describe, and in fact the category might be more important for its relation to the 'normal' case of nationality; accordingly, its form is as important as its content. Bhabha discusses this citizenship in terms of what legal theory calls 'effective nationality', which is adjacent to 'formal nationality' (see Aleinikoff and Klusmeyer 2001, 75). This nationality has status in the context of international rights legislation, and although it appears dependent or subservient to formal nationality its adjacency makes it a necessary supplement to the latter category. The term captures the sense in which the global citizen is necessarily disjointed, and not quite at one with itself. Effective nationality is contiguous, and its relationship with formal nationality is one of metonymy. The repeated reference to metonymy allows us to understand Bhabha's introduction of Antonio Gramsci at this point. Of course, Gramsci is most closely associated with the idea of hegemony (e.g., Gramsci 1992), an idea that emphasizes the ways power is not only a matter of domination but also of consent. As is well known, according to Gramsci, in trying to create consent, hegemony encounters inevitable dissent, meaning that cultural meaning is negotiated, and is not something that can be simply imposed by predictable ruling classes. To answer the question of who exactly conducts these negotiations under globalization, Bhabha evokes a 'philosophy of the part', a philosophy given institutional expression in the 'the cultural front', which evolves a non-totalizing world-view. The cultural front transforms the meaning of hegemony, because it undermines the idea of pre-given political identities. The relationships of hegemony may be complex negotiations, but they are still complex negotiations between fairly stable classes. This stability might appear to have been undermined by the shift to postmodern social conditions, but political collectivities obviously retain their importance. It is just that there is a need to imagine collective subjects, and not simply reduce these subjects to effects of rational contracts between fully conscious individuals; in other words, a cultural front is an alliance that is narrated, and indeed is explicitly so. Rather than resorting to simplistic polarities, the cultural front places itself in a relationship of negotiation with the status quo, meaning that it does not simply reject the status quo. Instead, there the cultural front as an idea demands the recognition of process and partiality. The metonymy that Bhabha apparently privileges over metaphor is here reframed as subaltern contiguity, or a translation between political contexts that is always provisional and ongoing.

This translatability is what allows so many different experiences to be called 'postcolonial'. The category does not reduce these experiences to instances of an overarching framework, but instead recognizes that translations and affiliations between contexts can be expedient in political transformation. Grouping these examples together constructs a form of counter-hegemony; such a postcolonial cultural formation must be constructed with care, but its potential justifies that effort. This is because the postcolonial perspective has so many insights into the experiences that characterize the present. So, Bhabha suggests that the feeling of time in the contemporary moment is best imagined through the examples given by partial milieus, meaning those subjects and collectives who experienced histories of slavery and colonialism. These subjects' feelings of partiality and transition should, he argues, be built into the idea of global citizenship, in that the subaltern negotiates from a position of partiality and hybridity, without the guarantees of rootedness. Only through emphasizing the interconnectedness and incompleteness of our identities can we construct a model of citizenship that will not revert to default assumptions about the permanence and pre-eminence of national identity. Languages might appear to be 'naturally' the preserve or property of such national identities. If we wish to offer a corrective or (more reasonably) supplement to such a perspective, then World Englishes provide a starting point. Indeed, through foregrounding what I am calling a postcolonial conception of global citizenship we can begin to discern a very different picture, and one that might have a place for World Englishes as languages of global citizenship. That is the case in spite of the evident difficulties in adapting Bhabha's conception of citizenship to contexts of actual governance. Indeed, while it is difficult to make Bhabha's sense of global citizenship fit the context of global governance, in terms of understanding the role of Englishes it might also be essential. World Englishes might be the languages of at least some 'emergent, undocumented lifeworlds' (2007a, 39). However, the role of World Englishes in the realm of global institutions is as yet limited if not non-existent, and we remain in a situation where English in the (apparent) singular is a controversial institutional presence, as we will now see.

English in/as the Global Institution

This discussion of models of global citizenship emphasizes that the philosophical abstractions are very much connected to international governance and institutional practices. Such is also the case with English, which is often discussed (as here) in highfalutin terms but is also a matter of everyday use. Much of the activity in English on an inter- or supranational level is of course witnessed in formal institutional practices. Such practices are themselves difficult to view dispassionately, and are often the source of controversy. If nothing else, these practices can feel divorced from the citizens, whether these citizens feel global, regional, or, more likely still, local. Will Kymlicka, political theorist specializing in liberalism and minority rights, observes an 'obvious fact'; he writes that '[W]e need international political institutions which transcend linguistic/national boundaries. We need such institutions to deal not only with economic globalization, but also with common environmental problems and issues of international security. At present, these organizations exhibit a major "democratic deficit"' (2001, 324). Restricted as they are to national contexts, national political institutions seem inadequate to the tasks of governing economic globalization, international security, and related issues such as the environment. Such an assertion sounds rather obvious, although it is of course not obvious to everyone. Kymlicka, however, takes it to be obvious; if we accept this obviousness, we might then focus on the question of transcending specifically linguistic boundaries. Kymlicka's assertion is far-reaching, and in the context of language raises one question immediately: does an institution that transcends linguistic boundaries need to conduct its business in multiple languages, in one language, or in some combination that oscillates between multi- and monolingual working practices? Of course, English often in fact appears to dominate many international institutions, and so, keeping this first issue in mind, we can move on to a second issue. If we accept Kymlicka's assumption, we need to ask: despite the fact that it is at the moment the language most transcendent of boundaries, is English in fact one of the aspects of globalized institutions that contributes to this 'democratic deficit'? Perhaps it might be counter-intuitively argued that not only does English not transcend boundaries, it in fact still operates to bolster certain national interests and privileges. Does English necessarily privilege its so-called native speakers, thereby undermining not only global institutions but also the very idea of global citizenship? One way to approach this question is to consider the connection between global citizenship and cosmopolitanism. In his study of cosmopolitanism, Stan van Hooft expresses the basic alternatives in familiar terms: 'One could ask of [the spread of English] whether it occurred because of a newly emerging sense of global solidarity and cultural understanding or whether it arose because of the hegemony of English-speaking peoples in the world' (2009, 10). He suggests that Esperanto may be the only language that is genuinely cosmopolitan in spirit. That emphasis on *spirit* indicates again the significance of splitting global citizenship between institutional and metaphorical levels, and in the situation raised by Kymlicka the emphasis is clearly more on the institutional (although he does, it should be noted, decouple global citizenship from direct accountability), perhaps suggesting that English is even less appropriate. The following section addresses this issue, although, as my earlier discussion of 'the' global citizen indicates, English's role cannot be understood purely in institutional terms.

Discussion of global linguistic realities certainly frequently coincides with discussion of global governance or citizenship. The speaking of a language around the world (however limited in specific contexts) is clearly connected to the development of global institutions (again, however limited). In each case, the existence of the global scale can be understood to be (and is often desired to be) supplemental in the Derridean sense, meaning that it is both a superficially unnecessary addition and also something fulfilling a fundamental need. Exploring contemporary cosmopolitanism, David Held argues that global governance is being realigned with democracy and social justice, but that this does not necessarily imply the shrinking of state power: 'it seeks to entrench and develop political institutions at regional and global levels as a necessary supplement to those at the level of the state' (2010, 177). During certain phases of colonial control, and in certain contexts even after independence, the spread of the English language has appeared to demand the exclusion or at least marginalization of local languages (for a famous example, see Ngũgĩ wa Thiong'o 1981). In his dissection of linguistic imperialism, Phillipson (1992) argues that post-independence African states show evidence of the hegemonic role of English, with ELT being an instance of ongoing structural domination. Clearly enough, from any perspective interested in global justice, such a language has no place as the language of global citizenship. However, it is at least a possibility that English understood as supplemental, and diversified beyond the direction of native-speakers, *could* be very different.

Before discussing the assumption that there ought to be a language of global citizenship, it will be useful to understand how the apparent need for it arose. Much has been written about the Universal Declaration of Human Rights and similar international documents, for example debating their ethnocentrism (for an overview see Morsink 1999; on the philosophical background see Morsink 2009), but in any case the period following 1945 saw the foundation of key international and often *supra*national institutions. The United Nations began in 1945, along with the World Bank, UNESCO and UNICEF in 1946, the World Health Organization (WHO) in 1948, and the International Atomic Energy Agency (IAEA) in 1957. In addition, other groupings have maintained or intensified their importance, often in quite different ways, as can be seen in the examples of the Commonwealth and the European Union (EU) (currently posed by UKIP [United Kingdom Independence Party] as alternatives for the UK; see Nuttall 2008). All such institutions (and others such as the Association of Southeast Asian Nations (ASEAN)) have discussed and acted on demands for official languages, and have tended towards accepting the need for 'working languages'. While it is controversial, English remains important to all such institutions, and, as David Crystal (2003) has pointed out, a significant proportion of their institutional running costs necessarily covers translating documents and interpreting debates and discussions. Nonetheless, multilingualism is a political, practical, and philosophical necessity in international institutions, and can be a key element in their identities, as in the EU. The example of the EU is interesting, in that it appears to be a test case for multilingualism, as Phillipson (2003) suggests. Today the respect for and learning of multiple European languages is understood to be vital in uniting the varied countries constituting the Union, and yet the Directorate-General for Translation (DGT) has published its own study of the implications of lingua franca usage, focusing in its second half inevitably on English (European Commission, Directorate-General for Translation 2010). However, we cannot focus only on the present state of multilingualism alongside English as a lingua franca, as the EU has a long history that provides some important context for how its languages are conceived today. In 1958, the official and working languages were those of its founding states: Dutch, French, German, and Italian. Today it has twenty-three official languages, some of which are shared by more than one state, with some states operating in more than one of those languages. EU law is binding on states and accordingly states must have versions of individual laws in their national languages, demanding at least that much translation. Then there is the question of what the DGT refers to as the *natural justice* of each member state playing its own linguistic part. However, practically speaking, this multilingual emphasis is potentially onerous. In 2003, the EU population was 379 million, and expenditure on translation by all the EU institutions came to 549 million euros, out of the total EU budget for that year of 98,300 million euros. Translation by DGT on its own cost 230 million euros. Accordingly, for translation, each EU citizen paid 1.45 euros (all institutions)/0.60 euros (DGT only). After 2004's enlargement, the EU had a population of 453 million and the cost of translation at all institutions was estimated to be 807 million euros per year including, for DGT, 320 million euros (1.78 euros and 0.70 euros respectively, per citizen). This was from a total EU budget for 2004 of 99,806 million euros and for 2005 of 105,221 million euros (figures from European Commission, Directorate-General for Translation 2012). There has been further enlargement since 2004, and as of 2013 countries such as Iceland and Turkey seem likely to add to the translation costs. In times of economic certainty, such costs might be warily accepted; those times have at least temporarily passed for the EU. The DGT itself notes that financial constraints dictate that not all documents are translated into every language, and specifies English, German, and French as procedural languages. Potentially, it may be time to cease viewing such constraints as cultural and political as well as financial.

Much of this chapter seems to assume that global citizenship does in fact require a language, but the EU case suggests that this is not necessarily true. Indeed, depending on how we view translation, interpreting, and advances in machine translation, there may not be any need for linguistic compromise. While Crystal (2003) points out that the few professional translators and interpreters are overpowered and underpaid, Ostler (2010) has recently argued that machine translation has already fulfilled some of its early promise, and is therefore a capable aid to those who wish to read in languages they know little or not at all. Intriguingly, although mainly symbolically, in 2012, Esperanto became the 64th language supported by Google Translate. Such technology is cost intensive in development but cheap once running, although we remain far from perfection – should meaningful perfection be possible. Ostler claims that English will not be succeeded by any other lingua franca (obvious alternatives being languages such as Chinese or Spanish) because of these technological developments; he even suggests that people will simply speak to the world in their own language, depending on technological connectedness to guarantee communicative connectedness. According to this logic, language learning might well be perceived as decreasingly important (and English would certainly lose its current cachet), leading to a form of 'cosmopolitan deficit'. However the technology of machine translation develops, and it is developing rapidly, the fact remains that we *do* have a worldwide working language. However, the appeal of Ostler's vision of machine aided global communication is obvious, because it is far from clear that English can be described or accepted as the language of global citizenship, and there are alternatives that have been entertained.

Cosmopolitan Alternatives to English

The next context I will consider foregrounds democracy understood in less institutional and more metaphorical terms. This metaphorical level is that on which we might be said to have a world econoculture, and, as already mentioned, this culture functions as an extension of Anderson's idea of imagined communities. We certainly have the controversial use of English within supranational institutions, those institutions constituting one element of global citizenship. But, of course, there are other, less institutional ways of conceiving that citizenship, and these less institutional levels are more reconcilable with different versions of English. Indeed, we also already have a kind of relatively restricted use of English by global citizens; we just might need to have more such citizens. Furthermore, it is not clear that such citizenship coincides with cosmopolitanism. Indeed, the extent to which it does coincide depends on which definition of cosmopolitanism we are discussing, and it may be necessary to shift our focus to forms of what constitutes Bhabha's vernacular cosmopolitanism. It is certainly easy to conceive of cosmopolitans as fundamentally transnational or even supranational, as suggested by commentators such as Ulf Hannerz (1996). However, the freedom to be transnational, alongside a fluency in English, is also predictably associated with elite cultures of various forms. As one example of this position, we can consider Montserrat Guibernau's description of a cosmopolitan identity:

> By definition, a cosmopolitan identity is fluid, dynamic and a prerogative of a selected elite. Today's cosmopolitans belong to the middle and upper

classes, tend to speak English as a mother tongue or as a lingua franca, enjoy sufficient resources to take advantage of the goods and lifestyles associated with post-industrial societies and feel comfortable using the continuously emerging new ranges of sophisticated information technology and communications goods bombarding the market. Cosmopolitans transcend the limits of their national and local communities and enjoy travelling a world that, for them, has truly become a single place. (Guibernau 2007, 152)

Cosmopolitans are not global citizens necessarily, and emerging forms of cosmopolitanism certainly might be dismissed as restricted to a global elite. Indeed, it is clear that Guibernau's description shares many characteristics with certain understandings of postmodern identity, something that has long been argued to mark the limits of the practices and discourses of the colonial West (see McLennan 2003). If English is the language of *that* version of cosmopolitanism or postmodern fluidity, then again it is unsuitable for global citizenship, with those identities tending to mistake their own rarefied conditions for more general global conditions. It should, however, be noted that while Guibernau insists that a shared language is absolutely essential for a shared identity, her stated objection to English is that, despite its number of speakers, 'it is still far from being a *lingua franca* at global level' (2007, 155). Whether or not that is true, it is easier to imagine more political and cultural objections to English as having greater significance. We might understand English to be 'the cosmopolitan tongue', as McWhorter (2009) suggests, but he is dismissive when discussing widespread concerns about its spread, seemingly unable to imagine alternative perspectives. This limitation means that in the end the cosmopolitanism in question itself begins to appear very limited indeed. I earlier cited translation costs in the EU, but such costs are only one measure of linguistic issues or even risk; as the association of English with a limited cosmopolitanism implies, there are serious social costs, within individual states and across the world, and these costs can be understood in terms of *class-linking* and related categories. Perhaps it is impossible for English to overcome its association with wealth and privileged social strata, and perhaps the desire that it (or rather, its speakers) should overcome this association is somewhat naive, as English often continues to be associated with *aspiration* as such. However, without some reckoning with the restrictions and prejudices involved, English will remain the expression of a wealthy global citizenry.

We can consider this issue by thinking about the potential disadvantages soon to be clear for monolingual speakers of English. In terms of English speakers, the possible alternative ways of using English in Guibernau's description are important; she refers to speaking English as a mother tongue *or* speaking it as a lingua franca. As David Graddol writes in a report for the British Council, the spread of English worldwide does not necessarily mean that 'native-speakers' can relax and enjoy an arbitrary but nonetheless assuredly real advantage. Indeed, according to Graddol, the monolingual

English speaker is likely to find himself or herself at a disadvantage in the near future, particularly in relation to an English-using global 'elite': 'we must not be hypnotized by the fact that this elite will speak English: the more significant fact may be that, unlike the majority of present-day native speakers, they will also speak at least one other language – probably more fluently and with greater cultural loyalty' (1997, 63). Graddol's reminder comes from a report for the British Council, which of course has its own angle and emphasis, while the commissioning body has its own investments. These contextual points have not compromised Graddol's acuity, and his point is very significant for thinking about English today; the question of cultural loyalty seems to be central to any use of English (or any other natural language) as the language of global citizenship, as once again the historical contexts and present-day realities assert themselves and inevitably challenge English's pre-eminence. We might wonder, however, if there has been some form of qualitative change in values and attitudes vis-à-vis English, particularly if English is understood as blurring into Englishes. We might also wonder about the definition of the 'global elite', apparently coinciding with Guibernau's cosmopolitans. Who speaks Englishes, and how do they feel about that act of speaking? English speakers are most often not *only* English speakers, but bi- or multilinguals, in much the same way that global citizens will not only act as or feel themselves to be global citizens.

That last point is important when understanding the emotional connection felt by speakers of English to the language. Again, this analysis draws in theories of hegemony, but in this case specifically that of Laclau and Mouffe in their critique of politics (see, for example, Laclau 1996; Laclau and Mouffe 2001). Laclau and Mouffe employ an anti-essentialist approach that assumes that the meaning of any given identity is not contained within itself, but is always different from itself and deferred. And yet this does not mean that social identity does not exist, just as it does not mean that society itself does not exist. Being, understood in this anti-essentialist way, the being of any social identity, is a matter of *articulation*, which is the combination of two elements within a differential signifying system. The two elements that are combined (for example, in terms of the global spread of English, *Anglophone* and *French*) clearly produce a new meaning, a new social identity, and they importantly emphasize that this meaning is very much a *production* rather than an originary essence. For Laclau and Mouffe, we need to conceive society itself in the same way, which is why hegemony is used. Although society is not an objective totality, and indeed is a production, that does not make it any less real; hegemony is the ongoing process that produces the meaning of society. To return us to the question of English, we can then argue that one need not think or identify as an English speaker, even when one is a native speaker, all of the time. And even those who have little allegiance to English, due to historical or cultural distance, may align themselves with the language more in certain contexts.

Being an English speaker, or a speaker who switches between English and Englishes, alongside other languages, is a common enough practice and experience. English is one language amongst many, just as global citizenship is one form of citizenship amongst others (at least it could be, or should be). One key move towards accepting English and Englishes worldwide will have to be its displacement from an unthinkingly privileged position. That displacement would simply be an acknowledgement of the reality of the majority of linguistic ecologies in which English holds a place. Few indeed believe that global citizenship will replace other forms, but that does not mean it will not continue to have an important role to play. The same ought to be true of English, for as long as its use makes sense for its worldwide users. Considering the contingent relation between national community and citizenship, Held discusses the potential for understanding global citizenship as one form of citizenship amongst others: 'people would come, in principle, to enjoy multiple citizenships – political membership, that is, in the diverse communities which significantly affect them' (2010, 101). To some extent this understanding of global citizenship describes what we usually think of as contingent identities. However, while Held puts stress on citizenship as a question of political identification with multiple foci, global citizenship could perhaps more often be understood outside narrowly political terms; in other words, it could be understood in terms of cultural politics. Such diversity of communal identification implies contingency, and perhaps also different ways of thinking about English. Should we think about English as a unitary phenomenon, within reason, one to which speakers around the world aspire, frequently despite themselves? If we think of English in this way then the objections we have already considered are raised, and we ought then to seek alternative languages. Looking back at various attempts to produce and or impose such an alternative also provides evidence as to why no alternative language currently seems plausible. It might indeed be the case that, in terms of lingua francas, English will be the last, as Ostler suggests. Yet what we also have in Englishes is a series of languages that eludes the status of one language among others. It is that plurality that signals the potential of English as languages of global citizenship. Nonetheless, the alternatives are real and worthy of serious consideration, as we will now see.

One alternative to English that appears to avoid cultural and historical associations (desirable or, more likely, not) is Esperanto, the best-known international artificial auxiliary language. As is well known, Esperanto's creator Ludwig Zamenhof wanted to devise a language that was not only easy to learn but also that would assist in achieving world peace. As Kep Enderby (cited in Al-Dabbagh 2010) suggests, Esperanto is still being used, has a literature of its own, a significant number of translations, and George Soros as a prominent (native) speaker (although one who apparently believes that Esperanto had its chance and failed (see Okrent 2009)). However, despite its apparently neutral identity, there are obvious limitations to Esperanto. One limitation is practical, as, with only approximately two million speakers, it does not exert the same powerful pull as a widely spoken language. Nor, arguably, does it evolve through the concerted everyday use that leads to so much development of a natural language. Finally, and importantly, it is distinctively European (hence, perhaps, Google Translate's facility with the language, despite the small amount of available data), and so is not necessarily easy to learn for speakers of non-European languages, and perhaps not so neutral as its proponents advertise. Another alternative to English (whatever its name states) is Basic English, as devised by C.K. Ogden and championed by I.A. Richards. As Colin MacCabe suggests, although Richards is better known for his involvement in shaping practical criticism, he pursued literature to 'ensure optimum forms of communication' (1999, 165), particularly as a response to war. Basic is an aspect of Richards's pursuit of this communication, and he took it to China, during his time at Tsinghua University. With its strictly limited vocabulary and apparent ease of learning, it seemed ideal for bringing the country within the realm of international communication. Commenting that there were simply so many Chinese that it would become imperative that they be brought into the international community, Richards (1943) suggested that Basic English could be a key force in creating or fostering the supranational impulse. By contrast, Richards noted the limitations of Esperanto, specifically its artificiality. He further warned that the supranational language could not be a 'denatured' form of an already existing language (some who encounter Basic may find this warning amusing and even bemusing). Finally, he placed emphasis on avoiding any feeling of imposition of the language, implying that English *per se* could not but feel imposed, for all the reasons we have already mentioned. Basic English, in a way comparable to Esperanto, is utopian; the product of a committed pacifist, it lives on in the form of the Simple English version of Wikipedia (although it allows 1,000 most common words rather than Basic's 850). Making English basic, simplified, international, or some other variation, appears to reduce the seemingly inherent advantage of English native speakers. However, it ought to be remembered that Basic was championed by Churchill, implying that Ogden and Richards, however much they sought to avoid imposing any language on any speaker, were somewhat naive (see Tong 1999; Koeneke 2004). As another more recent alternative, Marko Modiano's models of English as an International Language (EIL) are concerned to move away from any stress of native speakers (and so can be compared to airline English, other English for Specific and Academic Purposes (ESP) versions, and recent attempts to imagine teaching English as a Lingua Franca (ELF)), but still centred on a privileged version accessible to some but not all (see Modiano 1999; Jenkins 2009). Finally, we can consider Jean-Paul Nerrière's Globish as an alternative, from its name onwards designed to avoid associations with the flag-waving implicit in celebrations of global English (both American and British; see Nerrière and Hon 2009). Extending to its logical conclusion Modiano's position in support of his idea of EIL, Globish is challenging in its argument that native speakers are simply too good at English to be good speakers of English internationally.

Each of these alternatives to English (understanding Basic, EIL, and Globish to be in various ways meaningfully distinct from English) appears to be a singular phenomenon (consequences of a homogenization that is another myth analysed by Watts (2011)). But, of course, it could be argued that the alternative ought to be marked by both centripetal and centrifugal forces (an idea drawn from Bakhtin, but with precursors; see Bolton 2006). It is desirable that an alternative has some of the features of a single language (communicative practicality, global consciousness, and so on) with some of the features of multilingual reality (distinct identity, resistance to ideologies of transparency, etc.). These paired features are at least tentatively discernible in World Englishes. The pluralization of English reminds us that the range of other languages impacting on English is too great to pretend that fragmentation is not already under way: Singlish and Spanglish, if understood as connected, and products of similar linguistic processes, must also be understood as deriving from *very* different contexts. And this tension (fundamentally, a series of tensions between centripetal and centrifugal, visible in linguistic, political, cultural, and other domains) is what allows World Englishes to function as languages of global citizenship. The outline of an explanation for this perhaps counter-intuitive claim is as follows. We need to begin by recalling the social, political, and cognitive implications of the diversity of World Englishes. Tom McArthur (2002) makes a heavily qualified claim for the potential of such a family of English languages, knowingly risking the charge of wide-eyed idealism. If we shift our rhetoric somewhat, and imagine the World Englishes as instances of a language of global citizenship, then we gain something as much as we lose the obvious transparency of an international standard. If global citizenship shadows formal citizenship then it does not subsume all its linguistic resources in the drive to fit an ideal communicative situation. If that is the case then the Englishes that increasingly mark informal global or supranational belonging are quite properly distinct from the English that is used in international institutional contexts. This distinction can be understood through shifting our attention to versions of communication found in the philosophical work of Habermas and Derrida. Habermas is well known for extending a Kantian vision of global institutions and citizenship, as that vision might be realized in the twenty-first century. In an interview entitled 'America and the World', he raises the question of whether people can be made to care beyond the social solidarity of a national identity (2004); he wonders if national social rights can be expanded to supranational communities, and so about the possibility of a world political community. Seemingly, a political community depends on an insider/outsider distinction, and so there would have to be large regional communities interacting rather than a world community; for example, European citizenship might well be viable, but according to this logic not world or global citizenship. If there was to be a 'parliament of world citizens' (a second chamber, shadowing the General Assembly), Habermas notes that it would need to be *negative*, based on avoiding atrocity and conflict. He suggests that such an assembly could not be held together by *positive*, thick traditions. However, we might wonder if this is *necessarily* still the case, insofar as World Englishes provide the semblance of a thick linguistic family tradition.

Paradoxically, perhaps, such a thick tradition may well exist to the extent that Englishes imply not consensus (as McArthur appears to suggest), but *dissensus*. As I mentioned at the beginning of this chapter, Oakeshott (1962) has something like this emphasis in mind when he suggests that poetry has its place in a conversation that, while it may have passages of demonstration or argument, is fundamentally aiming at something other than truth and something more like 'simple' continuation. Certainly it is understandable that a conversation understood to be aiming for truth would demand that its participants be speaking their own tongues, however that category is understood (in fact, this would not be a conversation at all, according to Oakeshott, but instead inquiry or debate (1962, 198)). In a debate, the hegemonic properties of English might well be understood as an insuperable problem. Perhaps, however, certain (metaphorical) aspects of global citizenship are better understood as a conversation than a debate, and accordingly there is a place for English. Indeed, as already indicated, the numerous commentators who criticize English for its hegemonic properties are very much using the appropriate terminology; however, it is necessary to take the next step, which is to recall that hegemony's persuasive elements, its need to produce consensus, entail the possibility of dissensus. Indeed, we can argue that there is only communication to the extent that we do not in fact agree. Habermas is well known for the idea of the ideal speech situation, a non-coercive and rationally consensual communicative interaction (this idea has been superseded in his own work, it should be said). But it has been argued that implicit in Habermas's work is that the goal of communication is its end; pursued to its conclusion, in the truly ideal speech situation nothing is said. Ultimately, our speech acts involve us in disagreement from the beginning. As Geoffrey Bennington suggests, 'If the end of communication is the end of communication, then the closer you get to the end, the nearer you are to its end. The fact of communication means that communication is not perfect' (2001, 54). As a development of this counter-intuitive position, we might explore the following challenging suggestion from an interview with Derrida:

> we cannot, and we *must* not, exclude the fact that when someone is speaking, in private or in public, when someone teaches, publishes, preaches, orders, promises, prophesies, informs or communicates, some force in him or her is also striving *not to* be understood, approved, accepted in consensus – not immediately, not fully, and therefore not in the immediacy and plenitude of tomorrow, etc. (Derrida 1997, 218)

'Communication' is the last term in Derrida's list, and is arguably the master term underlying the others. To communicate, to be understood, is to become fully present, but also to vanish. It is to make ourselves fully transparent to the gaze of others. If we take this thought and extend it to the discussion of global citizenship understood beyond strict institutional rationality, then we might well find that Englishes allow us both to have our transparency and also to reserve our opaqueness and cultural specificity. As we have seen, language rights inevitably tend towards clearly defined languages (which in a sense do not actually exist, being rather effects of stabilization), and most likely defend minority languages against certain rapacious majority languages, the principal being English. A global citizenship would on one level seem to require the incorporation of this kind of right, in order to preserve the diversity of voices necessary for conversation not to become argument. Yet, perhaps, at least intermittently, World Englishes, without either a nation or a national minority identity, can offer much of what global citizenship seems to desire.

Conclusion

In their mobility and difference, World Englishes can function as languages of a metaphorical global citizenship, and in many cases already do so, if always alongside other languages. To that extent they act as a force resisting global English's centralizing and homogenizing pull. But neither the centripetal nor centrifugal has any necessary meaning outside the many contexts in which we already participate, and which will call us forward in the future. Those contexts are stretching the meaning of a postcolonial reading further and further. This chapter's initial discussion of Obama's invocation of global citizenship in addressing a European audience, as well as my use of examples drawn from EU practice, seem to have taken us far from meaningfully postcolonial contexts for English; indeed, perhaps we would be better focusing on other examples, such as how English functions in ASEAN (see Kirkpatrick 2008; 2010; 2012). Yet, at the same time, any extension of postcolonial studies into engagement with globalization studies will inevitably address such contexts, just as anti-colonial thinkers situated themselves against and alongside global traditions in thought (see, for example, Young 2001); certainly, any absolute division is rather artificial, particularly when it comes to thinking about Englishes today. Indeed, as this chapter has shown, postcolonial perspectives on issues relating to global citizenship and cosmopolitanism necessarily become involved in studies of globalization and so on, as part of a project of provincializing Europe. If, as this chapter has argued, it is appropriate to consider encouraging or at the very least tolerating an already existing language of global citizenship, then we might discuss World Englishes as languages of cosmopolitanism 'from below' rather than 'from above' (see Appadurai 1996; Bhabha 1996), hence my interest in global citizenship as cultural and also metaphorical rather than necessarily institutional and political. It is necessary to consider the more nebulous realm of popular global citizenship, rather than remaining restricted to governance, a sphere in which the spread of English will necessarily continue to be a controversial issue. That being said, the next chapter will bring together the analysis of political constitutions, specifically declarations of independence, with the cultural object most intuitively authoritative over language, the dictionary. It considers the extent to which dictionaries necessarily prescribe as well as describe. It also warns against a continued defaulting into familiar and reified varieties-based approaches to Englishes, which in the end is a defaulting into ideas of cultural and linguistic ownership quite inimical to any idea of global citizenship.

CHAPTER 4

Declarations of Linguistic Independence: The Postcolonial Dictionary

When in the course of human events, it becomes necessary for a people to improvise new words to catch and crystallize the realities of a new land; to give birth to a vocabulary endowed with its creators' irrepressible shapes, textures, and flavors; to tell tales taller and funnier than anyone else ever had thought to before; to establish a body of literature in a national grain; and to harmonize a raucous chorus of immigrant voices and regional lingoes – then this truth becomes self-evident, that a nation possesses the unalienable right to declare its linguistic independence and to spend its life and liberty in the pursuit of a voice to sing of itself in its own words.

Richard Lederer, 'A Declaration of Linguistic Independence'

Introduction

Crack open the pages of *The Coxford Singlish Dictionary* (2002) or browse the rather different pages of *TalkingCock.com*, specifically its dictionary section, and you enter a world of proudly if (to non-Singaporeans) frequently opaque cultural identity and satire. Arguably, these two sources amount to one dictionary, available in print but more accessible online, and standing as an amalgamation of satirical comment on Singaporean society and a source of linguistic data. There you can learn the proper pronunciation of the world's premier fast food restaurant ('Macnoner' or 'Mehnoner'), the nature of the advice, 'Don'ch play-play' (a warning against hubris, derived from Hokkien), or perhaps just remind yourself of the meaning of 'kiasu'. Of course, this is 'Singapore's premier satirical humour website!', and, as a colleague suggested to me, it is accordingly 'for fun', and perhaps should not be taken too seriously. Indeed, before you click through to the main site, you are encouraged to

75

note the following: '1. WE MAKE STUFF UP … 2. WE ARE NOT A POLITICAL SITE … 3. WE USE SOME STRONG LANGUAGE … 4. IF YOU DON'T BELIEVE IN FREE EXPRESSION OR OPINION, GO SOMEWHERE ELSE'. The warning not to be too serious serves its own function, and numbers 1 and 4 tend to undermine number 2; it all rather depends on how you define 'political'. In addition, as has been widely argued, one of the key components of ownership of a language, particularly perhaps in the context of World Englishes, is the capacity precisely to take it *un*seriously, to be playful, in short to be *ludic* in its use (see Y. Kachru 2006). In fact, this satirical dictionary indicates one of the ways in which speech-linked writing increasingly cuts across our distinctions concerning traditional authorities, literary or otherwise. Now, of course, in one sense this book recommends focusing attention on non-written culture. In particular, it explores the sense in which looking at World Englishes forces postcolonial approaches to move beyond specifically literary culture. Indeed, much of the research on World Englishes requires focus on many different forms of evidence. It may be assumed that literary culture is not a particularly good guide to the ways in which World Englishes are evolving, partly because of the startlingly rapid pace of that evolution. That being said, there are many ways in which written culture is obviously still key to understanding the worldwide spread of English, some of which relate precisely to that speed; writing, as is well known, is argued to be increasingly speech-linked, most notably perhaps in online discourse.

This chapter focuses on a rather different written object as a source of authority (see Wells 1973) and 'violence'; it focuses on the 'postcolonial dictionary'. On one level, World Englishes constitute challenges that have been taken up by traditional authoritative dictionaries, with at least some success. If English is truly the world's lingua franca, then, as Susan Kermas argues in relation to the *Oxford English Dictionary* (*OED*), 'lexicographers need to address the culture-specific dimension of knowledge sharing in today's global village and broaden their cultural viewpoint' (2012, 75). As Sarah Ogilvie (2012) has suggested, also in relation to the *OED*, there is a reasonably long but actually rather complex history of such broadening. At the same time, these traditional authorities have been joined by more recent projects which can be interpreted as declarations of linguistic independence. This chapter broadly explores the complexities involved in claiming that World Englishes are independent of the authority vested in British, American, and other forms of native speaker English, including an existing or projected Global English. In particular, this chapter considers the role of dictionaries as constituting declarations of such independence. Dictionaries appear authoritative in describing what has been or what is rather than what ought to be, yet their authoritative status is often translated in order to make claims about the latter. Accordingly, this chapter will explore the implications of this unavoidable tendency to what might be called 'violence' in the context of World Englishes. One case study it considers is the *Macquarie Dictionary*, first published in 1981, which on one level challenged more entrenched authorities but which inevitably (and presumably *desirably*) has evolved its own form of authority. The chapter also touches on Samuel Johnson, Noah Webster, the *OED*, and others. Each has something to teach us about how independence is declared, how violence is done, and how expressiveness is authorized. In juxtaposing them, this chapter puts in communication their forms of authority and symbolic value, considering, for example, what they indicate concerning influence between Englishes. Indeed, this chapter argues that postcolonial dictionaries force us to rethink relations between Englishes.

In order to understand the structures at work in such shifts in authority, this chapter again develops implications of Jacques Derrida's work, particularly relating to the idea of the performative. 'Addressing' the editors of Chambers, concerning its definition of 'deconstruction', Nicholas Royle makes the following observation: 'Constative language is language when it is supposedly simply stating something: your language, the discourse of the dictionary, is a conventional and very powerful example of this' (2000, 9). Of course, Royle is concerned to question the distinction between constative and performative, and this questioning (drawing on both Derrida and J.L. Austin) is developed in one direction in this chapter. Dictionaries are indeed some of the most conventional and powerful examples of what is essentially linguistic authority. They are representative of what Deborah Cameron describes as verbal hygiene, an unavoidable tendency towards norms and values, found even (or perhaps especially) in avowedly descriptivist linguistics; Cameron illustrates this normativity through the specific example of the *OED*, arguing that 'most revered authorities are those that claim most unequivocally to be "descriptive", and therefore disinterested' (1995, 8). Of course, the linguistic authority is, in all cases, a kind of more general cultural authority, and that is obviously the case when we begin to think about English worldwide. That authority, as regards English, is something that has been challenged by historical and political developments, but those developments intertwine with more philosophical considerations, as we will see. Whether or not we subscribe to the philosophy and politics of the postcolonial paradigm, it is evident that on a descriptive level there has been a measure of what Kachru (1985) calls the 'decontrol' of English in the postcolonial period, which is of course a primary motivation for description and discussion of World Englishes. At the same time, in terms of stability, many of these Englishes appear wanting, their codification a work in progress at best; for example, until (and even perhaps after) the intervention of Cummings and Wolf (2011), it seemed that much attested Hong Kong English vocabulary was specific to the pre-1997 period (for example, 'astronaut' as a specifically Hong Kong usage, which also appeared in the *Encarta World English Dictionary* (*EWED*)). Accordingly, codification through dictionaries becomes a focus for World Englishes research, while lexicographers have often framed their studies in relevant ways. Henri Béjoint, for example, argues that cultural identity *depends* on the creation of local forms of linguistic authority: 'the compilation of a native dictionary is a symbolical act of independence' (1994, 83). More directly working in the terms of this chapter, Edgar Schneider, in his study of postcolonial Englishes, refers to the *Macquarie Dictionary* as 'an explicit declaration of linguistic independence' (2007, 125). While many dictionaries may well be at most unofficial sources of authority, they nonetheless do become and are received as authoritative; institutions like the *OED* have prescribed despite themselves, specifically despite their impossible statement of their pure descriptiveness. Accordingly, it can be argued that, in the same way as similar projects, the *Macquarie* intervenes as both a description and declaration of independence, working through what Derrida, famously writing on the American colonies' declaration of independence, calls a 'fabulous retroactivity' (1986, 10). On the one hand, these independent Englishes already existed, and on the other, they required the dictionary itself to make them happen; or, to put it another way, these Englishes both already *were* and yet also *ought to be*. The dictionary is a performative through which, as Les Murray has written (reviewing the *Macquarie*), 'our entire language is henceforth centred for us, not thousands of miles away, but here where we live' (1981). However, Murray's language explicitly raises the question of a newly centred English, a re-centring (although one among many, perhaps; elsewhere he specifically refers to, 'the wide acceptance of a polycentric view of the language' (1991, 8)). What is interesting about this re-centring is that aspects of the *Macquarie* itself appear to undermine centred-ness in general. There is a form of tension in the project, which is exaggerated by the incorporation of vocabulary from World Englishes. This chapter will later consider the codifying role of the *Macquarie Dictionary*, and raise the question of the relationship between the Australian declaration of linguistic independence, and the other declarations (for example, Singaporean) that became a widely discussed but perhaps uneasy aspect of the project.

Dictionaries: A Postcolonial Approach

In order to introduce this chapter's argument in terms of World Englishes, it is useful to begin with documents of forms of English most usually considered authoritative, traditional, and associated with 'native speakers'. The *Oxford English Dictionary* and the Declaration of Independence, in their different ways, provide a framework for understanding processes of codification in World Englishes, and to that extent the latter seems to be still in thrall to assumptions about which Englishes truly *count*. However, the two are not necessarily touchstones, against which other projects and documents are measured; instead, they offer hints about how to approach developments in World Englishes. For this chapter, the significance of the *Oxford English Dictionary* and the Declaration lies in their meaning to people at the time of their publication, more recently, and potentially into the future. We can think about these books as objects meaningful to individuals and broader societies, just as we can in the case of potentially or already authoritative documents of World Englishes. In their introduction to the field, David Finkelstein and Alistair Mcleery make the following observation about the practice of book history:

> Book historians try to understand what place books and reading had in the lives of people and society in the past, in the present, and even in the future. Grand projects like the *Encyclopædia Britannica*, the *Encylopédie*, and *The Oxford English Dictionary* have all had tremendous social and cultural effects, acting as guardians of accuracy, setters of standards, summarisers of important intellectual material. Equally, there are manuscripts and iconic documents that have become emblematic symbols for entire generations, cultures, and communities – witness the Magna Carta, the Declaration of Independence, or New Zealand's Treaty of Waitangi. (Finkelstein and Mcleery 2005, 4)

These two lists fascinatingly collide the two kinds of text that this chapter wishes to consider: grand projects like dictionaries, and iconic documents such as constitutional declarations. Revealingly, the political documents immediately direct us towards a postcolonial approach.

Many scholars have already developed our understanding in this direction. For example, in her study of the *OED*, Charlotte Brewer quotes Robert Burchfield (channelling Crusoe, and echoing Samuel Johnson) recalling his sense of the editorial task as one of colonial pioneering. Brewer observes that, 'Reading the *OED* in terms of such imagery – that of imperialism, conquest, and subjection – is the task of a separate book' (2007, 288 n. 1). That book has yet to be written, but there have of course been other attempts to understand dictionaries in these terms, and Brewer cites John Willinsky (1994) and Phil Benson (2001). Willinsky argues that 'The *OED* has taken up a new sense of World English, not […] as an expression of empire and an extension of Christianity, but as part of a redefined role for the United Kingdom and its venerable institutions in a postcolonial world' (1994, 175). He suggests that this role is one of authority and discrimination, with the potential meanings of authoritative discrimination, or discriminating authority, being exactly what is at issue in his book. The following questions arise: what kind of authority does the *OED* exemplify in a postcolonial world, and what kind *should* it develop? The ethical and political commitments of postcolonial studies are evident here. Alongside Willinsky's focused study of the *OED*, Benson more generally explores ethnocentrism in dictionaries, suggesting that, 'ethnocentrism is often most apparent in the bringing of the periphery to light as a reflection of the knowledge of the centre' (2001, 7). In particular, he considers the ways in which the *OED* incorporates 'China' as an example of this ethnocentrism, functioning according to a kind of orientalism. Additionally, there are other studies that use an explicitly postcolonial framework to position other dictionaries, such as Bill Ashcroft's comments on Samuel Johnson's preface to his famous dictionary. Drawing on Martin Wechselblatt (1996), Ashcroft argues that, 'almost before the English language had begun to be transported to British colonies, its vulnerability to change had already been described in terms of *the imagery of colonial contact*' (2008, 7). Johnson's language indicates his concern about the need to fix the language, but also the impossibility of doing so. The preface discusses the difficulties through a language of colonial contact, and, accordingly, Ashcroft suggests, 'the conflict between cannily recognizing the fluidity of linguistic meaning on one hand and protecting those meanings sent down from posterity by the greatest of English writers on the other, resolves itself in the colonial imagery of contamination and miscegenation' (2008, 8). Of course, that is actually a resolution without resolution, so to speak, and, as we will see, this is necessarily the case. Indeed, Ashcroft concludes that, 'The "Preface" is a deeply ambivalent moment in the institutionalization of the English language' (2008, 9). One might almost say, the preface is the first of many necessarily and even *constitutively* ambivalent moments of institutionalization or codification. Consider Johnson's comment about the necessary failure of his enterprise, but also the necessity of making the attempt, from his preface (1755):

> If the changes that we fear be [...] irresistible, what remains but to acquiesce with silence, as in the other insurmountable distresses of humanity? It remains that we retard what we cannot repel, that we palliate what we cannot cure. Life may be lengthened by care, though death cannot be ultimately defeated: tongues, like governments, have a natural tendency to degeneration; we have long preserved our constitution, let us make some struggles for our language. (Johnson 2009, 253–254)

Johnson brings together his attempt to preserve the English language with preservation of the constitution, and the connection is extremely suggestive.

A rather different example is that of Noah Webster, who in his linguistic declaration of self-determination appears to be such a 'good patriot' that he has been presented as a kind of unofficial signatory of the Declaration of Independence (see Kemp 1925). (Interestingly, Les Murray argues that Susan Butler is far more attracted to Johnson's rhetoric than she is to the polemical Webster; indeed, something like Johnson's concern underlies but also undermines Webster's apparent certainty.) Of course, Webster had two principal goals in his approach to the English language: helping to produce political uniformity via linguistic uniformity, and gaining linguistic independence. The first of the goals is outlined clearly in 'Dissertations on the English Language', when he writes that 'Small causes, such as a nick-name, or a vulgar tone in speaking, have actually created a dissocial spirit between the inhabitants of the different states, which is often discoverable in private business and public deliberations. Our political harmony is therefore concerned in a uniformity of language' (1789, 20). For Webster, political unity, apparently partly imperiled by miscommunication, implies the goal of linguistic unity. The second goal follows soon after:

> As an independent nation, our honor requires us to have a system of our own, in language as well as government. Great Britain, whose children

we are, and whose language we speak, should no longer be *our* standard; for the taste of her writers is already corrupted, and her language on the decline. But if it were not so, she is at too great a distance to be our model, and to instruct us in the principles of our own tongue. (Webster 1789, 20–21)

Here Webster emphasizes something that I will discuss later: the question of distance and relative influence between varieties of English. In addition, Webster also focuses on the limits of English in Europe, compared to endless possibilities in America, where he argues it will be spoken by a quarter of the world's population: 'Compare this prospect, which is not visionary, with the state of the English language in Europe, almost confined to an Island and to a few millions of people; then let reason and reputation decide, how far America should be dependent on a transatlantic nation, for her standard and improvements in language' (1789, 21–22). Vast distances are no longer an impediment to influence, if they ever were; indeed, Webster's concern indicates a clear anxiety that this influence is to some extent unavoidable.

In terms of his first goal, it can be argued, Webster's concerns about linguistic influence imply an ongoing anxiety about potential political harmony. Returning to the second goal, that of independence, Webster expresses the desire in terms of an inevitability:

Let me add, that whatever predilection the Americans may have for their native European tongues, and particularly the British descendants for the English, yet several circumstances render a future separation of the American tongue from the English, necessary and unavoidable. The vicinity of the European nations, with the uninterrupted communication in peace, and the changes of dominion in war, are gradually assimilating their respective languages. The English with others is suffering continual alterations. America, placed at a distance from those nations, will feel, in a much less degree, the influence of the assimilating causes; at the same time, numerous local causes, such as a new country, new associations of people, new combinations of ideas in arts and science, and some intercourse with tribes wholly unknown in Europe, will introduce new words into the American tongue. These causes will produce, in a course of time, a language in North America as different from the future language of England, as the modern Dutch, Danish and Swedish are from the German, or from one another: Like remote branches of a tree spring from the same stock; or rays of light, shot from the same center, and diverging from each other, in proportion to their distance from the point of separation. (Webster 1789, 22–23)

There is simply no doubt, according to this view, that 'natural' political and historical developments will lead to an independent language. English in contact with Europe will head in one or more directions, while in America it will, under pressure from local natural and cultural causes, head in other directions. This already is the case, or at least already *will be* the case. What, then, would be the point in *not* declaring it to be the case, or *not* making it happen? Such a logic can be found elsewhere, but for this chapter Webster is the most unavoidable example, precisely because the issue is the American language's connection with the constitution of the American people. That the more 'British' version of Webster's work which eventually became standard owed much to its conflict with Joseph Worcester's rival *Anglophile* dictionary tells us a great deal about how different the perception of a dictionary might be from its reality, and in this case it was and is perceived as a parallel declaration of independence (see Green 1999). Interestingly, as Martin Kayman notes, such declarations of independence as Webster's are also found for British English itself, although Kayman gives a later example, and perhaps all such examples do come later, it requiring the first modern declaration of linguistic independence to enable other comparable declarations. Kayman quotes Edwin A. Abbot's 'On Teaching the English Language' from 1871, in which Abbot addresses his audience on the need for English to be independent from 'foreign influence' such as Latin: 'I will ask you to consider this Lecture as a kind of declaration of independence on the part of our mother tongue, a protest that the English language ought to be recognized as requiring and enjoying laws of its own, independent of any foreign jurisdiction' (2004, 4). Developing Cameron's notion of verbal hygiene, Kayman continues to argue that linguistics itself functions, as a theory of language, to *legislate*: indeed, it performs 'the imagining of linguistic constitutions' (2004, 4). Kayman's choice of words here is highly suggestive, as we will explore later, and he is developing the explicit intention of a central figure like Webster.

To Constitute and to Prescribe

Already my comments on Webster give an indication of how this chapter will develop. In particular, there is in Webster a clear sense that the American language already *was* but also *ought to be*. This chapter approaches the roles of dictionaries through a framework based on analysis of a political constitution. That analysis is no doubt familiar, but will be introduced here as necessary context. Constitutions, in brief, seem simultaneously to describe a pre-existing state of affairs and produce it. In suggestive and familiar terms borrowed from J.L Austin, constitutions are, then, both constative and performative. Writing about the 'travels' of the theory of the performative, Jonathan Culler writes that 'the act of constitution, like that of literature, depends on a complex and paradoxical combination of the performative and constative, where in order to succeed, the act must convince by referring to states of affairs but where success consists of bringing into being the condition to which it refers' (2007, 152). In fact, this appears to be a form of impossibility. Fundamentally, the same structure is at work in Bhabha's previously mentioned postcolonial analysis of 'the people' as both pedagogical and performative, objects and subjects of the narration of their history and identity. Culler, of course, is discussing Jacques Derrida's brief but challenging and extremely suggestive discussion of the American Declaration of Independence. Derrida's analysis of the Declaration invites us to think about any act of constitution in a comparable way, even a constitutive 'act' such as the accumulative codifying acts leading to the event of a dictionary's publication (although the acts and events are not easy to differentiate, and 'event' as it features in Derrida's work is not a thing that happens at one time, then being over and done). Some of the explicit and important themes of Derrida's brief essay include the performative, the other, responsibility, the promise, the event, and the signature. It is also the case that the entire essay presumes an understanding of Austin's 'theory' of the performative, although that theory (which never aims to be and never becomes a theory) is not discussed, and so it is necessary to cross-reference the essay with some of Derrida's other works, particularly 'Signature Event Context' (in Derrida 1988) and other works relating to the performative.

No doubt Derrida's discussion of the Declaration was counter-intuitive on its initial presentation. Nonetheless, particularly in its analysis of the famous *are and ought to be* moment ('these United Colonies are, and of Right ought to be Free and Independent States'), Derrida's reading has proven fertile. However, given the kind of constitutional document at issue in Derrida's essay, it might seem difficult to 'apply' it to the dictionary's own institutive and constitutive acts, even if such an application has intuitive plausibility. The difficulty is that a written document that enables the people as origin of political power to define the nature of their self-government is superficially unlike a dictionary. Nonetheless, if we follow the intuitive plausibility through to some logical conclusions, the beginnings of a case become evident. Other aspects of political constitution include the possibility that they give expression to already existing forms of identity, cultural in addition to political desires, and so on. These broader aspects of constitution imply the intersection of political and linguistic constitution given expression by Webster. In each case, however, we find the implicit distinction between the pre-existing content and its form given by the constitution or dictionary itself. A slightly different way of expressing this logic is to say that language is used as a tool to assert or describe a state of affairs (e.g., this language exists, *here* we collect and categorize it). Yet this apparently common-sense understanding of the distinction is one that cannot hold, and Derrida's introduction of speech act theory complicates matters immediately. Austin, as is well known, rejects the *assertionalist* or descriptivist paradigm in language philosophy; when he focuses on declarative statements, he argues that in their expression of states of affairs they are but one aspect of language use. Of course, Austin is interested in theorizing the ways in which language is constituted by acts, successful or otherwise. Such acts include promising, betting, and so on, and are something that language philosophy for a long time tended to ignore. Indeed, declarative statements are ultimately not only statements of affairs but also acts themselves. Taking this sense of language as performative and 'applying' it to a political constitution, Derrida makes a striking argument about the Declaration of Independence as both statement and action. Instead of being 'merely' supplementary, and an expression of a pre-existing foundational identity as well as political and cultural desires, the written constitution becomes the 'foundation' itself. 'The people' is not a foundation given expression by the constitution, but instead is an effect. As Derrida argues, 'The signature invents the signer [...] in a sort of fabulous retroactivity. [...] This happens every day, but it is fabulous' (1986, 10). This signing creating the signer cannot happen; it is impossible in one sense, which is why it is fabulous. Yet of course this impossibility takes place on a daily basis. And, as Culler suggests, the impossibility is a necessary part of the happening. There is a necessary non-presence involved in the apparent act of making happen.

Derrida's short piece, which is an 'introduction' to a longer very different talk, opens many possibilities for development, and not everything relevant to dictionaries can be covered here. There are, however, other points that are highly suggestive; for example, Derrida suggests that the act of signature cannot be reduced in a constitution, and is not to be dismissed as a simple 'empirical accident'. However, other kinds of text, like dictionaries no doubt (numerous anecdotes about the history of the *OED* notwithstanding) at least must pretend to perform this reduction. Derrida writes the following about the act of signing: 'This attachment does not let itself be reduced, not as easily in any case as it does in a scientific text, where the value of the utterance is separated or cuts itself off from the name of its author without essential risk and, indeed, even has to be able to do so in order for it to pretend to objectivity' (1986, 8). Institutions, like scientific discourses, must become independent of the empirical individuals who produce them. However, instituting language structurally indicates that institutions keep the signature within themselves. Can we understand the general editor of a dictionary as a representative? And, if we can, a representative of whom – the other editors, the contributors, or of the community of users whose usage is apparently recorded, but whose usage is also and unavoidably thus prescribed? Derrida's essay puts in question representation as such (Jefferson, the others, the people, God). The people's independence is neither simply stated nor simply declared by the declaration. Are they already free, and simply stating this state of freedom, or are they making themselves free via the declaration? This series of questions does not indicate a set of problems that could be resolved, in order fully to comprehend the apparent impossibility that Culler summarizes so concisely; instead, the impossibility is itself constitutive. As Derrida continues: 'It is not a question of a difficult analysis which would fail in the fact of the structure of the acts involved and the overdetermined temporality of the events. This obscurity, this undecidability between, let's say, a performative structure and a constative structure, is *required* in order to produce the sought-after effect' (1986, 9). Again, the repeatability that we would casually say is introduced here is what enables the people who are yet not exactly there, not exactly present, and always in a sense to come.

Derrida's reflections must seem very abstract; the question for this chapter is partly what this non-presence indicates about dictionaries in general, and partly how exactly postcolonial dictionaries are exemplary of the kinds of structure Derrida analyses. In terms of the first issue, there is a danger of formalism in applying Derrida's analysis. According to Benhabib (1994), discussing Derrida alongside Jean-François Lyotard, it appears that in thinking about the limit cases of political constitutions the two thinkers have become stuck in a kind of linguistic formalism. According to Benhabib, they show little interest in the content of the constitutions in question. Indeed, she argues that in focusing on limit cases they neglect the extent to which mere routine politics is not mere or routine at all, but is instead an endless contestation and potential expansion of the political identity (the 'we') that is initially constituted. Benhabib's criticism is significant for this chapter, because while it may appear strange to apply such a criticism to a specifically linguistic context there is clearly a danger that such an analysis as this one may remain stuck in a kind of linguistic formalism, without discussion of specific examples. Meanwhile, the second issue can be refined in terms of how we might rethink the authority of dictionaries in the age of World Englishes, but might better be framed in terms of what should be called a post-varieties approach (something gaining prominence in World Englishes studies). There is a kind of 'illegitimacy' to foundational acts as there is no preceding state of existence to which they refer back. But that is not to suggest that the Declaration of Independence is illegitimate. Nor should we imagine it to be, when applied to this chapter's focus, an attack on the authority of dictionaries as such. Following Cameron's idea of a *necessary* verbal hygiene, a more fundamental level of 'violent' prescription, we should then be seeking the lesser violence. What would that mean in the context of the postcolonial dictionary and World Englishes? It seems at least arguable that the act of constitution inherent in something like the *Macquarie Dictionary*, drawing in vocabulary from across Asian Englishes, is appropriate for the development of World Englishes, which are increasingly clearly not discrete varieties. At the same time, such an approach holds off the moment at which a general global English is apparently described or declared, a declaration evident in the example of *EWED*. Holding on to these two levels of description, capturing both connectedness and separateness, is to seek the lesser violence. To explore this on a less abstract level, we can return to Edgar Schneider's work on the development of postcolonial Englishes.

Authority and Epicentre: Postcolonial Declarations

As mentioned at the beginning of this chapter, Schneider formulates an important model for the development of postcolonial Englishes (PCEs). He warns that the developmental process does not account for every instance in every context, but nonetheless suggests that 'there is a shared underlying process which drives their formation, accounts for many similarities between them, and appears to operate whenever a language is transplanted' (2007, 29). This complex process involves five diachronic stages: 1. foundation; 2. exonormative stabilization; 3. nativization; 4. endonormative stabilization; and 5. differentiation. In each stage Schneider focuses on each side in the communicative situation, i.e., both colonizer and colonized. This complicates the process through four different factors in each stage: 1. extralinguistic factors leading to; 2. identities forming on each side, leading to; 3. sociolinguistic constraints that cause; 4. specific linguistic structures. We can summarize this process in the following way. The settlers begin by considering themselves part of the 'us' of their origin, and so separate from the 'other' of the indigenous population they live alongside. Over time bonds with origin weaken, and that origin itself becomes an 'other'. Accordingly, a new 'us' begins to evolve, an identity incorporating the indigenous peoples. Meanwhile, that process occurs 'in reverse' for the indigenous peoples. Schneider explains the significance of his model as follows: 'to a considerable extent the emergence of PCEs is an identity-driven process of linguistic convergence (which [...] is followed by renewed divergence only in the end, once a certain level of homogeneity and stability has been reached)' (2007, 30). In short, linguistic developments follow a drive towards convergence which is led by pressures relating to identity. Once convergence has been achieved, the space for divergence is opened. Authority prescribes convergence followed by divergence, once certain conditions have been met.

However useful or accurate this developmental model may be for specific instances (and Schneider is surely right that it is more useful for some than others), it is clear that it works to understand changes within a particular context for individual postcolonial Englishes. This perhaps necessary or at least strategic limitation raises the question of what we might discover if we lifted it. Indeed, lifting this limitation is inherent to World Englishes studies, particularly perhaps in its post-varieties developments. In any case, a specific historical example with continued relevance and effects is useful here: Australia as a 'regional epicentre' of developments in World Englishes. Discussing Australian English as an epicentre, Pam Peters cites Schneider's model for the evolution of these Englishes, taking in fully fledged varieties, early stage nativizations, temporary fossilizations, and so on (Peters 2009). Peters continues to claim that little attention has been given to the *interaction* between these Englishes. Her focus is on the influence of Australian English (AusE) on New Zealand English (NZE). Peters builds her case through reference to several accounts of English that utilize related terminology. If, after Clyne (1992) and many other commentators, we utilize pluricentricity to understand English today, we can then think about distributed regional centres, which can be outposts of a primary centre or instead can be independent centres. Again, like many other commentators, Clyne thinks of English as centrifugal.

The choice of language is instructive, and hardly accidental or clumsy, no matter what some commentators may believe. Likewise, in her reference to Gerhard Leitner (2004), who proposes the term 'epicentre' for a regional standard, Peters is concerned to pursue the implications of such words. Epicentre implies the possibility of the variety (endonormative and stabilized) influencing other varieties, and this is what Peters calls 'epicentric influence', referring specifically to semantically transferred usages found in NZE based on convict settlement, and accordingly necessarily deriving from AusE. As has obvious plausibility, parallel political and cultural developments in the two countries have led to a range of linguistic connections. Peters argues that AusE and NZE have also developed in parallel, but with AusE providing the ground, through such texts as Edward Ellis Morris's *Austral English* (1898); as Peters suggests, there is, 'varietal difference, grounded in Australia' (Peters 2009, 115). Tracing later developments, Peters suggests that NZE often shows evidence of a tension between AusE informality and BrE formality, concluding that perhaps AusE is reinforcing NZE's evolution in the direction of greater informality (the divide between speech and writing still being much stronger than in AusE). Drawing broader conclusions, Peters argues that 'Mutual influence among emergent regional varieties should be factored into the evolutionary model for pluricentric languages, though it is more likely to come from settler than indigenized varieties of English' (Peters 2009, 122). That may well remain the case, and it will be a difficult violence to avoid, although one that World Englishes studies is already questioning.

It is revealing, I would argue, that Morris is one of Peters's examples, as it suggests the significance of such authoritative texts. Further, in spite of her suggestion (plausible enough in itself) that such mutual influence is more likely to *come from* settler varieties, the authority exerted by Australian English or the mutual influence could well be directed towards indigenized varieties, given a certain set of codifying contexts. That is where the *Macquarie Dictionary* is an interesting example, as we will consider later; for now, let us focus on Morris's contribution to the history of codification. Morris relates that the accumulation of material began as a response to James Murray's call for *OED* contributions, but that 'when my parcel of quotations had grown into a considerable heap, it occurred to me that the collection, if a little further trouble were expended upon it, might first enjoy an independent existence' (1898, x). His explanation of just how Australasian English differs from American English is instructive, and fits well a familiar framework for understanding the former's wealth of vocabulary items. Morris notes that the difference between the North and South Temperate Zones meant that users of English in Australia needed that much more new vocabulary to describe new flora and fauna: 'It is probably not too much to say that there never was an instance in history when so many new names were needed, and that there never will be such an occasion again, for never did settlers come nor can they ever again come, upon Flora and Fauna so completely different from anything seen by them before' (1898, xii).

American English is certainly distinct, with the American climate and animal life requiring English's adaptation; as Whitman's 'An American Primer' (1904) famously suggests, a 'new tongue' is required for 'new vistas'. However, according to Morris, the independence this new tongue apparently demonstrates is not as ample or even complete as that which arises from encountering kangaroos and other radically unfamiliar fauna as well as flora. Giving a twist to the familiar connection between climate and language, Morris suggests that the different 'zones' lead to quite different demands on languages, and accordingly that English was less 'stretched' in North America than it had to be in Australia. Furthermore, this stretching is entirely appropriate and worthy of being recorded. Morris does acknowledge the possibility that the usages recorded by his dictionary might well be dismissed: 'It may be thought by some precisians that all Australasian English is a corruption of the language' (1898, xvi). However, he is of course not prepared to accept such dismissiveness. At the same time, there are elements of embarrassment and condescension in his own reflections. For example, Morris sadly says that 'the man in the bush' has ended up naming many things. Bush dwellers' pidgin English (which Morris insists on calling 'pigeon' English, apparently as a way of resisting the very processes that led to it) is dismissed as obviously 'a falling away from the language of Bacon and Shakespeare' (1898, xv). This process is distinguished from what Morris calls, referring to Yule and Burnell's famous Anglo-Indian glossary, 'the law of Hobson-Jobson', which he defines in the following way: 'When a word comes from a foreign language, those who use it, not understanding it properly, give a twist to the word or to some part of it, from the hospitable desire to make the word at home in its new quarters, no regard, however, being paid to the sense' (1898, xv). *Hospitality* is an intriguing term here, fitting a long discursive tradition of linguicism in which English is more open than other languages. Morris analyses this apparent hospitality, and identifies two principal sources of new vocabulary, the first being altered English, meaning kinds of re-application. The second source is Aboriginal languages (including Maori, which Morris notes is much better studied than the Aboriginal languages of Australia). The hospitality he identifies implicitly foregrounds the second source. This becomes clear in the following passage, which expresses very concisely several aspects of the ideology of English uniqueness: 'English has certainly a richer vocabulary, a finer variety of words to express delicate distinctions of meaning, than any language that is or that ever was spoken: and this is because it has always been hospitable in the reception of new words. It is too late a day to close the doors against new words. This *Austral English Dictionary* merely catalogues and records those which at certain doors have already come in' (1898, xvi). In claiming that he is merely recording, Morris sidesteps the question of the connotations of his project, and the possible influence it might have. The connotations and broader influence are what Peters explores; perhaps we can explore them still further here, and take them in a rather different direction.

Regional and Global: Competing Authorities

As has already been mentioned, the *Macquarie Dictionary* is cited by Schneider as itself a form of declaration of linguistic independence. Such a description of the dictionary implies that the dictionary itself was not quite descriptive, or rather was not received as being descriptive. While it might embody a kind of democratizing spirit, challenging sources of 'imperial' linguistic authority, it also seems to have been received as, and intended to be, a prescription that such a form of English *ought to be*. Furthermore, as is well known, the *Macquarie* pays attention to other varieties of English, in particular Asian Englishes. Susan Butler makes the following claim in her discussion of the dictionary's geographical and cultural range:

> Our Australian experience has given us a sympathy for other varieties which have, as we have had, to make elbow room for themselves between the prestige forms of American and British English. It is our aim to give some account of these Englishes as faithfully as we can while acknowledging that our efforts can only produce an interim record and that we must await the definitive account undertaken by the speakers of these varieties. (Butler 1997, 285)

It is, then, not just a question of adding 'exotic' vocabulary; indeed, putting it like *that* is to voice exactly the sort of attitude against which the dictionary argues. While acknowledging the simple interest in vocabulary, Butler suggests that many terms were previously only covered from an imperialist perspective, but gradually lost their place. Echoing Robert Phillipson, Butler suggests that the older imperialism has been replaced by that of English as a second language (ESL), which fears recognition of such vocabulary. But Australian English itself is here imagined to be similar to various Asian Englishes, and the *Macquarie* is then a sympathetic form of linguistic authority. Indeed, Butler suggests that these Englishes are oriented towards American English in much the same way as Australian English, particularly through borrowing and redefinition. While there may be an inevitable re-centring involved (as Les Murray suggests), the dictionary is also concerned to think regionally about English, as well as maintaining an emphasis on local context: 'We hope to promote discussion of the role of English in the region, not focussing, just as so often happens, on its utilitarian purpose, but on the role that each regional variety of English has in reflecting the culture of the language community which speaks it' (1997, 285). While this is no doubt a more difficult balance to maintain than it sounds, it is surely preferable to these Englishes being swallowed up by either American English or a monolithic Global English.

Focusing on these Asian Englishes draws our attention to the fact that, in many ways, the Australian declaration of linguistic independence has been immensely successful. The 1988 publication of the first edition of the *Australian National Dictionary: A Dictionary of Australianisms on Historical Principles*, would appear to be confirmation of that independence. Indeed, for Bruce Moore, the battle to make Australian English independent has been long won, and this victory was one part of the end of the 'Cultural Cringe'. However, for Moore, the focus on independence has meant that all energy was expended on declaring that independence, with surprisingly little vocabulary deriving from more recent transformations in Australian identity: 'just as in the nineteenth century the babel of voices produced few borrowings into Australian English, the massive post-war migrations have produced no borrowings from migrant languages into Australian English' (2001, 55). The English makes happen a kind of Australian identity, a fundamentally white male identity that no longer exists. In terms of how Australian English makes Australian identity happen, there is a kind of lag here, or even a crisis, according to Moore: 'The irony is that while nationalism gave the language its confidence, the language now voices a crisis of identity. *Currency* no longer needs to define itself in relation to *sterling*. That is the end of the cultural cringe for Australian English, but perhaps only the beginning of the "re-casting" of the currency of national identity' (2001, 57). One way of addressing this crisis, and re-casting that identity, is of course to extend that identity across different varieties of English around Asia, and to orient Australia towards that continent instead; that, as is evident in Butler's formulations, is something the *Macquarie* was already addressing or perhaps helping to make happen.

A very different kind of project aiming to incorporate vocabulary from a range of Englishes is *EWED*. Published as part of a complex collaborative enterprise, and famously involving Microsoft (which published the *Encarta Encyclopedia* until 2009), *EWED* was announced as a radical break; as Tom McArthur writes, 'In a serious sense, and whatever its fate as both an electronic and a paper dictionary, *EWED* changed the rules of the game' (2004, 7). His comparison with the *New Oxford Dictionary of English* (NODE) and other projects suggests that *EWED* is part of a broader development that recognizes the possibility of a standard core that will enable a general worldwide competence. As he notes,

> We have never had uniformity and/or neutrality in English, and it would be perverse to expect it to emerge in the rough and tumble of today's eclectic usage. Yet, as CNN, the BBC, and even Microsoft suggest, the community of English users may have fewer problems at the world, international, or global level than in past national levels. There may now indeed be more conformity than less. (McArthur 2004, 15)

While McArthur may well be correct, that does not mean that *EWED* is without its problems. Some of those problems are practical, as diagnosed by Sidney I. Landau: 'If EWED had somehow managed the feat of using a form of international English for its defining vocabulary that worked equally well in the U.S. and Canada, Britain, Australia, New Zealand, and South Africa, we should be amazed and have to confess that a world perspective had been achieved. But no such effort has been made' (2000, 12). Instead, Landau notes that the dictionary has coverage of restricted terms, and essentially is published in two different forms, the British edition being significantly longer. These problems would tend to undermine claims to global coverage. Other problems are more political, but remain connected with the practical level. For example, Kayman (2004) notes that *EWED* specifically cites the symbolic value of the fall of the Berlin Wall, and accordingly we are invited to put it in the context of the so-called New World Order. For him, this is a salutary reminder of the ongoing connection between English and specific cultural forms. Meanwhile, Benson thinks critically about the supposedly post-imperial version of English the dictionary contains. He writes of a 'tendency to submerge the imperial origins of English as an international language within post-imperialist notions of "overlapping standards" and English as "the language of the world"' (2001, 121). For Benson, this tendency does not leave behind the imperial vision of English, as is evident in the failure to revise words from earlier dictionaries that were perceived as part of the periphery being 'discovered' by the centre (to illustrate, he gives definitions of 'durian' that betray an earlier imperial perspective). But perhaps the other limits to any such project, limits that extend beyond these seemingly empirical 'accidents', are the more significant. Re-centring may well be an unavoidable aspect of codification, even in the context of dictionaries that are avowedly regional, but dictionaries of global English mask this re-centring, disclaiming their hegemonic effects. *Macquarie* has been alive to these hegemonic effects, and so represents a far better authoritative practice than *EWED*.

I began this chapter by discussing the *Coxford Singlish Dictionary*, and in closing I would like to return to issues that arise from thinking about that dictionary seriously. Those issues are to do with technology, but not the kind of technology that drives something like the idea of global English encountered in the *EWED*. Of course, codification has its locations, institutional and otherwise. The fact that writing is increasingly speech-linked focuses our attention on the mechanisms and motivations for this relative shift. It becomes clear that the same technological shifts leading to speech-linking also enable accelerated attention and access to codification. Codification is, therefore, shifting according to the same set of factors that is making its target move with increasing speed. Codification might be expected to reduce complexity and standardize the non-standard, in this scenario, yet the *OED* just as much as other repositories of authority is edited on the basis of lexicographic democracy and objectivity implicit in the very idea of descriptiveness. Accordingly, while fluid authority is still authority, we must qualify this statement with the observation that codifiers increasingly seek the lesser violence in recognizing the diversity of Englishes. The technology involved points us towards an essential aspect of this lesser violence: that it recognize a certain post-varieties reality to Englishes, a recognition that must retain an understanding of the importance of national varieties while also building upon a supranational understanding that carefully resists Englishes being subsumed by a hegemonic global English. This balance already appears a most difficult one to achieve, yet the reality of World Englishes is increasingly forcing it upon our understanding.

Conclusion

It is impossible for dictionaries, or any other form of codification, to avoid doing a certain kind of violence to that which they record, and in turn to those who consult them as authorities. That has not stopped some commentators attempting to celebrate an apparently innate hospitality demonstrated by the English language, which presumably accompanies its lack of authoritative academy, allowing its adoption and adaptation throughout the world. Writing with a breezy optimism about the power and potential of Global English, McCrum describes the difference between the grand projects that codified English and French:

> In France, an authorised process of writing a national dictionary codified, solidified and ultimately fossilized the language. For English, the dictionary process achieved the exact opposite: it gave expression to its contagious adaptability, catchy populism and innate subversiveness. French might be the language of international relations, but its potential as a world language would remain circumscribed by custom, temperament and philosophical preference. (McCrum 2010, 145)

McCrum is summarizing the state of affairs in which Johnson's work intervened, and also the distinctly national achievement for which it was celebrated by Garrick and others. But, of course, as Mugglestone demonstrates, even the context for the *OED*'s specifically historical and scientific method was one in which so-called national honour was at stake (2000, 4). These contrasting histories seem to have led us to our current situation, according to McCrum, with *Francophonie* becoming an apparently ever more 'minor' aspect of international linguistic relations, and English seemingly unassailable as the lingua franca of globalization. Of course, dictionaries are somewhat more complex than they seem, and codifying efforts for English are hardly limited to the UK and the US. McCrum presents us with a 'Globish' that remains tied to histories and controversies remarkably distant from many of our concerns. Questions about the codification of Englishes are now questions that involve varieties and speakers across the world, acting to declare their independence, however uneasily or incompletely. These other acts of linguistic self-determination demand our attention, as this chapter has explored.

What this chapter has shown is that in the context of World Englishes dictionaries have exaggerated the tendencies identified by Webster's approach to American English. As commentators such as Cameron (1995) have pointed out, there will be a necessary element of 'prescription' to dictionaries; as she suggests, 'there is no escape from normativity' (1995, 10). However, what the dictionary prescribes is not only usage, but also that something exists, whether 'English' in general, or 'American English', or some other variety of English, including indeed a 'World English' as found in *EWED*. That is a strange way to phrase it, of course, and necessarily so; to prescribe that something exists, rather than to describe that it exists, captures the sense that it both *should* and somehow already *does* exist. As Royle suggests, some dictionaries, perhaps those associated with established, native speaker Englishes, simply say that *this language exists*. The postcolonial dictionary, meanwhile, goes further in declaring, through a 'fabulous retroactivity', both that *this language exists,* and that *this language ought to be.* Yet that is not quite the full story, for the postcolonial dictionary also says that this language exists *and therefore its speakers ought to be.* That is explicit in Webster's discussion of the need for American English, which is a need both to be independent from British English and to be aligned to a common American English, thereby to a common American identity. Yet, as Webster astutely observes, the danger of being influenced from afar (from Britain and Europe more generally) is both a possibility and a kind of absurdity. That distance seems too great, to Webster, for any real influence on American English to continue for any length of time, and he thinks it inevitable that future divergence would be significant. However, as the example of Australia and New Zealand indicates, once you have one break, you can obviously have more, perhaps indeed many more, and then there arises once again that question of influence. As Peters argues, Australian English may well have functioned as a kind of regional epicentre. The implications of that example, in the context of World Englishes, are hinted at by the incorporation of Asian English vocabulary in a project such as the *Macquarie Dictionary.* However noble the motivations, the move to re-centre is always possible in such an undertaking, and reinstates a varieties-based paradigm. But influence is far more far-reaching and interconnected in the world of World Englishes, meaning that dictionaries need to come to terms with a post-varieties context, and act within a post-varieties paradigm. However, that does not necessarily lead us to something like a dictionary of global English, as might be found in the example of *EWED*, which, however well-meaning its conception, really might be described in terms of linguistic imperialism. It appears that a proliferation of dictionaries, postcolonial and otherwise, is both *what ought to be* and, of course, *what is.*

CHAPTER 5

Writing after the End of Empire: Composition, Community, and Creativity

Suppose we come across someone who looks to us subordinated and oppressed but who does not give us any signs of being in that state, at least signs that we would recognize?

Dipesh Chakrabarty, 'A Correspondence on Provincializing Europe'

Whoever teaches without emancipating stultifies. And whoever emancipates doesn't have to worry about what the emancipated person learns. He will learn what he wants, nothing maybe.

Jacques Rancière, *The Ignorant Schoolmaster*

Introduction

It is arguable that cultural studies as a discipline has both broadened the scope of literary studies and simultaneously placed its privilege in question. Nonetheless, the study of World Englishes, despite its institutional location in linguistics, continues to give a certain privilege to literary creativity, elevating this creativity in the classroom and in research. As evidence of this continued privilege, recent issues of key journals such as *World Englishes*, and also newly established programmes in relevant institutions (for example, the City University of Hong Kong's MFA in Creative Writing, launched in 2010), give emphasis to creative writing in World Englishes. In fact, there are even efforts to transform aspects of composition along lines broadly influenced by this emphasis, and if those efforts have begun in the North American context they will perhaps flourish even more readily in the numerous contexts of World Englishes. Indeed, this continued emphasis has intuitive plausibility, with literature seen as the natural focus for the true linguistic innovation characteristic of an owned and localized variety of English. Indeed, in an obvious example such as Indian English, its historical depth is partly exemplified by its long literary tradition, including English language writing's acknowledgement by the Sahitya Akademi. Many of the categories of cultural studies might themselves play into this continued privilege, deriving as they appear to do from literary theories (which were, perhaps, themselves more often than not adaptations from varieties of linguistics). And, after all, in the study of World Englishes we are focusing on linguistic change, so what could seem more natural than to privilege literature? Perhaps what cultural studies can offer us when we focus on World Englishes is a series of corrective perspectives that help us understand quite why these Englishes are to a great extent not understood as continued forms of linguistic imperialism. Cultural studies perspectives, in putting the English language (and English literature) alongside other cultural forms (and priorities), help us understand World Englishes in terms of the central category of hegemony; consensus implying dissensus, globalization implying glocalization. This chapter considers how creativity and creative writing come to be understood as (and *taught* as) drivers of dissensus.

Such creative dissensus is clearly a challenge (however partial) to the assumption that English around the world operates as a form of ongoing linguistic imperialism. The usefulness of hegemony, central to cultural studies, obviously supplements the way commentators such as Robert Phillipson use the term. Cultural studies takes the Gramscian understanding of the term and extends it, and that extension has great relevance to World Englishes. Gramsci was interested in the counter-hegemonic utterance, an utterance that works against the common-sense understanding of the world that is produced by hegemony; it concerns, then, meaning that is supposedly excluded from our thought. For Gramsci, we are free to speak, to interpret, or to refuse to give our consent. When we respond to cultural texts, our production of meaning is not preordained, contained and conditioned by the text's structural and semiotic elements; instead, there are alternative meanings, which we can both find and produce ourselves. If we are interested in the connection between World Englishes and hegemony, then we are interested in the *reception* of English; we become interested in audiences, and what they do with the culture around them. One such audience is obviously found in the classroom, where students of English around the world often find themselves faced with learning not just the language but also the literature of the traditionally English-speaking world, as well as extending their abilities through creative writing of various kinds. While it may seem that the ongoing privilege of literary studies is a problem, maintaining a gap between learners and the mighty native speaker creator (whether that speaker is a writer or not), it can instead be argued that literary studies is part of a general stress on a creativity that is implicitly political, and that the creativity of Englishes is an aspect of resistance to a monolithic and imperialist English.

Apparently paradoxically, that resistance is also directed towards the celebration of difference. The discourses of World Englishes and postcolonialism share an emphasis on the liberation of difference. When transferred to the context of composition studies, this emphasis appears to demand that, on an abstract level, composition should assume qualities associated with creative writing. Application of the postcolonial paradigm to the US composition context is under way, but this chapter makes a comparison between that context and Hong Kong in order to understand attitudes of partial resistance to the embrace of World Englishes and their processes of cultural translation. It considers possible explanations for such resistance, and speculates about wider issues concerning postcolonial theory and the legitimate application of its concepts, specifically difference and cultural translation. The potential blending of aspects of creative writing and composition is one way that the privileges of literary study might be indirectly defended in a foreign language context. In arguing for the continued importance to language students of studying literature, emphasis is clearly placed on the significance of linguistic innovation. The discourse of World Englishes invites teachers to shift (to some extent, in certain parts of the curriculum) that emphasis away from 'distant' creative writers (still most frequently native speakers, conventionally understood) to the students' own creativity. Furthermore, such creativity does not have to remain confined to the creative writing course, but can also be found and encouraged in composition, as well as, by extension, critical writing about literature. In this way, the distinction between error and innovation is demonstrated to be less clear than students assume. It has even been argued by some commentators that linguistic facts imply an *obligation* not only on the teacher but also the student. Describing the pedagogical issues arising from English's status as a formerly colonial language now dominant under globalization, Christine Pearson Casanave notes that English's association with economic, cultural, and political dominance demands that its role in education is considered very carefully indeed. One aspect of this consideration is, she suggests, students' own understanding and application of their insights into English's roles: 'Teachers who hold strong beliefs about the inseparability of language and politics claim that L2 writing students need not only to be aware of the ways that the English language is implicated in issues of power but also to recognize that they have the right, or perhaps the obligation, to question, resist, and challenge the status quo' (2004, 197). I cannot see any objection to the idea of it being a right, but Casanave's hesitation in reporting it as an obligation is appropriate, as it is obviously not the teacher's role to dictate what should and should not be concluded, or what should and should not be then done. Nonetheless, it is often the case that postcolonial studies tends towards prescribing a course of action for students. The inseparability of language and politics to which Casanave refers can be framed in various ways, but there is no doubt that postcolonialism has become one of the most widely utilized frameworks. Furthermore, 'obligation' is an apt way to describe the way some commentators conceive the situation described above. According to some perspectives, postcolonialism is not only a possibility when we are discussing creativity and composition; a postcolonial perspective appears to be a *necessity*, and is a perspective that students themselves hardly seem allowed to remain indifferent to, let alone reject entirely. It is not only a question of how to discuss the teaching of English around the world, or to rethink the teaching of composition. It seems to be obligatory to bend English itself into new shapes, and so to embrace the diversity of Englishes available to different audiences and writers around the world. In a way, it begins to seem obligatory not only to understand and accept World Englishes, but also to write in them.

However, this laudable emphasis on English being or becoming Englishes (i.e., potentially the 'property' of language students, wherever they may be) inevitably comes into conflict with the demands of local educational institutions (both universities and governments) as well as students (and also indeed parents). Against the discourse of World Englishes practising the political and philosophical assumptions of postcolonial studies, there are powerful countervailing forces that demand less liberation of difference and more bolstering of sameness; indeed, it is demanded that the distinction between error and innovation is not only maintained but also strengthened, explained by teachers in greater depth, and fully respected by students. Creativity in such a context might appear, depending on one's perspective, a laissez-faire acceptance of the blending and blurring of properly distinct linguistic and cultural identities. These general points about the tensions deriving from the teaching and researching of World Englishes will be explored in relation to Hong Kong, understood primarily as postcolonial and a context in which English is a foreign language, even if Hong Kong is one of many contexts in which the English as a second language/English as a foreign language (ESL/EFL) distinction is less obvious than it seems. It will be compared with Singapore, a context in which a stress on creativity makes more immediate sense, in that Singaporeans (depending on age, class, and other factors) might well self-identity as native speakers, and are operating in a multilingual context in which English is termed a second rather than foreign language. It is arguable that the situation in Hong Kong is changing, and is hardly uniform across even tertiary institutions (with two of eight such government-funded institutions incorporating Chinese-medium instruction), but even so the desire to discuss its English as one of the World Englishes is symptomatic of the political and philosophical investments of postcolonial studies, perhaps telling us less about the demands and expectations of the postcolonial subjects themselves.

Fretting in the Shadow of Language

The creative writer's expression of anxiety concerning the English language is a familiar postcolonial element. Stephen Dedalus's soul fretting in the shadow of the dean's language is perhaps only the most famous representation of a postcolonial predicament in which even the most adept and innovative stylists fail to escape entirely the sense in which they should not be using the language at all. Indeed, this anxiety applies even to writers who speak only English. If even these often game-changing creative writers have wrestled with that language, it might seem strange to want to encourage all learners of English to embrace their creative capacity. That would be surely to generalize the anxiety, to deepen uncertainties in use of a language that teaching might be expected to alleviate to some extent. Nonetheless, in English studies there has been a shift from getting it right to getting it wrong in your own way. A shift of emphasis has indeed taken place, and that is one thing I want to focus on here. My focus will also be not only on how World Englishes help us understand the spread of English but also on how the category 'World Englishes' itself betrays its reliance on certain assumptions that can be problematic, depending on context. Those assumptions I will call 'postcolonial', but they are hardly shared by all the writers and critics associated with that term. Instead, they are the assumptions of postcolonial theory, even if that is itself an imprecise generalization. The discourses of World Englishes and postcolonialism share an emphasis on the liberation of difference. As I have already suggested, when that emphasis is transferred to the context of composition studies, it entails that composition should assume qualities associated with creative writing. However, this chapter assumes that transferring these qualities is often highly problematic, which becomes clear through comparing composition practices in different contexts.

Whatever our perspective on this cultural translation, it has implications for the practice of English composition in the postcolonial classroom. These implications derive in particular from the blurring of the distinction between error and innovation; in the context of widened 'ownership' of English implied by World Englishes, it is difficult to justify all the corrections inherent in some versions of composition studies. Needless to say, however, there is no single postcolonial classroom, and no abstract model of cultural translation can help us understand all the instances of World Englishes. It seems necessary, then, to compare instances in which cultural translation is embraced with those in which it is to some extent rejected. In order to make this comparison, we can put postcolonial theory and World Englishes in the context of composition studies, which in some traditions and in certain contexts (particularly the North American context) has in more recent times conceived its role as one of liberating potential difference rather than policing the sameness of standards. Both postcolonial theory and World Englishes have much to offer the theory and practice of such a composition studies. Indeed, it is increasingly common to find composition theorized in terms of being postcolonial (see, for example, Lunsford and Ouzgane 2004). Additionally, the acknowledgement that error and incipient innovation are inherently indistinguishable, an acknowledgement that drives certain perspectives on World Englishes, has clear relevance to any composition practice that would seek to embrace *creativity-in-difference*. Nonetheless, before we embrace a postcolonial composition that coincides with the presuppositions of World Englishes it is necessary to consider the counter-arguments that might be marshalled in the service of *the same*. Composition studies obviously have an institutional grounding, and a geographical location. Furthermore, composition is distinct from creative writing, and it is not something to be found in all English-language-medium tertiary institutions, not even in all native speaker contexts. The specificity of composition as pedagogical object might help us understand its political and philosophical openness to postcolonial theory and World Englishes, but might also demand that we reassess the application of these fields' insights in other contexts.

My approach is to consider some of the arguments for a postcolonial composition studies, and then, in order to avoid context-stripping, to re-contextualize them in terms of a historically postcolonial context (what Terry Eagleton (1998) and no doubt many others would call a 'real' postcolonial context). That context is my own, a trilingual university in Hong Kong, which, while even in local terms atypical, is revealing when the most familiar political-philosophical postcolonial perspective is brought to bear on it. Before getting to that specific context it is necessary to be selective (but not simply partial) in order to grasp issues in composition studies. There is, of course, a huge range of material on which to draw in composition studies, which in turn draws on a range of complex thinkers, sometimes from other fields, sometimes working within composition itself. However, in order to understand postcolonial composition it is possible to pick out certain trends that have been evident for some time. Much contemporary composition, in common with thinking about pedagogy across many disciplines, owes a great deal to the work of Paolo Freire. Freire (1970) distinguished the *banking* concept of education, in which there is no encouragement of critical thinking (possibly even discouragement), and no place for the student voice, from *problem-posing* education, in which the student voice is encouraged, and the aspiration is to critical consciousness. Composition has converted this emphasis into an emphasis on process rather than product, although reintegration of the two has also been important. Much of the work relevant to a postcolonial composition draws on this emphasis on process, and frames it using a range of theorists such as Bakhtin, Derrida, and even Deleuze. For example, discussing what she calls a pedagogy of possibility, conceived in terms drawn from Bakhtin, Kay Halasek stresses the importance of student agency, resistance to norms, and holding open the possibility of becoming. Composition needs to hold open the possibility of ideological understanding and then change: 'The student as author is an agent in her own ideological becoming, a person whose intentions and responsibility for learning determine and define what personal and cultural structures she chooses to resist and transform. Students and writing instructors who take seriously their own, and one another's, ideological development restore the possibility for cultural and political change' (1999, 193). Unsurprisingly, a composition drawing on Bakhtin's work seeks to enable a diversity of voices in the classroom. Composition studies indeed appears well placed to put into practice discourses concerning cultural change because in the composition context, as Halasek suggests, the student is an author. However, as she makes clear, the range of different authorial voices in the composition classroom is at least as important as the individual voice. Only through engagement and dialogue can the individual become, and presumably continue becoming.

To some extent, drawing on Bakhtin in this way is a way both of describing classroom practicalities and of philosophizing concerning linguistic-political fundamentals. Accordingly, it is unsurprising that composition addresses issues relevant to postcolonial and World Englishes sites that are found outside the North American institutional context. It also important to stress that the diversity of student populations has raised the question not only of different voices but also of different languages, and of code-switching and code-mixing. To the extent that composition has challenged myths concerning monolingualism, it fits well far-flung and wide-ranging discussions. As Paul Kei Matsuda suggests, however, this monolingualism is something that continues to require challenging: 'It is important for composition scholars, regardless of specialization, to reexamine how and to what extent the monolingual assumption pervades the field and its intellectual practices, and to consider ways of moving beyond those unexamined assumptions' (2012, 49). On one level, this challenge is necessary in order to avoid prejudice against multilin-gualism, which has so often been viewed as an impediment, whether to educational opportunity or cultural 'integration'. But we can be more 'realist' and argue that, if nothing else, this challenge is necessary in order to rise to the demands of globalization. Students are not merely preparing for professional life within a well-bounded nation, and so composition must be partly, 'about preparing students – both domestic and international – for the increasingly globalized world that has always been, and will continue to be, multilingual' (2012, 36). As Matsuda implies, monolingualism has been historically rare. The question of whether or not we should be buying into the myth of language as commodity, or education as commodity, in order to educate global citizens as global entrepreneurs, is one on which I have already commented, and I am sure that Matsuda is not making that argument anyway. Even outside the realm of neo-liberal educational realism, we should continue to make the case that multilingualism is an advantage and asset. This is certainly the case for those working in North American composition, and Matsuda insists that 'the question is no longer limited to how to prepare students from around the world to write like traditional students from North America; it is time to start thinking more seriously about how to prepare monolingual students to write like the rest of the world' (2012, 50). And how do students write in the rest of the world, assuming he is not referring to other nations stereotyped as monolingual Anglophone contexts? Again, in raising such questions composition draws inevitably close to the concerns of World Englishes. Matsuda is alive to the need to pay attention to the differences involved in studying this broad spectrum of English language contexts: he stresses the different language situations, the different forms of English, and of course the different politics of languages to be found in different contexts. All of these differences are directly relevant when we consider Hong Kong, as this chapter will do later.

These suggestions about composition are important, and are given shape through stress on particular aspects of class, sexuality, ethnicity, gender, and so on. What is most relevant to my concerns, of course, is the already mentioned interest that composition has shown in postcolonial studies. The collection *Crossing Borderlands* (Lunsford and Ouzgane 2004) brings together many perspectives on postcolonial studies from composition specialists (one of the complaints to which I will return is that the interest is rarely returned). In their introduction, the editors suggest that making the connection is important because both disciplines interrogate the production of a certain kind of obedient subject, and seek forms of resistance to that production. Accordingly, it is surprising that connections have been limited, although composition's struggle for institutional recognition was a distraction, and it tended to essentialize the student writer. Additionally, they suggest that postcolonial studies has focused on Europe and ignored the postcolonial nature of the US. Finally, they suggest that postcolonialism has spoken for students (at best, as students are often not mentioned at all). Seeking to make the connection more clearly, scholars cover various points of convergence, as well as divergence. In terms of convergence, and what postcolonial studies can offer composition, there are some strikingly clear statements. For example, Gary A. Olson argues for the potential benefits of adding a postcolonial perspective to composition. He suggests that it works to empower students, by giving them an agency usually denied by teachers, who, despite their best intentions, tend to marginalize students. Postcolonial theory tells us about relations of power between students and teachers, but it also illuminates, as we would expect, relations between different racial and ethnic groups. As Olson suggests, it demonstrates how colonial structures frame 'how learning occurs, or doesn't, how students relate to peers and to teachers' (2004, 89). We can agree that postcolonial theory provides conceptual frameworks for understanding both what composition does and what it fails to do, often in spite of itself. While postcolonial studies may well have focused too much of its attention on Europe and its former colonies, one outcome of turning attention to the North American university context is to subject it, including composition, to rigorous critique. Olson is clearly concerned about how composition falls into various rhetorical, pedagogical, and political traps, even when it apparently already comprehends those traps all too well. So, it appears that the conceptual and political traffic is unidirectional, with composition in the position of being corrected by the superior theoretical perspective afforded by postcolonial studies. Nonetheless, as already mentioned, there are numerous moments when apparent weaknesses of postcolonial studies come under scrutiny, and these moments will be key to my discussion of Hong Kong.

One criticism levelled at postcolonial studies is that it is a species of rhetorical conflation of very different political and economic positions. Once again, it is necessary to remember that there is postcolonialism and 'postcolonialism' (even if this distinction will not always be as obvious as it seems). Deeprika Bahri makes this argument in a way familiar from the discussion of cultural translation as a concept: 'In effect, the easy recourse to postcolonial tropes and concepts dehistoricizes the local struggle and prevents the development of specific strategies to cope with the particularities of the moment, whether in the classroom or in theory' (2004, 80). Postcolonial theory's seductive vocabulary of the hybrid and the marginal distracts us from the necessary task of contextualization and specification. Postcolonial theorists often speak from somewhat privileged positions, something which should be recalled each time we wish to apply their vocabularies elsewhere. But, even if we accept the validity of their terminology, we would do well to heed Susan C. Jarratt's implicit warning that there is a difference between what teachers argue that students are *capable* of doing, and what they actual *will* do or *desire* to do. After exploring the complex rhetorical substitutions used by Spivak and others, Jarratt writes that 'Imagining students capable of inscribing multiple selves could be an important reading posture for teachers concerned with subject construction in a post-colonial era' (2004, 122). The stress here is on imagining, rather than speaking *for* or demanding *from*, students. Indeed, Jarratt emphasizes that students are unlikely to employ consciously the forms of rhetoric found in the work of, for example, Trinh T. Minh-ha. There is a definite danger in imposing expectations, and being disappointed when they remain unfulfilled.

Following such critical remarks, it is clear that the connection between postcolonial studies and composition is hardly as unidirectional as it superficially seems; indeed, it might only seem unidirectional to those outside or unfamiliar with the institutional and intellectual contexts. In fact, the most trenchant discussion of postcolonial studies is found in Min-Zhan Lu's chapter immediately following the introduction. She seeks to question composition's position as grateful recipient of gifts from theory and literary studies more generally (and, in this, postcolonial studies' supposedly superior position is not alone in being questioned). Surveying other chapters in the collection, she makes some very challenging arguments. For example, she contends that everyone expects you (whoever *you* may be in English studies) to know theory, or know theorists at least, even if you have little interest in theory as such. By contrast, no one has any such expectations regarding composition studies. Postcolonial specialists simply do not seem to have any sense of what goes on in composition teaching or research. Furthermore, by sharp contrast with composition, postcolonial studies appears to have little understanding *of* or even interest *in* the students in the classroom. Nor, Lu argues, does it have much interest in the materiality of writing (I am less convinced on this point, particularly as Lu is specifically targeting Spivak, who often gives us too much sense of materiality and too little actual writing). From Lu's perspective, postcolonial studies has much to learn from composition, particularly when it comes to being situated and attentive to the dangers in assuming that we teachers know better than students. As she writes, 'We cannot speak *for* the student writers – legislate what they can, want, or need to do – but only *to* them in an *imagined* conversation *across* social, historical, and institutional divisions' (2004, 27). This last point echoes Jarratt, in reminding us not to feel too confident that we have the political and philosophical answers that students simply need to internalize, and then put into practice. Postcolonial composition cannot in all seriousness aim to save its students from themselves, as we will explore in some detail later.

While the postcolonial tendencies in composition studies are certainly most appropriate, it is already clear that we should not conclude that composition was *destined* to be drawn into postcolonialism's orbit, at least partly because composition has been on many occasions deemed secondary and supplementary, as Lu's intervention makes clear. Discussing this apparent relegation, Sidney I. Dobrin discusses writing about composition studies in terms of ideas about supplementarity drawn from Derrida. Seeking a postcomposition, Dobrin is careful to note that it will forever remain *post*, and will never be realized in a future present. Composition is not something that is perfectible, and on one level cannot be conceived in terms of a checklist of concrete practices. In fact, there is a danger in postcolonial composition placing a demand on both professorial practitioners and students. Postcolonializing composition seeks to resist one hegemonic composition, but intuitively postcolonial composition might in turn appear a form of hegemony, and that is inevitable, particularly if we view it as a necessary realization of political goals, with a checklist of beliefs and consequent pedagogical activities. Disciplines come into being as a consequence of a process of stabilization, placing limits on the play of hybridity and flux. While that is inevitable, it needs to be engaged and recalled by any composition that desires to be open to *possibility*, as Halasek and many others understand it. Attempting to write in a manner that is appropriate to this openness, Dobrin suggests that composition is necessarily hegemonic, defining itself as open but in spite of that rhetoric retaining a divisive and exclusive institutional and intellectual identity: 'Composition guards its places by presenting a discourse of inclusiveness, by making that discourse seem a natural part of the field's discourse. But that diversity, that openness to dissent, must share occupation within composition's places' (2007, 30). For Dobrin, it could not be otherwise, but the situation he describes raises important issues about composition as an oppositional field. If we follow Dobrin's argument, the evident problem is not solely theoretical, however abstract my discussion here. The situation he describes is partly a matter of students being expected to take responsibility for their product, however central composition studies might make the process that leads to it. But, on a theoretical level, which is the level Dobrin explicitly addresses, there is a concern that composition studies functions as a discipline with clearly demarcated territories, despite its theoretical commitments to diversity and its institutional experience of external assault (that assault coming particularly perhaps from literature departments, but also elsewhere). The theoretical issue might appear to be an inevitable outcome of both intellectual engagement and negotiation, and of institutional self-protectiveness. But I think the key is that it only becomes a real problem if the state of composition studies is understood to be final, or even perfected.

That danger is what drives Dobrin and others to conceive composition studies in terms of postcomposition. As already discussed, Dobrin does not believe that postcomposition can ever be brought into being; it must forever be open to revision, and always be on the verge, to come. Of course it is hardly possible to reject disciplinary stabilization, just as languages or cultures have centripetal as well as centrifugal tendencies. If nothing else, composition has, like many other disciplines, defined itself in order to defend itself. Composition has standardized itself, forming boundaries around itself, and defining a group of practitioners, students as well as teachers. As Dobrin puts it, 'This is what We do; everything else falls outside our governance. Standardization makes validation easier, but standardization is always a reduction, not an elevation' (2011, 103). There are various reasons why boundary formation frequently feels necessary. Composition studies has itself had moments of institutional anxiety, and such anxieties often demand a healthy dose of certainty and decisive framing. Utilizing Mark Taylor's ideas concerning complexity, Dobrin thinks about composition in the following way: 'It is specifically in spaces at the edge of chaos where the potential postcomposition lies, where spaces of complexity, ecological relations, and posthuman agents begin to expose the dynamic facts to the phenomena of writing. It is in and through such spaces we engage postcomposition's becoming' (2011, 159). Dobrin's suggestions are again, according to his logic of the post, not spaces that would lead to a (cultural-political) realization or completion of composition. Indeed, there is something *spectral* about it (as indeed there ought to be in any discipline). Citing Derrida and Geoffrey Bennington, Dobrin explicitly discusses postcomposition as concerned with *composition studies-to-come* that will never be achieved, over and done with, in some future present. With this in mind, the postcolonializing of composition studies should be seen as no different from any other process or adaptation of composition studies; it will not lead to a product (a *properly* postcolonial composition, as it were) that would be the fulfilment of the political destiny of composition studies, however urgent the issues raised by global English and World Englishes. Indeed, writing after the end of empire shares something of the *post-ness* of postcomposition as Dobrin outlines it, and we should perhaps desire a generalization of Stephen Dedalus's fretfulness. That generalization could only be highly abstract, and difficult to put into practice.

Bilingual Creativity and Composition Studies

We can now move on to re-contextualize the arguments in favour of a postcolonial composition studies in terms of World Englishes, and later our historically postcolonial context. The ways in which composition has been rethought are fascinating, but such work requires specificity and location. As Powell and Tassoni remind us, 'In each different place we have experienced, not only does the broader landscape shape specific, local academic practice – from research to teaching to service – in distinctive ways, but the academy shapes the local landscape in particular, site-specific ways as well' (2009, 3). Site-specificity, implying the necessity of ethnographic perspectives, can help us guard against context-stripping. But if we enter that ethnographic perspective specificity can begin to seem irreducible, and it might be wondered if there is any good reason to expect perspectives developed in the context of the North American composition classroom to have relevance in a different context such as Hong Kong. Of course, there is an immediate if perhaps only superficial plausibility in attempting to apply some of composition studies' insights in a postcolonial context, particularly now composition studies have postcolonialized themselves to some extent. Yet there are limits to that applicability, particularly given the transformations undergone by postco-lonial theory in other disciplinary contexts. Accordingly, it will be necessary to make this next translation carefully, paying attention to Hong Kong's resistance to certain implications of the postcolonial paradigm. The first thing that must be noted is that despite its relatively small number of institutions, and the superficial emphasis on English medium instruction, there has been significant diversity within the Hong Kong university system. Furthermore, that system is in a state of flux, and not entirely due to the symbolic and practical consequences of 1997's 'Handover'. Bolton (2003) writes optimistically about the possibilities for English in a Chinese Hong Kong, and certainly there have been developments over the last decade. They have not all been predictable, and certainly have not been consistent across different institutions. For example, writing about Lingnan University, Meaghan Morris observes its state of partial triglossia, with English increasingly ascendant, and insists that the linguistic politics of the institution must be understood as local choice rather than external imposition: 'This Anglophone event in our institutional life is a locally motivated, practical Hong Kong response to the globalizing policies aggressively pursued by the PRC' (2010, 188). For Morris, English may well be becoming more important at Lingnan University, but diagnosis of linguistic imperialism will take us only so far. Meanwhile, the Chinese University of Hong Kong has been, from its foundation (with moments of controversy, becoming perhaps more frequent; see Lin and Man 2011) a multilingual tertiary institution. Within that context, an English department has a peculiar role, particularly given that the university was initially partly defined by its difference from the Anglophone University of Hong Kong. Within that even more limited context, the role of English-language creativity for local students becomes rather interesting, and can act as a measure of the instantiation of values and attitudes vis-à-vis English in the Hong Kong context. According to commentators such as Phillipson (1992) and Pennycook (1998), postco-lonial cultures should retain (at the least) a healthy scepticism with regard to the ongoing presence of English in their educational institutions. With some hesitation and uncertainty, the Hong Kong university system (at least, elements of that system) has begun to embrace a 'realist' vision of international or globalized tertiary education, one aspect of which is a multilingual vision of curriculum delivery (as well as other aspects of education). In embracing this vision, it has acknowledged the fact that monolingualism has been rare, historically speaking, and the further conclusion that bi- or (more likely) multilingualism will be the global norm in the relatively near future. That fact raises the question of what will derive from this multilingual education, particularly with regard to the future varieties of English. It also raises the question of the ongoing political implications of such educational practices. World Englishes, as a philosophical-political framework, tends towards celebration of the potential of such education, and in this celebration it coincides with postcolonial theory in many of its guises. Such a position appears to celebrate cultural translation as such for its inherent creativity. There are, however, possible limitations to this position that need to be considered.

Such limitations are frequently obscured by the celebration of World Englishes' cultural translation that coincides with the basic assumptions of postcolonial theory. Returning to Kachru's argument concerning bilingual creativity, it is one with very interesting implications for the teaching of composition, wherever the students may be. If bi- and multilingualism have at best been ignored in composition studies (specifically in the US context), or perceived as a problem to be overcome (sometimes even through teaching students in separate classes according to linguistic background), Kachru's argument clearly suggests that we instead view multilingualism as an advantage. Again, it should be clear that in making this argument Kachru approaches a position familiar from traditions in postcolonial studies. As I have already mentioned, postcolonialism tends towards a critical view of monolingualism as convergent with or consequent upon imperialism, and I quoted Michael Holquist's argument about monolingualism's passion for wholes over parts or fragments. Liberationist linguistics seem bent on embracing fragments over wholes, it might be argued, and while it is impossible not to have sympathy with this position, there are clearly problems that arise when we apply this abstract perspective to specific linguistic contexts. For example, in the context of composition, there is a clash between postcolonial theory's political pronouncements in favour of difference and actually existing postcolonialism's often clear demand for sameness. This is to recall Bruce Horner's point about marginality: 'Of any seemingly "marginal" tradition we need to ask what it is marginal to, to what effect, in what social historical circumstances, according to whom. We cannot simply label cultural practices marginal or central, dominant or residual, outside history and circumstance' (2000, 180). Of course, as many critics have pointed out over the last twenty years, postcolonial theory can be criticized precisely for embracing difference beyond history, circumstance, and context in general.

Accordingly, Badiou (2000) and Hallward (2001) offer an important philosophical corrective, providing tools to help reconfigure postcolonial studies so that teachers do not demand difference from students, and become disappointed when it is withheld. There is no doubt that difference can go unquestioned, in the context of English studies generally, but now specifically in the study of the English language around the world. There are obvious political and cultural grounds for the celebration of difference, largely deriving from the colonial histories that enabled the spread of English. For example, Kachru writes the following: 'The impression now is that with the diffusion of and resultant innovations in English around the world, universally acceptable standards are absent' (1985, 242). Kachru is himself clearly identified with this position, which can be understood as a form of postcolonial linguistics. De-control removes English from the 'tyranny' of standards; alternatively, it could be argued that it liberates differences from the tyranny of the same. A long story, or stories; David Crystal (2004) writes in terms of the 'kaleido-scopic diversity' that is sadly if necessarily reduced to the sameness of 'English' as such. That kaleidoscope is undoubtedly often tyrannically reduced to a monochromatic sameness. We can understand such a conclusion as another celebration of cultural translation as found in the varieties of English found around the world. Of course, this celebration has been contested, with numerous commentators challenging its assumptions. Quirk writes the following about standards of English in a global context: 'ordinary folk with their ordinary common sense have gone on knowing that there are standards in language and they have gone on crying out to be taught them' (1985, 6). Certainly, postcolonial linguistics can be quite disappointed when (some of) the people it has liberated (in theory) to use their own Englishes demand (in practice) the perceived native speaker standard. It is not that Quirk's comments are opposed to postcolonial theory, more that postcolonial theory ought to rethink its reading of its philosophical framework, at least partly in order to be able to think about difference and sameness together, drawing meaning from their *relation* in specific contexts, rather than locked in abstract immutability. Cultural translation can be something to celebrate, but not always or everywhere; indeed, postcolonial theory is missing a great deal by not really thinking about the same. This constitutes a most difficult task: to articulate ontological universality and the singular, i.e., to think together the economy of sameness and difference.

Sameness and Difference: 'The' Classroom

A specific example will indicate what postcolonial theory is excluding. The questioning of the postcolonial paradigm, particularly in relation to the English language, is relevant to how teaching is conducted in a postcolonial classroom, although this does not apply to all such contexts, or for all teachers. In certain contexts there is ambivalence concerning the idea of the 'death of the native speaker', and not all students will readily embrace challenges to the 'myth of the native speaker'. This resistance can lead to a kind of infelicitous performative, as I will explore in the following theoretical example drawn directly from discussion of World Englishes. Seargeant taxonomizes World Englishes studies' nomenclature, keeping in mind the fact that 'an act of naming can be both a theoretical and a political tool, and it is in cases of this sort where a wider dissemination of the name is necessary, so that the idea of the language can be taken up as a marker of identity' (2010, 110). The discourse of World Englishes studies is an academic discourse, and certainly aspires to a certain level of scientific rigour appropriate to linguistics. Accordingly, Seargeant is interested in how the naming acts characterizing the discourse function analytically. However, he also draws attention to the wider circulation of such acts beyond the academic community. Accordingly, he continues to argue that 'the act of naming in effect creates an imaginary community of the users of the variety that it identifies' (2010, 110). This act could be an authoritatively academic one, or it could be (also) an aspect of extra-academic discourse. What strikes me about Seargeant's discussion is the mismatch between the *possibility* of such acts of naming being taken up as markers of identity and the certainty that they actually *do* create communities of users. In terms of a specific example, he specifically discusses classroom contexts, where the users are understood from a theoretical perspective to constitute a community: 'from the analytical perspective of the theorist, at least, they constitute an emergent community [...] Within classroom contexts these notional communities can then become actual, as students are grouped together according to the variety they are considered to speak or need' (2010, 110). As Seargeant suggests, the naming act categorizes according to linguistic behaviour, but as we find so often with categorization it also functions to frame social reality in a way that also changes it. However, we should remember the extent to which the act of naming does not *necessarily* lead to the creation of the community. This is because that act can be refused, especially in a classroom context, where the analytical perspective of the theorist meets hard reality. The naming act describes something that was in some sense already there, and perhaps also brings into being something that was not already there, but that second aspect of the act does not necessarily receive acceptance, and so does not necessarily do any work whatsoever, or at least not the work it was intended to do. Beyond the limits of the academic discourse (which are of course uncertain, but at least partly fall 'within' the classroom context), the performative can fail. Specifically, to tell a student (or a classroom of students metonymic of a community) that they are a 'native speaker' always might fail due to the previously mentioned, context-specific resistance or ambivalence towards the theorist's analytical perspective.

Before discussing that resistance or ambivalence to the 'death of the native speaker', specifically in the context of Hong Kong, it is helpful to revisit the idea and explore how it has been understood in composition studies. Ben Rampton argues that the categories of native speaker and mother tongue have tenacity partly because 'political interests often have a stake in maintaining the use of these concepts' (Harris and Rampton 2003, 108). Rampton proposes that we displace the genetic, naturalized assumptions behind these concepts with ideas of *expertise* and *symbolic allegiance*. Following a different logic, with similar intentions, Kingsley Bolton (2008) argues that by using the category of 'native speaker' for speakers of, for example, Indian or Philippine English, we may better comprehend the category as applied to speakers of American or British English. Clearly, then, the category of the native speaker is one that has become increasingly open to adaptation or re-invention. As an example concerning composition, John Trimbur, discussing the territorialization of language and the 'geohistory' of the native speaker, analyses the place of the Dartmouth conference of 1966 in the development of US college composition. In fact his analysis is relevant to and owes much to contexts outside the US–UK axis. Trimbur calls the native speaker 'an ideological and political problem', that implied 'cultural and linguistic homogeneity' and functioned increasingly as 'an emblem of threatened national unity' (2008, 144). Despite the spread of English, the assumption continued that it belonged in the Anglo-American centres. Native-ness was fundamentally naturalized, and while this process appears dubious outside the context of the so-called native speaker centres, it is hardly any more obvious within the US itself. Trimbur discusses Joshua A. Fishman's contribution to Dartmouth, which argued that 'Anglification does not amount to a simple triumph of monolingualism' (2008, 162); he concludes that we need to remember and explore the ambivalent US linguistic history in more depth.

This ambivalence has been historical fact, and the situation today builds on this history with further immigration and necessary shifts in attitude for the composition teacher. The situation demands, Horner argues, 'a radical shift from composition's tacit policy of monolingualism to an explicit policy that embraces multilingual, cross-language writing as the norm for our teaching and research' (2006, 570). Accordingly, one way in which postcolonial studies and composition might come together is to recognize difference; alternatively, we might recognize a *fuzziness* to the distinction between error and innovation. It is certainly possible to imagine composition studies 'becoming' creative writing. With the necessary qualification that 'composition studies' and 'creative writing' mean different things in different contexts, what we call composition studies might become creative writing, if not at an institutional then at a philosophical level. We might then say that composition studies, in a postcolonial context, now assumes that error and innovation are indistinguishable at the origin. This truth is evident at the level of student writing, and can be given theoretical coherence through postcolonial theory. At the same time, postcolonial theory will have to be revised and enlarged to be adequate to the level of the individual instance of writing, lest it indulge its tendency to speak for the postcolonial subject. The issue of subaltern 'voice' has often been considered, and postcolonial theory can seem to efface identities, or at best speak for them (as perhaps here). Accordingly, there is an urgent need to attend to some specific writing beyond literary works. In reading examples of this non-literary writing, of course, we might find that postcolonial subjects see no need for the postcolonial philosophy of difference. My concern is to explore the challenge to postcolonial theory embodied by the classroom experience of Hong Kong, particularly its ambivalence towards the death of the native speaker. In this ambivalence, there is resistance to a postcolonial philosophy of difference, and the assumption that cultural translation is an undifferentiated good. However, it should be emphasized that this is a description of one example, and does not necessarily have general relevance. The indistinguishability of error and innovation is acceptable in some postcolonial contexts, but not in others, and postcolonial prescription is not going to persuade those who resist the philosophy of difference that they should start using English in any way they see fit. Composition can become creative in specific political and cultural institutions, and some places see no need for this blurring, and no need to embrace a postcolonial English, or the multiplicity of World Englishes – at least, not yet.

Of course, this raises the question of what exactly constitutes a postcolonial context, either in terms of philosophy or history. It further raises the question of whether composition is actually practised in historically postcolonial contexts. As already mentioned, the Chinese University of Hong Kong was founded (during British rule) as a bilingual institution, as an alternative to the Anglophone University of Hong Kong. The different possibilities for curriculum delivery (Cantonese, English, and Putonghua) are kept separate, so on one level multilingualism is being held at bay. However, within the Department of English matters are less controversial and apparently much more straightforward. There is a composition stream, which is distinct from the university's general English programme that all other students go through, and there are also creative writing courses. As Shirley Lim (2001) has argued, such courses provide evidence that Hong Kong students do not fit stereotypes about materialism and pragmatism. However, it is possible that such courses could provide a designated space for certain forms of creativity deemed unacceptable elsewhere. Indeed, these courses are options, distinct from the composition classes. This separation is something that fits students' general theorization of their relationship with English, which is something I engage with in a mandatory course, 'World Englishes and their Cultures'. Students are capable of recognizing the innovative vitality of, as examples, South Asian Englishes and Singlish. However, it appears that they distinguish themselves as Hong Kongers from this stream of creativity in World Englishes, and do not identify themselves as practitioners of bilingual creativity. Instead, they seem to agree with David Bunton, author of *Common English Errors in Hong Kong* (1989), who wants to distinguish error and innovation as clearly as possible, and assumes that native speakers have the authority to make this distinction. His book is still in print after two decades, offering superficial confirmation that many Hong Kongers agree with its perspective.

The responses encountered in the classroom are perhaps unsurprising, and Horner reminds us that we should not equate official pronouncements about language with students' actual attitudes. He further reminds us of the consequent dangers of essentializing the student writer: 'Such an approach assumes a false uniformity to student consciousness: it overwrites the articulation of any emergent oppositional consciousness by tuning in only the voicing of official consciousness' (2000, 38). This warning is particularly useful for a context often compared with Hong Kong: Singapore. But I am attesting that my students recognize the partiality of institutional pronouncements about English, without making the next step that postcolonial theory seems to demand, to embrace marginal expressiveness. There is a distancing of English in Hong Kong, qualifying its status alongside the other World Englishes. This means that although Hong Kong English is itself highly innovative in its blending of different forms of Chinese and English (as evident from a cursory investigation of students' online presence), the students themselves would want to reject its validity beyond the most superficial or 'non-serious' uses; they would never want their study in composition to blur into creative writing. It is important to consider why this resistance exists, even if some of the reasons might seem obvious (emotional distance, motivations in learning, etc.). In general terms, Ackbar Abbas's comments prior to 1997's 'Handover' to China remain important: 'Of all the binarisms that keep things in place, perhaps the most pernicious in the Hong Kong context is that of East and West. This is not to say that there are no differences, but that the differences are not stable; they migrate, metastasize' (1997, 117). This binarism is not only institutional, but is also often maintained at the level of everyday practice. Abbas's general point informs the more specifically linguistic issues, although it cannot account for all cultural practices; indeed, outside the university classroom, English is everywhere used creatively, clashing with, transforming, and being transformed by Cantonese. However, it might be a useful point for the specific case of the university classroom, given the relatively restricted context that the university is in Hong Kong (approximately 18 per cent of high school leavers study at university). However, it does not explain everything about resistance to ownership of English.

One complementary explanation would be psychoeconomic; students are conditioned to value investments (of time and money) that are less risky than creativity, especially creativity in English. Discussing creativity more generally, Mark Runco makes the point that 'Different cultures value different things and some of these values directly influence the development and expression of creativity' (2004, 12). Different cultures frame our sense of the appropriateness of deviation and creativity; accordingly, such creativity in English might appear inappropriate. Perhaps creativity is kept quite distinct from the mainstream 'seriousness' of our language-learning. In any case, Runco's point is made in the context of the study of creativity in the Asian classroom, and he wishes to tweak certain stereotypes; for example, he argues that 'Western individualism', although quite possibly real, is not necessarily more conducive to creativity than 'Asian emotional control'. More generally, his argument is important, and complements critiques of attempts to foster creativity in the Asian classroom. Aik Kwang Ng and Ian Smith describe the paradox of promoting creativity in the Asian classroom: 'the more creative a class of students becomes, the more undesirable their behavior appears to the teacher' (2004, 87). If that is the case, attitudes are not changing fast enough to foster the desired creativity. Indeed, creativity may be desired for reductively instrumental reasons, and this again may result in inadequate economic and attitudinal resourcing for the creativity desired. This factor might be persuasive, although of course some of its assumptions would not hold true for all teachers; for example, local, native, and non-native teachers of English composition might hold different attitudes, and be perceived differently by students, parents, and so on. Indeed, the university teacher cannot be essentialized any more than can the students (see Braine 2010).

In any case, the above explanation is of course not only a psychoeconomic explanation. It is a realist explanation, one that recognizes the global linguistic situation, not to mention Hong Kong's place as an international financial centre (like Singapore). Kingsley Bolton, considering English in the light of the 1997 handover of Hong Kong, suggests the following: 'Offered a choice between affirming Hong Kong's identity as a southern Chinese city or as a "global" city, Hong Kong's Beijing-vetted government has opted for the latter. Such an identity choice inevitably involves the retention of English, if only for "pragmatic" and "business" considerations' (2003, 200). English might be a colonial legacy, but that is hardly the whole story. With some freedom, but also hard-headed practicality, English has been fostered for access to the global economy, something clearly essential for a financial hub. As in other contexts, an international English has been imagined in terms of a standard form, and accordingly English in Hong Kong is exonormative. Innovation will not be valued when it can be written off as error, and so students have a practical reason for resisting the death of the native speaker. However, as Bolton's final clause invites us to recall, this is not the end of the explanation.

That is because, as I have already suggested, a Hong Kong English really does exist, one that extends beyond accent to the grammatical and lexical specificity that defines a variety. However, this variety is not accepted by the general population, and is not a viable expressive medium in the university classroom. As has been suggested by Terence T.T. Pang, Hong Kong English is *localized* but not *indigenized*: through relexification, regrammatization, and rediscoursalization, Hong Kong users of English incorporate the language into their own. As Pang suggests, 'Such language use is not only indicative of an inventive and dynamic culture, but also various pragmatic norms and conventions' (2003, 17). The innovative dynamism and perhaps inchoate codification are linguistic facts, but they are not necessarily accepted or desired, and the values and attitudes leading to the failure of indigenization cannot be ignored or belittled. As Pang indicates, there is a dynamic, hybridizing, postcolonial vitality at work, which evinces cultural translation. In fact, this translation is one that might be harnessed even at an official level in future. However, currently there is not even any official recognition, and although there have been shifts in education policy governmental recognition remains lacking. Despite its existence, the local population does not accept Hong Kong English; indeed, it appears to be largely non-local linguists who celebrate its dynamism. Pang himself records the non-acceptance of the local population with a certain neutrality, but it seems that cold-eyed objectivity is the best that Hong Kong English can hope for at present, even a decade later. The cultural awareness that must follow codification is not in place (see Poon 2006). In the context of a general societal disinclination to accept Hong Kong English it is difficult to imagine promoting the sense that the local variety is valid for university composition.

World Englishes: The Promise of a Term

Ultimately, various explanations of resistance to creativity in World Englishes offer useful ways of accounting for the resistance of actual creators to a postcolonial injunction to embrace difference in English. Each explanation is valid and persuasive for specific contexts. None can be dismissed from the vantage point of a theoretical perspective that accounts for their mistaken assumptions. Nonetheless, postcolonial theory, with its paradigm of difference, appears impatient with the realities of postcolonial situations. Real postcolonial situations, as critiques of postcolonialism have long pointed out, are various, and cannot be accounted for by a theory, however useful that theory may be in certain contexts. There are distinctions to be made between a fundamental level of cultural translation that is always present, and actual instances of that translation, and resistance to it, that we find in everyday life in different contexts. Postcolonial theory cannot afford to tilt toward 'creating' at the expense of 'creators', and sometimes, when it appears most alive to the creators (e.g., students) it is in fact seduced by creating – in short, difference.

The danger of a quasi-philosophical explanation of the kind put forward here is clearly the possibility of careless generalization or essentialization. If 'the student writer' has sometimes been essentialized, it is also possible to find an essentialization of 'the native speaker'. I do not want to essentialize either again, but there are clear dangers that this might occur. Comparing student writers in Hong Kong to, for example, student writers in the US, is problematic. On one level it can be argued that the postcolonial rethinking of composition in the US identifies a more thoroughgoing philosophical postcolonialism than can be found in the historically postcolonial Hong Kong classroom. In fact, de-essentializing the native speaker for the Hong Kong classroom, while something that students can understand, is not quite something they can accept, at least not for themselves. The idea of the native speaker, with all its privileges, may be something they question, but what replaces it cannot be a wholehearted embrace of difference. It is, instead, a restrictive and simultaneously broadened sense of sameness; this could be understood as English in Hong Kong as an international language. Indeed, although some studies (Lai 2005) have found that postcolonial Hong Kong students value English more highly than Putonghua in terms of its integrative function, it remains the case that for obvious reasons they value Cantonese more highly than English. Indeed, in terms of English, students appear relatively uninterested in symbolic allegiance, and almost entirely focused on expertise or instrumental function. In understanding their own pragmatic motivations, I would imagine that they retain an assumption that cultural identities are things that exist first, and are then translated; that would be a plausible and seductive interpretation of the cultural translation that evidently does exist in Hong Kong identity, partly expressed in its specific usage of English.

Despite the evident drift of my argument, the idea that globalization poses a risk to the localized production of knowledge is understandable. Globalization is assessed as generally standardizing, and in the specific case of language use (particularly for the non-native speaker) implies restriction, the exonormative, the instrumental, and the emotionally distant. That we might want to liberate difference, against this globalizing linguistic force, is also understandable. This desire assumes the prior dissolution of the native speaker, and the elevation of non-native creativity, understood as a form of cultural translation. These two things are key factors in some contexts, but not in others. Kachru, like many who write on both World Englishes and postcolonial studies, elevates difference in practice; the postcolonial paradigm does so as philosophical precondition, of course. Arguably, 'we' are disinclined to revisit the paradigm of difference itself, even when to follow it to logical conclusions would be to override the desire for sameness found in students (from any context) we feel we are liberating. In other words, the emphasis on difference in theory, when met by sameness in practice, leads to a pedagogical disappointment; this is not an autobiographical assessment only, I would suggest, but a general comment on the postcolonial paradigm. It may be the case that in (to return to the comparison) Singapore there is a threat to localized knowledge production, and that this threat is embodied by the Singaporean government's 'hard' and 'soft' attempts to rid itself of Singlish. In the case in Hong Kong, for the moment at least the assumption of 'native speaker–non-native speaker' communication retains pragmatic validity.

Conclusion

While this chapter may seem pessimistic about the space for creativity in English in the university classroom, perhaps that pessimism will be overridden by developments in the medium term. On that question of space, and writing about Hong Kong generally, Bolton has suggested that 'Until recently, at least, the space available for English – for business, government, international communication, law – has been usually defined in pragmatic terms alone, but attitudes here also seem to be changing' (2010, 465). It is certainly the case that the Hong Kong government has begun to place emphasis on creativity and language arts, including in English, and so perhaps a shift from pragmatic assumptions is under way (see Burton 2010). In any case, my argument is obviously not that idiom needs to be barred from English language expression in university contexts, not even (in the postcolonial context, least of all) in a place such as Hong Kong. As Elaine Ho has recently argued, 'For a long time, anglophone Hong Kong writing has been triply marginalized, labelled as elite discourse, as the specialized language of literature divorced from the pragmatic adoption of English by the majority of locals, and as written rather than spontaneous oral performance' (2010, 435). I do not intend to contribute to further marginalization of English, particularly the Asian Englishes to which Ho convincingly argues recent Hong Kong creative writing is increasingly oriented. However, as Brian Chan (2007) suggests, and despite ongoing cultural and linguistic unrest, increased integration with China may well lead to closer identity and linguistic ties, in which case Hong Kong English may remain forever larval.

In any case, focusing on composition rather than creative writing suggests that we would do well to defer the former becoming the latter. The hard lessons of language-learning and use are not amenable to political and philosophical impositions. That warning applies equally to postcolonial theory and World Englishes, if they unquestioningly assume the desirability of cultural translation. In each case, one set of assumptions has replaced another. For postcolonial theory, the displaced assumptions concern the politics of English-language use, and appear to reserve creativity for the native speaker as such. For World Englishes, meanwhile, insofar as linguistics studies them to celebrate them, the displaced assumptions concern the pragmatics of interlocution. In neither case are we allowed to entertain a realistic acceptance of continuation of the displaced situation. That, I believe, can lead to a pedagogical pessimism. It is necessary to understand any resistance to the 'death of the native speaker' in the specific context it arises. Of course, in many postcolonial contexts there is such resistance, and any resistance to the full embrace of World Englishes is a residual reaction of a quasi-colonialist prejudice. However, each context demands its own response and its own neutral description, something that postcolonial theory is often unable to give. Ideally, in engaging with the study of World Englishes, postcolonial theory will become more attuned to the everyday politics and philosophies informing individual postcolonial contexts. It needs to develop its traditions of slow reading for broader and institutionally attentive purposes, as the next chapter will explore.

CHAPTER 6

Slow Reading: The Opacity of World Literatures

The majority of these students are never going to learn much literary English. It forms no natural part of their life needs.

I.A. Richards, *Basic English and its Uses*

[I]n order to do distant reading one must be an excellent close reader. Close reading for distant reading is a harnessing of aesthetic education for its own counter-example.

Gayatri Chakravorty Spivak, 'World Systems and the Creole'

Introduction

This series seeks to move beyond expected debates in postcolonial literary studies. In spite of that desire, in order to be adequate to what Wai-chee Dimock calls 'the planetary circuit of tongues' (2008, 142), postcolonial studies remain inevitably invested in forms of English literary studies. On one level, postcolonial literary studies continues to produce individual readings of literary works, writers, and national literatures. Perhaps some commentators argue that it requires no more readings of this type, but there are arguably new things to be argued, and in any case there will always be new works to be considered through the postcolonial paradigm. Alongside such literary critical readings, there is a postcolonial approach to the discipline of literary studies itself, considering the ways its histories have been part of colonial education, helping to frame the identities of the colonizing and colonized cultures. As probably the most influential example of this analysis, Ngũgĩ (1981; 1997) eloquently puts the case that European literary education restrictively frames the world for African eyes. This historical and cultural framing helps to explain, for Ngũgĩ, the institutional and symbolic value attached to the English department. Accordingly, the obvious extension of his case is for the English department's abolition (1972). Others have probed the historical details of the literary critical project. In a more narrowly British example, Chris Baldick (1983) examines the ways in which literary criticism through the Victorian period into the 1930s was a response to a never-ending *crisis* of culture. As mentioned earlier, from a specifically postcolonial perspective Gauri Viswanathan (1989) explores in detail the famously tangled history of English literary studies in the colonies. The incorporation of English literary culture into the civil service examinations throughout the empire becomes a revealing indication of the work for which literary studies was intended, but which it has (hopefully) transcended. These indications still perhaps leave us a little wary of the ongoing role of literary studies, and it can certainly be argued that 'literary English' (by which I.A. Richards did not exactly mean *literature*) is no longer always a major part of teaching English around the world, whether or not it would be a part of the 'life needs' of students. Considering the age of Global English, Martin Kayman argues that 'the modern tendency in the teaching of English to speakers of other languages to teach "the language" divorced from its "literature" is a way of disavowing the latter's original ideological mission and presenting "English" as free from imperial contamination' (2004, 6). The cultural politics of English is disavowed through this insistence on divorcing English from culture, particularly literary culture. In certain contexts, this divorce is not only attempted by teachers and institutions; as Eva Lam suggests, there is a conflict between intercultural communication and ethnolinguistic integrity, which means that 'Some students seek to reconcile these conflicting feelings by separating language learning from cultural learning' (2000, 380). However, this attempted divorce is necessarily a failure, as Kayman rightly argues, and English is by no means divorced from its cultures; indeed, my own department is not so rare in continuing to bring together literature and linguistics in teaching English to speakers of other languages (see Tam and Weiss 2004). Furthermore, the notion of World Englishes forces us to broaden our sense of which cultures we associate with English, which can be expressed by English, and so on.

It quickly becomes clear that literature is not viably excluded from the discussion of Global English and World Englishes. In fact, it can also be argued that some of the discussions in this specific book are connected to important changes, mooted or under way, in literary studies 'itself'. Partly that is the case due to connections between literature and literacy which seem inevitable in the histories leading up to World Englishes. Of course, those histories may be losing their pull on users of English today, literary writers or otherwise. If nothing else, focusing on postcolonial literature immediately raises the question of whether or not that literature (which is at best a valuable construct) has come to an end. Perhaps we ought to write in terms of global literature, or world literature, or even World Englishes literature. As mentioned in Chapter

1, it has recently been suggested (Dawson Varughese 2012) that we focus our attention on the ways World Englishes literatures are quite distinct from the postcolonial literatures that essentially pre-dated them, prefigured them, and in some ways have *restricted* them, at least in terms of broad international perceptions, particularly perhaps those of literary studies researchers. This shift in attention in literary studies is certainly welcome, but while context-based (or one might say *varieties*-based) approaches will remain important, it is also necessary to consider the extent to which postcolonial literary studies are in the process of becoming, or have already become, globalized, transnational, and otherwise *connected*. This chapter puts this emphasis on World Englishes literature alongside recent transformations in comparative literary studies that have led to different versions of world literatures. Some of these transformations have begun with the insight that postcolonial studies has established grounds of comparability quite different from those underlying earlier versions of comparative literature. On one level, then, this chapter seeks to focus less on the content and themes of World Englishes literature, which may indeed be different from those in postcolonial literature (although, of course, postcolonial writers often hated the label 'postcolonial', and their themes were diverse, often ranging far beyond those implied by the restrictive title). Instead, it focuses attention on the question of *how* we read, and in focusing on this question it shares an emphasis with the category of 'World Englishes literature', a category that implies nothing about the content of the literature in question. On the one hand, this chapter looks at this question through debates concerning forms of 'distant' reading enabled by technological advances, for example, in the analysis of corpora. On the other hand, in common with John Miedema (2009) and Simone Drichel (2011), I am here concerned to address the ongoing significance of forms of 'slow' reading, forms that imply the continued importance of a literary education.

Comparatively Slow: The Speed of Postcolonial Reading

Whether understood as 'close', 'distant', 'superficial', 'symptomatic', or some other form, postcolonialism as a form of academic discourse has involved a mode of reading global connections. It promises a way of reading the connectedness of the imperial experience, taking in different patterns of economic and political domination, different modes of cultural expression and different disciplinary methods. Programmatically, postcolonial literary criticism, as perhaps the primary example, positions itself close to the literary text in order to trace the ways it reflects, or reflects upon, these broader and more distant connections. Accordingly, Edward W. Said asks the following question about interpretive practices: 'Are there ways we can reconceive the imperial experience in other than compartmentalized terms, so as to transform our understanding of both the past and the present and our attitude toward the future?' (1994, 17). This question reminds us that Said was a comparative literature scholar; indeed, *Orientalism* (1978) itself was a kind of comparative study, and Said is well known for the place that Erich Auerbach occupies in his thinking. Said's work has long served as a model for how to read the imperial experience, beginning with literature but inevitably ranging wider. Yet it might seem necessary to ask if the resources provided by his work, and others in postcolonial theory, have reached the point of exhaustion.

Fundamentally, it seems that the kinds of connectedness evident in the imperial experience no longer obtain in the globalized experience. Under globalization such connectedness has not only been extended. Its quality has undergone a profound shift, due at least in part to new technological forms; as has often been argued, imperialism was unquestionably global, yet, counter-intuitively we have become with globalization more than or other than global. It is arguable that such a qualitative shift has important political implications. Postcolonial reading obviously imagines itself as a political act, in one way or another. However, postcolonial theory arose in a particular context, and as a response to certain specific historical situations. Evidently it can be argued that the context no longer governs our thinking; accordingly, if reading, and reading literature in particular, is to have ongoing relevance it might seem that new models of reading are necessary. As critics such as Rey Chow suggest, models of close reading or hermeneutics deriving from literary studies may appear limited, unduly bolstering the cultural capital of a specific scholarly community; it has been suggested that literary studies ends up offering far less potential for political intervention because of its complexity, by comparison with other cultural forms. Yet, as James Steintrager argues, 'we might still see hermeneutics as wrapped up with institutional prestige and a high, scholarly culture carved out of a no-longer dominant print culture and yet love this historically contingent, exposed form' (2010, 300). In such a situation, literary scholars, while continuing to be unapologetic close readers, would have to recognize their practice as having been superseded as a consequence of qualitative shifts brought about by globalization. Further, any scholars deriving a method from literary close reading would then have to re-evaluate their practice carefully.

Whether or not conditions have really changed in order to produce such a qualitative shift, it can certainly be argued that the central figures in postcolonial theory have much to offer, and part of their ongoing relevance derives from their disciplinary background. Jonathan Culler has suggested that 'The question of comparative literature has become everybody's question' (2006, 255); if this is true, postcolonial theory could plausibly be argued to have played a central role in the process. That is because the theorists most closely associated with the postcolonial paradigm were trained in the comparative literature tradition. In particular, Said and Gayatri Chakravorty Spivak have been very much part of this tradition, and so their reflections on the practice of reading are relevant to both postcolonialism and comparative literary studies. Culler himself identifies postcolonial theory as central to the creation of a context of global *comparability*: 'What has made possible much recent work in comparative literature has been the identification, largely by postcolonial theory, of a general postcolonial context within which comparabilities can be generated' (2006, 263). Comparative approaches, struck by the specificity and complexity of each discursive location, might once have seemed impossible: it appeared that with increasing knowledge of each (national) discursive context came the awareness that comparison as such dealt in superficialities. Indeed, new discursive contexts beyond the national have become increasingly important, and postcolonial theory has been one driver in reconfiguring meaningful comparison across literatures and cultures. As Roland Greene suggests, postcolonial studies is one approach that emphasizes elements that are in fact central to comparative study as such: 'Not literature but literatures; not works but networks' (2006, 214). The connection between comparative literature and postcolonial theory lies in their shared emphasis on the spaces between.

Despite the new perspectives generated by the two fields, the connection between postcolonial theory and comparative literature may have come to seem a liability in recent times. Interestingly, and perhaps unsurprisingly, just as comparative literature has continued to re-imagine itself alongside area studies and a return to world literature, so has postcolonial theory had to reconsider its relation with its others (see Spivak 2003). When once 'postcolonialism' promised new frameworks for understanding old traditions, it has increasingly appeared out-of-step with times of technological instantaneity and multilingual realities. It has begun to seem that postcolonialism is very much yesterday's news – a necessary phase, perhaps, yet still only a phase on the way to more fully global (and globalized) critical practices. Taking individual literary texts as examples of larger structures of cultural difference is no longer much of a contribution to the ongoing story of critical discourse. Indeed, with its often unspoken reliance on the assumptions (and critical objects) of literary studies, postcolonialism often seems leaden-footed. Nonetheless, as has already been suggested, there is a great deal still to value in the measured approach that the best of postcolonialism has offered and continues to offer, not least its emphasis on a particularly *slow* reading, a form of reading that in some ways coincides with close reading as traditionally understood in literary studies, but in other ways responds to certain specific critical contexts that are certainly new (or at least are newly felt).

Postcolonialism has, however, appeared in need of a defence; for example, Robert Young has offered a re-statement of the histories and theories that inform his vital work on the history of anti-colonial and postcolonial thought (2001). His title, 'What is the Postcolonial?', is a pointed response to suggestions that the postcolonial, as a theoretical movement, has been exhausted. Young suggests that so long as the 'impoverishments of global power' (2009, 25) continue, there will be a need for the postcolonial. He explains this continuing need by showing how the postcolonial evolved through a network of genuinely transnational intellectual and cultural contexts. It would certainly appear that this network has only become more relevant under globalization. Young identifies postcolonial theory as a more specific phenomenon, with 'the elaboration of theoretical structures that contest the previous dominant western ways of seeing things' (2009, 24). It draws its energies from critical perspectives that evolved in the colonial and anti-colonial periods, and offers continued resources for understanding globalization. Accordingly, Young argues that postcolonialism as a cluster of concepts has not been exhausted by recent developments in politics, technology, and so on. Nonetheless, it is revealing that this defence has seemed necessary, and it is indeed the case that postcolonial studies have been made to look rather 'slow' in recent times. Globalization studies, increasingly prominent in many aspects of the humanities and social sciences, holds out the promise of more responsive, up-to-date, and speedy interpretative frameworks. It may seem that postcolonial literary studies must necessarily be drawn into the networks of a nimble and comprehensive *world* literary studies, if it is to recapture some of its vitality and relevance. However, as Said argued in his defence of humanistic criticism, the speed quite often simply indicates a lack of connection and a lack of thought; he writes that we live in 'the greatest age of documentary expansion and rapid, if flattening and one-dimensional, communication in history' (2004, 81). Following Said and the other major figures in postcolonial theory, it may be argued that postcolonial literary studies cannot be understood as simply one relatively small subcategory of world literature, and further that its lack of speed may in fact be one of the chief virtues of postcolonial reading.

How to Read Postcolonially

The meaning of slow reading, as distinct from close reading, for example, will no doubt appear vague. One way to begin to define this reading is found in discussion of postcolonialism's focus on the status and accuracy of representation, particularly as found in imperial and colonial literatures, but also contemporary work. The definition takes shapes in arguments that insist postcolonial theory must supplement its obsession with representation with emphasis on responsibility. The concern with representation is understandable, to the extent that many instances of Western representation are demonstrably inaccurate and prejudiced. Such representation has been put in the service of political and economic domination, consciously or not; that is a founding claim, if not the founding claim, of postcolonial studies. However, following Said's *Orientalism*, postcolonial studies has, much of the time, refined an argument about the impossibility of representing other cultures without bias or prejudice; it has seemed that historical fact has been converted into philosophical constant. According to Robert Spencer, 'we are left with a sort of separatist ideology which bears little resemblance to the goal of universal emancipation that has inspired – and, just as importantly, *continues* to inspire – anti-colonial theory and activism' (2009, 72). Spencer

focuses on the possibility of accurate representation, even if such representation demands that we readers step outside the literary text. Such texts are
inevitably partial, and often play with that partiality through devices such as
unreliable narration. Of course, unreliability implies a reliability against which
it can be judged, and so to read literature is far from being an experience of
irreducible perspectivism. In fact, in putting emphasis on the reader rather
than the writer, Spencer encourages us to recall our responsibility as critical
interpreters; he wishes to shift the act of representing or rendering from
being prior to the text to occurring during the reading process. Such responsibility is one aspect of slow postcolonial reading.

As an example of this slow reading that makes the connection with
comparative literature, Spivak argues that we must resist the seductions of
the rhetoric of the global, and instead focus our attention on the uneven
realities of the *planetary*. In order to be responsible to these uneven realities, it
is necessary for us to pay close attention to the textual. While this continued
focus may appear irresponsible in paying such close attention to that which
is apparently marginal or unimportant, Spivak argues that it is an important
aspect of unlearning our ignorance and becoming responsible to every other:
'In this era of global capital triumphant, to keep responsibility alive in the
reading and teaching of the textual is at first sight impractical. It is, however,
the right of the textual to be so responsible, responsive, answerable. The
"planet" is, here, as perhaps always, a catachresis for inscribing collective
responsibility as right' (2003, 100–101). Like Spencer, Spivak is clear that it
will be necessary to step outside the literary text in order to be responsible.
Indeed, it is difficult to see how anyone could argue otherwise. Unlike
Spencer, Spivak appears to be focusing on perspectives as irreducible. In
fact, the use of 'planet' is designed to combat the reduction or elision
of perspective implicit in 'globality'; in this emphasis, Spivak is drawing
on Derrida's distinction between the English 'globalization' and French
'mondialisation' (Derrida 2004), something touched on in an earlier chapter.
Meanwhile, and unlike Spivak, Spencer blames the postcolonial investment in
a radical perspectivism, and its apparent consequent political ineffectiveness,
on post-structuralist thought. At the very least, post-structuralism appears to
supplant Marxism in the conversion of anti-colonial to postcolonial thought.
It is necessary, it may then be argued, to make postcolonial studies respond
to possibilities that are beyond its current structure of thinking, in order to
sharpen the sense in which postcolonial criticism should be responsible. Like
other fields, postcolonial theory is often unable to think responsibly about
other paradigms, as Spencer suggests with regard to Marxist criticism. It is
necessary at least to supplement the postcolonial paradigm, because it might
seem that postcolonial studies produces a radically predictable knowledge,
one that is irresponsible to the extent that it confirms what its paradigm
already sets up as worth knowing or worth thinking. It is important, then,
that postcolonial studies should interrupt its own paradigm; its practitioners
must constantly interrupt not only those with whom they are impatient

because their perspective conflicts with their own, but also their own voices. Indeed, from another perspective, postcolonial theory can be seen as rather unpredictable, being the kind of *interdiscipline* that might result from this interruption, the kind of work that might disturb more traditional and stable institutional identities (indeed, as I suggested earlier, postcolonial studies must be interdisciplinary). While postcolonial theory may well make this kind of self-othering gesture, that still does not necessarily answer charges about the 'datedness' of the theory itself. It is still possible to argue that postcolonial theory has been left behind by political and technological developments, unable to get *up to speed* with our globalized times. Reading as practised in postcolonial studies seems much too slow, from such a perspective.

Reading Beyond the Fine Print

One example of this perspective is Chow's emphasis, already mentioned, on film and a kind of 'superficial' reading (1995). As another example, it is possible to see cheap global communications technologies as extending the idea of the imagined community, or fragmenting such a community still further. In each case, the nature of the technology appears to qualify if not entirely supersede Anderson's *Imagined Communities* (2006). Anderson's thinking was of course based on print technology, which he took to be essential in the imagination of modern national identities. In putting print so squarely in the centre of the story of the modern nation, and also at the heart of postcolonial studies, Anderson can be criticized for putting too much emphasis on one cultural mode – literature, and in particular the novel. By contrast, Paul Gilroy conceives expressive communities characteristic of the 'Black Atlantic' as being only one alternative to the print-based model, and takes Anderson to task for an emphasis on assumptions about the significance of writing and literature. Gilroy is discussing the specific example of the UK, but makes general criticisms of Anderson; for example, he argues against Anderson's 'privileging of the written word over the spoken word' (2002, 44). While it is still possible to sympathize with Gilroy's position on speech and writing, it is by now obvious that writing is increasingly speech-linked, particularly in its online variants, and so discussion of Anderson's thesis moves into another sphere. Instances of social networking indicate something of a paradoxical literalization of the idea of imagined communities, but Anderson's idea was never quite that of a virtual community, and so it is necessary to explore further possible objections to his position.

Other critics take shifts in technology as marking superficially different but fundamentally similar breaks with postcolonial theory, its emphasis on literature, and its consequent elevation of a measured reading practice. Michael Hardt and Antonio Negri (2000) provide a powerful argument against postcolonial theory as a mode of criticism appropriate to an earlier technological and political age in which difference could be seen both as unmitigated good and necessarily oppositional. However, it is not necessarily clear that our context is really so transformed; has technological change produced just a change in quantity, or has quality been transformed as well? When Hardt and Negri write of the potential simultaneity of revolution, they license others to imagine only technological utopia, even if more sceptical responses are increasingly evident (e.g., Morozov 2011). Older oppositional reading models, based on deliberative slowness and patient reconstruction of oppositional possibilities, inevitably appear inadequate to these new realities. Reading must be immediate and connective, based on networks and simultaneity, if not indeed becoming technological in the ways envisaged by Franco Moretti (2005); in this way, *close reading* becomes *distant reading*. Indeed, Moretti famously argues that we need to learn 'how not to read [texts]' (2005, 57), focusing instead on units of a size above or below the individual text. Technology enables us to ask very different questions, and offers accordingly the possibility of breaking out of our literary and cultural critical repetition. By contrast, Homi Bhabha, following Said, focuses on the dangers inherent in the technology, even if the main danger appears to be that it simply replicates older exclusive imagined communities (1999, xii–xiii). The problem is more than that, and is related to the very practice of connective reading. For a long time models of intertextuality have been central to literary studies, and those models of text have been increasingly understood as reflecting or even predicting reading models based on instantaneous communication. It is possible, however, that this increasingly frantic understanding of reading produces the very opposite of the revolutionary practice it apparently desires. If world literature, conceived in terms of graphs, maps, and trees (complex networks of various kinds), is speeding up, perhaps we need to slow down. In short, we ought to read comparatively slowly.

In theorizing the network society, Manuel Castells (2000) argues that technology is actually only one element in a wider process of social change. He suggests that networks constitute our environment, referring to our context generally. Such a shift in our fundamental context leads inevitably to social change through form rather than content. In fact, the social change in question is towards proliferation of networks; this is a change from one type of society to another. Before modern networks, Castells suggests (and in this his argument is comparable with Anderson's position on imagined communities), societies were ordered vertically, in hierarchies of power exercised by small privileged groups. The network, however, is a form of horizontal social organization; accordingly, the network is potentially a much more *democratic* form of organization. Networks of people, places, institutions, etc., have always existed, like trade networks throughout history. However, the network was always undermined and overpowered by the way that hierarchy was able to organize and use power; for example, organized religion is partly a very powerful form of hierarchy. Castells thinks there is a big difference in contemporary networks, deriving from what new technologies allow us to do. The speed of decision-making and reconfiguration made possible by new communications technologies means that networks are now much stronger than in the past. The internet is a very good example of how this works, being designed to be adaptable in just this way; it has also been a shaping factor in the development of new social movements, like anti-war and anti-capitalist movements, which do not necessarily have one single goal and certainly could not have one kind of organization. To follow this to a logical conclusion, in the work of Hardt and Negri we find an argument for an alternative kind of globalization; crucially, they argue that new technologies and networks have put in place all the necessary tools for a fully global revolution. Instead of being the source of our alienation, technology is really what will potentially free us from alienation on a global scale. As will become clear, it is this utopian vision of instantaneous revolution that interests Bhabha, although he is doubtful that it is necessarily revolutionary.

Of course, cultural theorists in multiple fields have long understood the domains of globalization to be irreducibly complex, as this book has already briefly mentioned. Arjun Appadurai famously argues that 'The new global cultural economy has to be seen as a complex, overlapping, disjunctive order, which cannot any longer be understood in terms of existing center-periphery models' (1996, 32). Different kinds of flow (such as money, information, or people) do not necessarily follow the same pattern or direction. There is, then, an element of unpredictability when we come to model global patterns and directions of power. Importantly, the direction of movement is not the only aspect of the global economy that has taken on new qualities under globalization. It is almost a truism that the speed of this newly complex system has increased, as John Urry argues: 'people, machines, images, information, power, money, ideas and dangers are all, we might say, "on the move", travelling at bewildering speed in unexpected directions from place to place, from time to time' (2003, 2). Such de-materialized movement is complex and for most purposes instantaneous. This characterization of our experience of the present (although importantly it remains very far from being a universal experience) is intuitively plausible. This plausibility derives partly at least from the increasing familiarity of technology that produces the effect of the instantaneous. Appadurai writes that 'technology, both high and low, both mechanical and informational, now moves at high speeds across various kinds of previously impervious boundaries' (2003, 41). Due to this technological speed, Appadurai suggests we need to think about globalization in terms of two related categories. The first is fractals, which are of course repeating geometric patterns, irregular or fragmented geometric shapes that can be repeatedly subdivided into parts, each of which is a smaller copy of the whole. Less familiar is the second category Appadurai introduces to help us understand globalization – *polythetic* resemblances. A polythetic category has a large number of members who share many similar characteristics, and though the category shares various common characteristics, none is essential for membership. These two categories emphasize that while globalization may appear to be chaotic in our everyday sense of that word there *are* discernable patterns to be found.

Switching the context to the practice of reading literature, specifically in a global context, draws attention to the question of the adequacy of close reading; are reading methods associated with postcolonial theory and comparative literature appropriate to fractal globalized patterns of culture? It has been argued, for example by Moretti, that new corpus-based models of reading are now most appropriate; as already mentioned, this reading can be conceived as distant. Despite the clear differences in emphasis, Moretti's argument seems to coincide with many of the assumptions found in Hardt and Negri, specifically about the adequacy of certain oppositional models of interpretation; it would seem that models that draw upon both comparative literature and postcolonial theory may well have been appropriate under earlier technological conditions, but their adequacy is now in doubt. It is not clear, for example, that the conclusions of postcolonial literary studies are any more general, any more adequate to historical realities of literary production and consumption, than those of any other apparently less political mode of reading. Whether we think about new ways of reading as fast or distant, it certainly seems that something new is necessary.

Speed and Simultaneity

It is revealing to consider how Bhabha, such a pivotal figure in postcolonial theory, has responded to some of the challenges posed by new ways of conceiving global connectedness and political conflict. In order to understand his response, it is necessary to return to earlier work focused on national identity. Indeed, Bhabha's analysis of national identity helps explain some of his doubts about digital technologies, and his suggestion that earlier models of reading are not yet superseded. As already discussed, Bhabha draws upon Anderson's work concerning the imagined power of national identities. Bhabha's central point is that 'the space of the modern nation-people is never simply horizontal' (1994, 141). Bhabha is borrowing the characterization of metaphor operating 'horizontally' (selection according to similarity) and metonymy operating 'vertically' (combination through contiguity). With industrialization and globalization, there has been a loss of simple community identity; according to Bhabha, 'The nation fills the void left in the uprooting of communities and kin, and turns that loss into the language of metaphor' (1994, 141). Given this emphasis, Bhabha is less interested in nationalism, which is on the side of metaphor, and therefore has a kind of 'contexture deficiency'. Instead, he is more interested in the unending ambivalent vertical shifts of metonymy; these shifts remind us that while national identity is an achievement, it is an ambivalent one, often excluding those to whom the nation owes much. Instead of progressing serenely and horizontally through Benjaminian 'calendrical time', nations are inevitably beset by vertical instabilities. Bhabha's fundamental point about nations is that they are structured by an ambivalent temporality: 'The language of culture and community is poised on the fissures of the present becoming the rhetorical figures of a national past' (1994, 142). He refers to 'the disjunctive time of the nation's modernity', suggesting that we are caught 'between the shreds and patches of cultural signification and the certainties of a nationalist pedagogy' (1994, 142). As argued in earlier chapters, national identities are both pedagogical and performative: the nation is something that is taught as a stable entity but is lived as a constantly changing process.

Such critical perspectives on the nation have led Bhabha to engagement with theories concerning contemporary culture as transnational. His engagement challenges critics like Hardt and Negri, who, as already mentioned, focus on Bhabha's work as an example of an earlier phase of progressive thought that celebrated difference in opposition to dominant forces of sameness. To recap, they argue that, as global capitalism itself now embraces difference and relativity, progressive thinkers must grasp the challenge of the same or simultaneity, which increasingly is enabled by developments in communications technology. From this perspective, technology now enables a potential simultaneity of global revolution. With his emphasis on hybridity, we might expect Bhabha to celebrate the transnational and the cosmopolitan, but also the kinds of technology that increasingly (and increasingly quickly) enable new forms of cosmopolitanism. However, for Bhabha, the situation is considerably more complex; in the context of comments on Derrida, Bhabha expresses reservations about what we could call the digital technological imaginary, which he believes shares the temporality of the modern nation: 'Although cyberspace communities do not have the territorial imperatives of nationalism, it is interesting how active xenophobic nationalists are on the Web, often in the cause of nations to which they no longer belong, but to which they now turn to justify their fundamentalist aspirations' (1999, xi). There is nothing inherently transnational about communications technology: even if its form seems so clearly suited for the creation of bonds beyond the nation state, its content can so easily fall back into easy yet misleading homogeneity. Bhabha is suspicious of the ideologies of digital capitalism, because those ideologies obscure homologies of temporality in principle entirely consistent with the repetition and extension of modernity's worst features.

In stressing temporality, however, Bhabha is not simply dismissing these ideologies. Much of the world's population may be digital nomads in some sense, but there continues to be much diversity and conflict and therefore multiple nomadic identities to be scrutinized: not all culture travels easily, or quickly, and some of the time at least culture simply stops. Bhabha does not consider 'the' exile to be a normative identity, and he certainly does not assume that all exiles are cosmopolitans like himself; indeed, he has written dismissively of 'a doctrinal espousal of global nomadism or transnationalism' (2006, 34). Elsewhere, responding to cultural anthropologist James Clifford, he emphasizes 'the place of a lack of movement and fixity in a politics of movement and a theory of travel' (Clifford 1997, 42), paying attention to those 'people caught in that margin of nonmovement within an economy of movement' (Clifford 1997, 43). Process and circulation actually come to a halt for many different reasons, and are sometimes halted by the marginalized out of necessity. National myths may desire a return to a 'golden age' that never existed, and so such myths can be criticized for their damaging effects. Refugees, by contrast, hold onto fixed symbols for their survival, and as a consequence hybridization and stability come together.

It is this kind of unpredictable and disjunctive stasis that continues to *short* the apparently open circuits of culture today. This stasis, of course, causes difficulty for any model of reading that steps back in order to understand the big picture of instantaneous cultural movement. Indeed, in order to see how and where networks become blocked, or nodes become isolated, requires the practice of slow reading. Accordingly, and against the ideologists of digital capitalism, Bhabha has recently developed his emphasis on slowness, something that can help us understand the stability of certain symbols of cultural survival. This slowness is positioned specifically as a counterweight to what he calls the 'digital impulse of acceleration and immediacy – the split-second, virtual transmission of messages, money, and meaning' (2006, 30). Writing in tribute to Said, Bhabha criticizes what he calls 'telegraphic forms whose rapidity renders the world one-dimensional and homogeneous' (2005, 11). Describing Said's critical practice as based upon a 'philological imperative' demanding close reading, Bhabha suggests that rapidity (or even simultaneity) has a tendency to totalize and therefore be uncritical. By contrast, when we slow down our reading and thinking, we can be truly critical and attend to the decisions and omissions that necessarily structure our knowledge but that cannot be allowed to go unconsidered and unremembered. Bhabha writes that 'The slow pace of critical reflection resists processes of totalization – analytic, aesthetic, or political – because they are prone to making "transitionless leaps" into realms of transcendental value, and such claims must be severely scrutinized' (2005, 12–13). Such leaps must be interrogated all the more when they occur in the context of well-intentioned attempts to right past wrongs and defend the rights of the greatest number.

Postcolonial Slowness: Between World and Globe

It is certainly not the case that Bhabha, or postcolonial theory in general, is dismissive of the realities and experiences that accompany the networks of globalization. If nothing else, the terminology of nodes and networks provides useful ways for reimagining a great deal of what occurs in his work. For example, in terms of other thinkers' influence on his work, he has suggested that 'influences are more like networks than total traditions of thinking' (Sheng 2009, 161–162). Imperialism was itself a network, or series of overlapping networks, and the models of textuality informing work such as

Bhabha's derive themselves from assumptions of intertextuality as network. However, it is clear that certain celebrations of the potential of globalization overlook many continuities with earlier forms of its network, and overstate the qualitative changes wrought by technological shifts. In this, such celebrations leap into new forms of rhetoric that are seductive but also dangerous. It is arguable that the discourse of globalization can, in many contexts, resolve or indeed dissolve the real tensions that continue to exist in spite of globalization itself. Reading postcolonially, or from a comparative perspective, by contrast refuses to ignore such tensions. The same logic is at work in Bhabha's analysis of multiculturalism, which he argues will be a failure to the extent that it imagines harmony and transparency as the goals of a process that will come to an end at some definite point. As he writes with regard to Said: 'Slowness is a deliberate measure of ethical and political reflection that maintains tension rather than resolves it' (2005, 11). Rushing to describe the networks of globalized culture, we are likely to miss the continuing blockages.

In place of the globe, then, it is increasingly clear that it is necessary to think of the world, or the planet, terms that come out of rather different discourses and that are not at all the same. Again, this is where postcolonial theory and comparative literature continue to make their contribution. Samuel Weber, for example, develops aspects of Derrida's thinking concerning the ways using the term 'globalization' implies that the globe in question is (as he says in a reading of *Hamlet*) 'homogeneous, uniform and pure' (2007, 63). Weber is concerned to defend what he terms 'reading over', a form of reading which 'repeats without returning to its point of departure' (2007, 67). Again, this reading is a form of slow reading: close reading in fact is slow reading to the extent that it is responsible to its other (the text in whatever form) and so opens itself to mutability. Meanwhile, as has already been discussed, Spivak insists on the value of the term 'planetarity': 'I propose the planet to overwrite the globe. Globalization is the imposition of the same system of exchange everywhere. In the gridwork of electronic capital, we achieve that abstract ball covered in latitudes and longitudes, cut by virtual lines, once the equator and the tropics and so on, now drawn by the requirements of Geographical Information Systems' (2003, 72). The false equality of GIS needs to be countered by an emphasis on complexity and disjuncture, as described by Appadurai and Urry. One example of this understanding can be seen in analysis of the worldwide literary system, a network that inevitably grants different nodes continued privileges. Following this analysis, it is necessary to understand the literary world as a system with exclusions and 'elected connectedness'. As Pascale Casanova has suggested, this world is a 'floral pattern' (2004, 20), a network of translators and other 'connectors' that govern circulation of the literary. Indeed, this emphasis is one aspect of the distinction between a global literature and a world literature. As David Damrosch has argued, world literature is not one thing, and cannot be understood in terms of an undifferentiated global literature. Further, distant reading and a perspective focused on connectedness give us only one aspect of any cultural formation: 'As with texts, so with cultures at large: individual cultures only partly lend themselves to analysis of common global patterns' (2003, 26). As with Culler's comments on comparativism, there is at least the possibility that increased knowledge leads to a form of paralysis, and inevitably so, given that each discourse is underwritten by a specific context, and that the identification of a more general context (say, the postcolonial context) is fraught with the danger of simplistic generalization. In any case, as Damrosch continues, we are not faced with a choice between close, slow reading on the one hand, and distant, 'instantaneous' reading on the other: 'we don't face an either/or choice between global systematicity and infinite textual multiplicity, for world literature itself is constituted very differently in different cultures. Much can be learned from a close attention to the workings of a given cultural system, at a scale of analysis that also allows for extended discussion of specific works' (2003, 26). Moretti's distant reading gives us much that has never been given to literary studies before, but it cannot be made to blur into a general technologically enhanced rupture with previous ideas of interpretation and politics.

Conclusion

The slow reading necessitated by the postcolonial context is, to return to an earlier term, a question of responsibility. That responsibility can now be understood as a responsibility to understand the diverse 'relatedness' of cultural contexts. As is well known, Said made the connection between his analysis of orientalism in history and more recent representations of 'the Arab', etc. The misrepresentations he found in much contemporary media discourse were partly a consequence of undue haste and a technological framing of information: 'We are bombarded by prepackaged and reified representations of the world that usurp consciousness and preempt democratic critique' (2004, 71). Revealingly, his concern about the jargon of theory in the humanities is partly phrased in terms of its own pre-packaging, and its inability of thinking outside its own paradigm: 'The risks of specialized jargons for the humanities, inside and outside the university, are obvious: they simply substitute one prepackaged idiom for another' (2004, 72). Postcolonial theory could be at risk of just such a pre-packaging, without interrupting its own paradigm and 'deranging' its own idiom. As has already been indicated, however, Said extrapolates some significant conclusions from this analysis of bite-sized information culture both outside and inside the university:

> the prepackaged information that dominates our patterns of thought (the media, advertising, official declarations, and ideological political argument designed to persuade or to lull into submission, not to stimulate thought and engage the intellect) tends to fit into short, telegraphic forms. [...] All the choices, exclusions, and emphases – to say nothing of the history of the

subject at hand – are invisible, dismissed as irrelevant. What I have been calling humanistic resistance therefore needs to occur in longer forms, longer essays, longer periods of reflection. (Said 2004, 73)

Unsurprisingly, Said wishes to defend the nature of what he calls philology. Such work ought to make clear all that has been excluded, how it was excluded, and why. In the end, this work is necessary in order to counter the glibness of official discourse, and that discourse is ultimately so swift that we barely notice its looseness, vagueness, or straightforward inaccuracy. We must, then, read slowly; this slowness is fundamental to responsible politics, postcolonial or otherwise. It may seem to be impossible to make such a connection between slow reading and responsible politics, and yet that is exactly what Spivak does in her own re-imagination of comparative literature: 'Of course, the literary is not a blueprint to be followed in unmediated social action. But if as teachers of literature we teach reading, literature can be our teacher as well as our object of investigation' (2003, 23). In order to have the general context of comparability, rather than have versions of it fed to us by self-interested informants of one sort or another, Spivak counsels that we learn again to read.

However, in learning to read again, which will be a never-ending process, we are not returning to an earlier phase of critical practice to re-learn something we have forgotten. In fact, it can be argued that postcolonial reading is not a phase of critical practice that we have passed through. It is not even the case that it is in the past, a critical mode to which we might return in order to maintain our understanding of the political contexts of literature and culture. Instead, it is a form of reading that continues to exist, or rather continues to be demanded. As Greene suggests, postcolonial studies constitutes, 'a limit-case that shows how inseparable works and networks are, how often works must be reinvigorated within networks even as the networks themselves are reinvented again and again – in the case of colonial networks, by restaging the conversations between past and present' (2006, 222). The general postcolonial context in which comparison can take place keeps our interpretation focused on the 'roughness' of the global space, while there is always the possibility that the globalized context vaporizes the complexity and disjuncture inevitably present, producing a misleading smoothness. The ideologies of digital capitalism, which accompany the dream of simultaneous revolution, produce an immediacy of superficial solidarity. Close reading, with literary study understood as fundamental to postcolonial theory, functions as a form of resistance to this ideology of immediacy, an ideology which in Hallward's terms is an ideology of the *non-relational* (2001). Further, as Said indicates, close reading necessitates a particular kind of writing to accompany it, tease out its most complex and paradoxical insights, and not least demand close reading in turn. One of the challenges posed by World Englishes is for postcolonial studies to recognize in 'itself' that which is most valuable, as this chapter and the Chapter 1 have argued. This chapter in particular suggests that only through slow and patient negotiations of reading and writing can we adequately relate the nodes that, with varying levels of connectedness, make up our world.

Conclusion: English Remains, Englishes Remain

The tensions in the use of a universal standard are seldom clear to those in a dominant position with regard to it for they do not need to suppress local innovation in order to participate in a universal network.

David Singh Grewal, *Network Power*

From a sceptical perspective, postcolonial studies remains locked into an oppositional framework. While that framework acknowledges that postcolonialism is in many ways about what Young calls 'unfinished business, the continuing projection of past conflicts into the experience of the present' (2012, 21), the need for new perspectives is also frequently expressed. This book has argued that one possibility for finally breaking out of that framework is to engage with World Englishes studies. In common with other approaches to aspects of globalization, World Englishes studies assume less a centre-periphery model, however valuable such a model may still be for some contexts, and more a dynamic network. Of course, the power of a node in such a network depends not only on what it is in itself, but also on how connected it is. However, connectedness still implies the potential significance of a node's self-identity, and there will still be moments when centre and periphery are the best terms to describe what is under consideration. David Singh Grewal (2008) writes of English in terms of *network power*, describing the fact that people are rational agents, to some extent, but also that the context in which they make a choice may well compel that choice, leading to a widespread feeling of being coerced. The process of tacit social coordination that 'decides' on global standards proceeds inevitably to eliminate alternatives capable of fulfilling the same function, and this seems to be the case with English understood as a global language. But, as is clear, there are other possibilities within World Englishes; the spread of Englishes and the increased acknowledgement of linguistic hybridization work alongside the tendencies of network power that favour a standardized global English.

Keeping this balance in mind, this book has argued the following: World Englishes demand that postcolonial studies look towards a future that, whether it 'speaks English' or not, will need to be characterized by a different idea of communication. Even when celebrating the use of English in, for example, literary texts, postcolonial studies has persevered with a notion of communication based on the assumption of native–non-native interlocution; that assumption is implicit in a notion such as 'writing back'. But, as World Englishes literature might suggest, and as World Englishes more generally prove, that assumption is no longer tenable. Nor is any model of communication that assumes smooth accessibility, transparency, and consensus; such a model of globalized imperialism will be experienced as, in important ways, imperialist. As the instances of China and India (often taken to be the future of English) in their different ways indicate, World Englishes imply a more diverse set of models of communication, models that linguistics has been theorizing for some time. But, logically, the Anglophone university, after which all similar institutions seem increasingly and myopically modelled, cannot be our only source of such theories, and the future of bi- and multilingual research will be key to new developments in postcolonial studies and beyond.

Engaging with such a multilingual future, and exploring some of its implications, paradoxically demands that we (some of us at least) also engage more fully with the English language as it was, is, and will be. As postcolonial studies has appeared to focus so much on forms of Anglophone literature, it would seem obvious that at the very least it had paid a great deal of attention to the English language, alongside other major colonial and postcolonial languages. It is the contention of this book that the attention it has paid English can be built upon, broadened, and extended in some surprising ways. Sometimes this book has argued that English is far more 'colonial' than has been allowed, and at other times it makes a more positive assessment of English's role and potential. The key distinction to be made, even if it cannot be made with any finality, is between English and Englishes. Ashcroft Griffiths, and Tiffin (2002 [1989]) long ago distinguished english from English, and in making that distinction they were following in a powerful tradition of colonial and postcolonial literary writing. But that clarification, enabling a clear sense of the independence of New literatures in English or postcolonial literatures, does not cover quite the same ground as that between English and Englishes. If nothing else, the later distinction is part of a disciplinary formation (see Seargeant 2012) that draws much of its energy from varieties of linguistics, with much overlap in cultural studies approaches, and so to some extent it implies a displacement of literary studies from the study of postcolonial language. Relatedly, it focuses our attention on narratives of contemporaneity (see Biccum 2009) that draw a fuzzy (and sometimes not so fuzzy) line between histories of empire and developments in globalization. That line enables a move 'beyond the postcolonial' (as in Dawson Varughese 2012), taking us away from the preoccupations that have animated but also possibly fixated postcolonial studies as a discipline or inter-discipline. Of course, as Biccum argues, these narratives of contemporaneity also imply that however English came to be so widely used it would be pointless to allow that firmly *complete* past to interfere with our smoothly communicative present. At the beginning of my introduction I quoted Randolph Quirk and Mario Pei, with their rather different views of English's position in the 1960s. Quirk's suggestion (1962) that English's wide usage owes nothing immediate to the dominance of the UK or US is more neutral than Pei's unashamed celebration of an American cultural imperialism (1967), but each certainly implies that 'we' best keep the past in the past, and focus instead on what it has done for 'us'. That sentiment is inadequate today, as it was when originally expressed.

Despite diverting attention from postcolonial literary studies, there is still much to be gained from keeping literature a central part of the postcolonial conversation, as I have already discussed at some length, and I would like in conclusion to use a literary example to explore some open questions concerning the future of World Englishes. That example is Ryszard Kapuściński's *Travels with Herodotus* (2007), a reflection on the important but troubling writer's journalistic career. Although of course Kapuściński must be a controversial figure from a postcolonial perspective, this book is very suggestive in taking us back to a recognizable but notably different international linguistic context. It begins with recollections of early reporting in India and China, two highly significant foci when thinking about English today and in the future (in common with many commentators, Graddol (1997; 2007) identifies the two as central to the future of the language). This example gives us immediate scope for thinking differently about English as a global language. Whatever perspective we adopt towards the English language's present scope, its preeminence and dominance can appear unchallengeable. Yet both preeminence and dominance are unlikely to be long-lived, and each is a relatively recent phenomenon. To take a key example, it is clear that despite Chinese having the greatest number of native speakers English has a very large number of learners within China itself, definitely in the order of hundreds of millions, and, according to recent statistics gathered as part of a national language survey, perhaps as many as nearly 400 million (see Wei and Su 2012). China may indeed have over a million English teachers of various types (McArthur 2003). While that may be the present situation, in the recent past the main foreign language learned in China was instead Russian (which is gaining some importance again), as Adamson (2004) demonstrates. Sudden switches between favoured foreign languages are hardly unheard of, and looking back to this recent past reveals both a very different global linguistic environment and the lineaments of the situation we currently inhabit. It may seem difficult to credit, at this point, but at the time Kapuściński was engaging with that China, as well as India, English was also supposed to be finally fading from postcolonial India's linguistic scene.

This strikingly different linguistic context should at least give us pause to rethink our sense of present and future Englishes. Writing a little later than Kapuściński's experiences, Pei discusses the potential future of English in the context of state communism, which already recalls a quite different context for discussing English's spread. In geopolitical terms, Pei is not very apologetic about anything, arguing that cultural imperialism, neo-colonialism, etc. are just what they are: backward nations submitting to the power of the forward-thrusting modernizers, and so on. In the context of this (to Pei) quite welcome if not indeed necessary ongoing domination, English ought to be central. As Pei writes: 'We, the speakers of English, should proudly flaunt the banners of cultural imperialism, neo-colonialism, and commercialism. The first places us in the forefront of intellectual and educational progress; the second proves that we are scientifically and technologically in the lead; the third points the way to a better material life for everybody concerned' (1967, 174). Forty years later, Pei's dynamic optimism and faith in cultural supremacy appear both disgraceful and surprisingly myopic. At the same time, English itself seems a clear case of a hold-out against all too obvious (if complex) shifts in power between West and East, particularly towards China and India, the rivalrous neighbours. Kapuściński's book transports us back to earlier European experiences of the two, and gives us insight into specifically linguistic issues that have become more and more central to discussion of English.

Setting out from Poland as a young and confessedly extremely naive reporter, Kapuściński travelled to India, China, and numerous other places both unfamiliar and wondrous. Of course, his writing has been long criticized for what Ryle (2001) calls 'gonzo orientalism', and his reputation for honesty concerning details of his experiences has come under sustained attack (see Domosławski 2012). Indeed, Kapuściński's travels through these powerful civilizations are no more immune to reductive racism than his works on Africa. Nonetheless, his reflections on English in India and China in particular give a revealing glimpse of a different linguistic world. A record of and reflection on his travels through India, China, and elsewhere, *Travels with Herodotus* foregrounds issues concerning language, although its frequent references to his lack of English betray the fact that it was actually published rather late in his life, three years before his death in 2007. Dwelling on his earliest foreign travels, he reflects on how poorly prepared he was for India, with no real contacts and very little knowledge of English. Early in the book he buys a copy of *For Whom the Bell Tolls*, in the hope that Hemingway will help him improve his English. Undoubtedly, Kapuściński is not the only learner of English who has felt, or has been instructed, that Hemingway writes with uncommon clarity and directness. Unfortunately, that particular novel seemingly had an effect opposite to that desired:

> The more I tried to understand this text, the more discouraged and despairing I became. I felt trapped. Besieged by language. Language struck me at that moment as something material, something with a physical dimension, a wall rising up in the middle of the road and preventing my going any further, closing off the world, making it unattainable. It was an unpleasant and humiliating sensation. It might explain why, in a first

encounter with someone or something foreign, there are those who will feel fear and uncertainty, bristle with mistrust. (Kapuściński 2007, 20)

These perhaps rather basic comments about language and intercultural contact need to be understood in the context of the young Pole travelling for the first time in the 1950s. Later he remarks that his first reaction was to flee to the familiar, and to forget India in particular, symbolic as it began to seem to him of personal failure. It is the specifically linguistic problems that seem most troublesome, and it is here that the focus on English makes more explicit sense. Thinking about how Herodotus himself might have handled this oppressive sense of linguistic materiality, Kapuściński remembers the status of Greek as lingua franca (in fact it is doubtful that Herodotus spoke *any* other language, even the Carian of his own background). But are these reflections on lingua francas supposed to comfort the young reporter (if indeed they could have occurred to him at the time)? As he remarks in passing, Greek was replaced by Latin, French, and ultimately English, and so he would seem to be back where he started.

Determined to be more positive in his approach, Kapuściński begins to engage India through the English that surrounds him. A world of astonishing sensual drama is focused (and perhaps reduced) by the language of the relatively recently departed colonial culture. This English constitutes a materiality that enables Kapuściński to grasp something of India's *ipseity*, however counter-intuitive that might appear. While he himself registers the problem in grasping the country through this foreign language, it is not exactly clear that passages such as the following allow him to deal with the political and cultural difficulties he is facing through his European partiality and its divide-and-rule approach:

I walked around the city, copying down signboards, the names of goods in stores, words overheard at bus stops. In movie theatres I scribbled blindly, in darkness, the words on the screen, and noted the slogans on banners carried by demonstrators in the streets. I approached India not through images, sounds, and smells, but through words; furthermore, words not of the indigenous Hindi, but of a foreign, imposed tongue, which by then had so fully taken root here that it was for me an indispensable key to this country, almost identical with it. I understood that every distinct geographic universe has its own mystery and that one can decipher it only by learning the local language. Without it, this universe will remain impenetrable and unknowable, even if one were to spend entire years in it. I noticed, too, the relationship between naming and being, because I realized upon my return to the hotel that in town I had seen only that which I was able to name: for example, I remembered the acacia tree, but not the tree standing next to it, whose name I did not know. I understood, in short, that the more words I knew, the richer, fuller, and more variegated would be the world that opened before me, and which I could capture. (Kapuściński 2007, 22)

There are a number of assumptions and elisions in this passage, of course, but it could be argued that Kapuściński's approach to English as an Indian language has received significant confirmation in more recent studies of English as it is used today (most influentially in Kachru 1986). But, to return to the assumptions and elisions, it is of course not a simple statement to say that Hindi is *the* indigenous language, even if it was the one given most prominence. Additionally, he appears to be making a claim for English as an indigenous language, while still accepting the usual assumptions about its status as a colonial tongue. Furthermore, the separation of spoken and written language from all the other languages of India (visual, olfactory, etc.) is rather simple-minded, even though it is a separation we may all assume from time to time. This passage is opaque in its reflections on language and its ability to grasp India, but it is nonetheless clear enough in some of its statements: English is Kapuściński's 'indispensable key' to India. As already mentioned, much of the recent discussion of English in India is explicit in its treatment of English as an Indian language. Despite the limits of his perspective, Kapuściński is perceptive in his treatment of English in India as one of the World Englishes.

However, in treating Indian English in this way, Kapuściński is of course also glossing over the many controversies that exist concerning the language today, and that were at least as significant at that early stage of independence. He is seemingly ignoring (or worse, condoning this ignorance when writing fifty years later) the cultural politics and linguistic imperialism that he is experiencing and taking part in. And yet he is not *entirely* ignoring these factors, as a little further on in his reflections we read the following:

> Only in India did I realize that my unfamiliarity with English was meaningless – insofar as only the elite spoke it here. Less than 2 per cent of the population! The rest some one of the dozens of other languages. In this sense, my not knowing English helped me feel closer, more akin to the ordinary folk in the cities or the peasants in the villages I passed. We were in the same boat – I and half a billion of India's inhabitants!

> While this thought gave me comfort, it also troubled me – why, I wondered, am I embarrassed that I don't know English but not that I don't know Hindi, Bengali, Gujarati, Telugu, Urdu, Tamil, Punjabi, or any of the many other languages spoken in this country? The argument of accessibility was irrelevant: the study of English was at the time as rare a thing as that of Hindi or Bengali. So was this Eurocentrism on my part? Did I believe a European language to be more important than those languages of this country in which I was then a guest? Deeming English superior was an offence to the dignity of Hindus, for whom the relationship to their native languages was a delicate and important matter. (Kapuściński 2007, 43)

To understate the matter, it seems unlikely that his apparently poor English really did bring Kapuściński any closer to the mass of India's population that did not speak English. However, he is at least showing a sense of what focusing on English ignores when approaching India. Again, though, his understanding of just why English might really be a useful and necessary aspect of Indian life (some or perhaps even many Indian lives) is lacking. His recollections are certainly confusing, perhaps even to himself, as it is hardly clear that believing English to be part of Indian life entails any form of belief in its superiority. Furthermore, it is not obvious that his generalizations about Indian culture are any less Eurocentric than if he believed English superior because it is identified as 'European'. Indeed, it seems likely that Kapuściński is projecting the concerns of *this* century back on his younger self.

Accordingly, it can be argued that Kapuściński's comments about English in India point to an awareness of the localization of the language while remaining caught in instructive and even perhaps necessary guilt. It might be argued that this combination is very much one we find today, whether in relation to English's roles in India or elsewhere. Yet it is perhaps the case that it is his trip to China that most clearly reveals the unspoken assumptions behind English as lingua franca. For the language Kapuściński speaks with the locals who are in effect managing his trip to China is of course Russian. Even at that relatively recent point when, according to many narratives of its rise, English was already well established as *the* world language, there was a very serious alternative. As already mentioned, Russian was the main foreign language in China for a long time. While this may have been an ideological choice, and was indeed subject to fluctuation according to changing political circumstances (as Adamson (2004) has shown), Russian's relatively recent high status in China focuses our attention on the fragility of languages that function internationally. For many reasons it is possible to predict that English will be replaced as a lingua franca. Alternatively, as already discussed, we might even think of English as likely to be the *last* lingua franca (see Ostler 2010). There is nothing dramatically distinct or unique about the English language *per se* that explains its seemingly meteoric rise, or that will insulate it from the political, economic, and cultural changes that will lead to a loss, however relative, of its international standing. Kapuściński evokes a world in which the possibility of this loss was clearer than it is today, partly because it might appear by now that the English language has triumphed as an international language. His own confusions are, I would argue, hardly his alone, and in plunging into the wide world of the postcolonial and Cold War period he raises many of the questions that continue to frame engagement with the politics of English.

Having said all of this, Kapuściński still manages to make an argument for English as the language of border crossing. India and China evoke similar feelings for him, and this is partly a matter of the meaningful qualities of writing systems in themselves. Referring to 'the Great Wall of Language', he observes that 'It was actually not dissimilar to how I had felt in India. There too I could not penetrate the thicket of the local Hindi alphabet. And were I to travel farther still, would I not encounter similar barriers?' (2007, 63). That would appear to be a good argument for sitting down and studying a language in some depth. Nonetheless, perhaps as a matter of temperament (as he reflects on Herodotus' ethnicity), he himself has become obsessed with crossing the border: 'Cultures are edifices with countless rooms, corridors, balconies, and attics, all arranged, furthermore, into such twisting, turning labyrinths, that if you enter one of them, there is no exit, no retreat, no turning back. To become a Hindu scholar, a Sinologist, an Arabist, or a Hebraist is a lofty, all-consuming pursuit, leaving no space or time for anything else' (2007, 71). It is no surprise, then, that despite all his knowledge telling against it, Kapuściński is so worried about the state of his English. But it is not just that border crossing is something that English does, or something that it enables an English speaker to do with greater ease than those who do not speak it. It is more that that border crossing, as in the case of the English that Kapuściński finds in India, is something that is found within the language itself, and within the linguistic ecologies that English affects and that affect English. India is in some ways an exemplary place to discuss these issues in that it is a central location for one of the World Englishes. And those Englishes prompt us to rethink (without rejecting) the numerous connections made between English and colonial legacies.

These examples of recent history also invite us to question the easy assumption of continuities between histories of empire and colonialism, and the shifting configurations of globalization. Indeed, whether focusing on Tibet, Xinjiang, various African countries, or any number of other widely scattered locations, commentators are increasingly likely to raise the issue of China as a colonial force itself – however, if that suggestion is accurate, perhaps a perceived contrast with previous colonizers is key. That being the case, attention is now being paid to the potential for Putonghua to become a world language (rather than the already massive regional language it is), or for it to be considered a colonial language. For example, the Confucius Institutes might be seen as not unlike *Alliance Française* or the British Council, but then, depending on your perspective, that similarity qualifies them precisely for suspicion and criticism. This issue is increasingly interesting at a time when English has been well established as a 'Chinese language' itself (see Jiang 2003), rather than simply being a language widely learned in China; as Kachru would make the distinction, English is now understood to be *of* rather than merely *in* China. Clearly these developments could be related, might be in conflict, and in any case ought to be articulated. Postcolonial studies, reconfigured in relation to World Englishes studies, as well as other currents in globalization studies, needs to play a role in making such articulations, given the well-developed and provocative conceptual apparatus it has developed.

As this book explores in different contexts, postcolonial studies already contributes to many of the discussions that arise from the present state of English, and it would be surprising if this were not so. It can be argued, however, that in extending itself postcolonial studies ceases to be the discipline we have known (if we have ever really known it to be 'one'), and becomes more an aspect of a broader perspective on the making of meaning in all media, in much the same vein as Miller recommends for the humanities as such: 'Here is the future for the humanities: comprehensive, omnibus survey courses about how meaning is made, circulated, and received in all media – running across science, capital, fiction, sport, news, history, and politics' (2012, 122). Obviously enough, the World Englishes will be for some time a central aspect of each of these media, and will be key drivers in the unpredictable transformation of each of these contexts. What exactly will a renewed postcolonial studies offer such shifting contexts? Through putting postcolonial studies into dialogue with World Englishes, this book has suggested different ways that it might participate in Glissant's 'theory of specifically opaque structures' (1989, 133). There are, of course, many possibilities that derive from the spread of a global English, but, as the diagnosis of linguistic imperialism suggests, a central possibility is that communication becomes a form of coerced accessibility to Anglophone globalization. World Englishes themselves are potentially rather *in*accessible, hence the frequently staged opposition between mutual intelligibility and cultural expressiveness. Ultimately, however, World Englishes reinstall the need for a labour of reading in our engagement with other contexts and cultures – whoever *we* may be. On the one hand, they hold out a greater facility for mutual engagement; on the other, they withhold the promise of transparency. It is necessary for us to analyse how they function, what they enable, and what they block, in diverse and specific contexts. In short, World Englishes have no *necessary* meaning, their potential and implications being ripe for direction and shaping; sooner or later, if not already, they will constitute a worldwide responsibility.

Bibliography

Abbas, Ackbar. 1997. *Hong Kong: Culture and the Politics of Disappearance*. Hong Kong University Press.

Adamson, Bob. 2004. *China's English: A History of English in Chinese Education*. Hong Kong University Press.

Ahmad, Aijaz. 1992. *In Theory: Classes, Nations, Literatures*. London: Verso.

Al-Dabbagh, Abdulla. 2010. *Literary Orientalism, Postcolonialism, and Universalism*. New York: Peter Lang.

Aleinikoff , T. Alexander, and Douglas Klusmeyer. 2001. 'Plural Nationality: Facing the Future in a Migratory World'. *Citizenship Today: Global Perspectives and Practices*. Washington, DC: Carnegie Endowment for International Peace. 63–88.

Alim, H. Samy, Awad Ibrahim, and Alastair Pennycook. Eds. 2009. *Global Linguistic Flows: Hip Hop Cultures, Youth Identities, and the Politics of Language*. New York: Routledge.

Alsagoff, Lubna. 2010a. 'English in Singapore: Culture, Capital and Identity in Linguistic Variation'. *World Englishes* 29.3: 336–348.

—. 2010b. 'Hybridity in Ways of Speaking: The Glocalization of English in Singapore'. In *English in Singapore: Modernity and Management*. Eds. Lisa Lim, Anne Pakir, and Lionel Wee. Hong Kong University Press. 109–130.

Anchimbe, Eric A., and Stephen A. Mforteh. 2011. *Postcolonial Linguistic Voices*. Berlin: Mouton de Gruyter.

Anderson, Benedict. 2006. *Imagined Communities: Reflections on the Origin and Spread of Nationalism*, 3rd edn. London: Verso.

Appadurai, Arjun. 1996. *Modernity at Large: Cultural Dimensions of Globalization*. Minneapolis, MN: University of Minnesota Press.

Archibugi, Daniele, and David Held. 1995. *Cosmopolitan Democracy: An Agenda for a New World Order*. Cambridge: Polity Press.

Asad, Talal. 1986 'The Concept of Cultural Translation in British Social Anthropology'. In *Writing Culture: The Poetics and Politics of Ethnography*. Eds. James Clifford and Geoge E. Marcus. Berkeley: University of California Press. 141–164.

Ashcroft, Bill. 2001. *Post-Colonial Transformation*. London: Routledge.

—. 2008. *Caliban's Voice: The Transformation of English in Post-Colonial Literatures*. Abingdon: Routledge.

Ashcroft, Bill, Gareth Griffiths, and Helen Tiffin. 2002 [1989]. *The Empire Writes Back: Theory and Practice in Post-Colonial Literatures*. 2nd edn. New York: Routledge.

Austin, J.L. 1961. *Philosophical Papers*. Eds. Urmson James Opie and Geoffrey James Warnock. Oxford: Clarendon Press.

Badiou, Alain. 2001. *Ethics: An Essay on the Understanding of Evil*. Trans. Peter Hallward. London: Verso.

Bahri, Deeprika. 2004. 'Terms of Engagement: Postcolonialism, Transnationalism, and Composition Studies'. In *Crossing Borderlands: Composition and Postcolonial Studies*. Eds. Andrea A. Lunsford and Lahoucine Ouzgane. University of Pittsburgh Press. 67–83.

Bal, Mieke, and Shahram Entekhabi. Dirs. 2005. *Lost in Space*. Documentary film.

—. 2007. 'Translating Translation'. *Journal of Visual Culture* 6.5: 109–124.

Baldick, Chris. 1983. *The Social Mission of English Criticism, 1848–1932*. Oxford: Clarendon Press.

Béjoint, Henri. 1994. *Modern Lexicography: An Introduction*. Oxford University Press.

—. 2011. 'Patrick J. Cummings and Hans-Georg Wolf, *A Dictionary of Hong Kong English, Words from the Fragrant Harbour*'. *International Journal of Lexicography* 24.4: 476–480.

Benhabib, Seyla. 1994. 'Democracy and Difference: Reflections on the Metapolitics of Lyotard and Derrida'. *Journal of Political Philosophy* 2.1: 1–23.

Bennington, Geoffrey. 2001. 'Ex-Communication'. *Studies in Social and Political Thought* 5: 50–55.

Benson, Phil. 2001. *Ethnocentrism and the Dictionary*. New York: Routledge.

Berns, Margie. 1998. '(Re)Experiencing Hegemony: The Linguistic Imperialism of Robert Phillipson'. *International Journal of Applied Linguistics* 8.2: 271–282.

Bery, Ashok. 2009. 'Response'. *Translation Studies* 2.2: 213–216.

Bhabha, Homi K. 1994. *The Location of Culture*. London: Routledge.

—. 1996. 'Unsatisfied: Notes on Vernacular Cosmopolitanism'. In *Text and Nation: Cross-Disciplinary Essays on Cultural and National Identities*. Eds. Laura Garcia-Moreno and Peter C. Pfeiffer. Columbia, SC: Camden House. 191–207.

—. 1999. 'Arrivals and Departures'. *Home, Exile, Homeland: Film, Media, and the Politics of Place*. Ed. Hamid Naficy. London: Routledge. vii–xii.

—. 2005. 'Adagio'. *Edward Said: Continuing the Conversation*. Eds. Homi K. Bhabha and William J.T. Mitchell. University of Chicago Press.

—. 2006. 'Another Country'. *Without Boundary: Seventeen Ways of Looking*. Ed. Fereshteh Daftari. New York: The Museum of Modern Art. 30–35.

—. 2007a. 'Notes on Globalisation and Ambivalence'. In *Cultural Politics in a Global Age: Uncertainty, Solidarity and Innovation*. Eds. David Held and Henrietta Moore, with Kevin Young. Oxford: Oneworld. 36–47.

—. 2007b. 'Global Minoritarian Culture'. In *Shades of the Planet: American Literature as World Literature*. Eds. Wai-chee Dimock and Lawrence Buell. Princeton University Press. 184–194.

Biccum, April. 2009. *Global Citizenship and the Legacy of Empire: Marketing Development*. New York: Routledge.

Bisong, Joseph. 1995. 'Language Choice and Cultural Imperialism: A Nigerian Perspective'. *ELT Journal* 49.2: 122–132.

Block, David, and Deborah Cameron. 2002. *Globalization and Language Teaching*. London and New York: Routledge.

Bokhorst-Heng, Wendy. 2005. 'Debating Singlish'. *Multilingua* 24.3: 185–209.

Bolton, Kingsley. 2000. 'Orientalism, Linguistics and Postcolonial Studies'. *Interventions* 2.1: 1–5.

—. 2002a. 'Chinese Englishes: From Canton Jargon to Global English'. *World Englishes* 21.2: 181–199.

—. 2002b. *Hong Kong English: Autonomy and Creativity*. Hong Kong University Press.

—. 2003. *Chinese Englishes: A Sociolinguistic History*. Cambridge University Press.

—. 2005. 'Where WE Stands: Approaches, Issues, and Debate in World Englishes'. *World Englishes* 24.1: 69–83.

—. 2006. 'Varieties of World Englishes'. In *The Handbook of World Englishes*. Eds. Braj B. Kachru, Yamuna Kachru, and Cecil L. Nelson. Oxford: Blackwell.

—. 2008. 'English in Asia, Asian Englishes, and the Issue of Proficiency'. *English Today* 24.2: 3–12.

—. 2010. 'Creativity and World Englishes'. *World Englishes* 29.4: 455–466.

—. 2012. 'World Englishes and Linguistic Landscapes'. *World Englishes* 31.1: 30–33.

Bolton, Kingsley, and Braj B. Kachru. 2006. *World Englishes: Critical Concepts in Linguistics*. London and New York: Routledge.

Bolton, Kingsley, and David Graddol. 2012. 'English in China Today'. *English Today* 28.3: 3.

Bolton, Kingsley, and Q.S. Tong. 2002. 'Introduction: Interdisciplinary Perspectives on English in China'. *World Englishes* 21.2: 177–180.

Bowman, Paul. 2007. *Post-Marxism Versus Cultural Studies*. Edinburgh University Press.

Braine, George. 2010. *Nonnative Speaker English Teachers: Research, Pedagogy, and Professional Growth*. London: Routledge.

Brewer, Charlotte. 2007. *Treasure-House of the Language: The Living OED*. New Haven, CT: Yale University Press.

Brumfit, Christopher. 2004. 'Language and Higher Education: Two Current Challenges'. *Arts and Humanities in Higher Education* 3.2: 163–173.

Bruthiaux, Paul. 2010. 'The Speak Good English Movement: A Web-User's Perspective'. In *English in Singapore*. Eds. Lisa Lim, Anne Pakir, and Lionel Wee. Hong Kong University Press. 90.

Brutt-Griffler, Janina. 2002. *World English: A Study of its Development*. Clevedon and Buffalo, NY: Multilingual Matters.

Buden, Boris. 2005. 'The Pit of Babel, or: The Society that Mistook Culture for Politics'. 14 December. http://translate.eipcp.net/strands/01/buden-strands01en. Web.

Buden, Boris, and Stefan Nowotny. 2009. 'Cultural Translation: An Introduction to the Problem'. *Translation Studies* 2.2: 196–219.

Bunton, David. 1989. *Common English Errors in Hong Kong*. London: Pearson.

Burns, Anne, and Caroline Coffin. 2001. *Analysing English in a Global Context: A Reader*. London and New York: Routledge in association with Macquarie University and the Open University.

Burton, Pauline. 2010. 'Creativity in Hong Kong Schools'. *World Englishes* 29.4: 493–507.

Butler, Susan. 1997. 'Selecting South East Asian Words for an Australian Dictionary: How to Choose in an English Not Your Own'. In *Englishes Around the World*. Eds. Manfred Gèorlach and Edgar Werner Schneider. Amsterdam: John Benjamins. 273–287.

—. 2012. 'A Dictionary of Hong Kong English: Words from the Fragrant Harbor by Patrick J. Cummings and Hans-Georg Wolf'. *World Englishes* 31.4: 549–551.

Cagliero, Roberto, and Jennifer Jenkins. 2010. *Discourses, Communities, and Global Englishes*. Berne: Peter Lang.

Cameron, Deborah. 1995. *Verbal Hygiene*. London and New York: Routledge.

—. 2000. 'Language: Difficult Subjects'. *Critical Quarterly* 42.4: 89–94.

—. 2002. 'Globalization and the Teaching of "Communication Skills"'. In *Globalization and Language Teaching*. Eds. David Block and Deborah Cameron. London: Routledge. 67–82.

Canagarajah, A. Suresh. 2013. *Translingual Practice: Global Englishes and Cosmopolitan Relations*. New York: Routledge.

Carter, Awena, Theresa Lillis, and Sue Parkin. Eds. 2009. *Why Writing Matters: Issues of Access and Identity in Writing Research and Pedagogy*. Amsterdam and Philadelphia, PA: John Benjamins.

Casanave, Christine Pearson. 2004. *Controversies in Second Language Writing: Dilemmas and Decisions in Research and Instruction*. Ann Arbor, MI: University of Michigan Press.

Casanova, Pascale. 2004. *The World Republic of Letters*. Trans. M.B. DeBevoise. Cambridge, MA: Harvard University Press.

Castells, Manuel. 2000. *The Rise of the Network Society*. 2nd edn. Oxford: Blackwell.

Chan, B.H.S. 2007. 'Hybrid Language and Hybrid Identity? The Case of Cantonese-English Code-Switching in Hong Kong'. In *East-West Identities: Globalization, Localization, and Hybridization*. Eds. K.B. Chan, Jan Walls, and David Hayward. Leiden: Brill. 189–202.

Chow, Rey. 1995. *Primitive Passions: Visuality, Sexuality, Ethnography, and Contemporary Chinese Cinema*. New York: Columbia University Press.

—. 2008. 'Reading Derrida on being Monolingual'. *New Literary History* 39.2: 217–231.

—. 2012. *Entanglements, or Transmedial Thinking about Capture*. Durham, NC and London: Duke University Press.

Clifford, James. 1997. *Routes: Travel and Translation in the Late Twentieth Century*. Cambridge, MA: Harvard University Press.

Clyne, Michael G. 2005. *Australia's Language Potential*. Sydney: UNSW Press.

The Coxford Singlish Dictionary. 2002. Singapore: Angsana Books.

Cronin, Michael. 2003. *Translation and Globalization*. London: Routledge.

—. 2006. *Translation and Identity*. London: Routledge.

—. 2009. 'Response'. *Translation Studies* 2.2: 216–219.

Crystal, David. 2003. *English as a Global Language*. 2nd edn. Cambridge University Press.

—. 2004. *The Stories of English*. London: Allen Lane.

Culler, Jonathan. 2006. *The Literary in Theory*. Stanford University Press.

Cummings, Patrick, and Hans-Georg Wolf. 2011. *A Dictionary of Hong Kong English*. Hong Kong University Press.

Dai, Fan. 2012. 'English-Language Creative Writing by Chinese University Students'. *English Today* 28.03: 21.

Damrosch, David. 2003. *What is World Literature?* Princeton University Press.

—. 2009. *How to Read World Literature*. Chichester and Malden, MA: Wiley-Blackwell.

Davidson, Keith. 2012. 'English, "So to Say"'. *English Today* 28.1: 58.

Davis, Kathryn Anne. 2011. *Critical Qualitative Research in Second Language Studies: Agency and Advocacy*. Charlotte, NC: Information Age Publishing.

Dawson Varughese, Emma. 2012. *Beyond the Postcolonial: World Englishes Literature*. New York: Palgrave Macmillan.

de Bary, Brett. 2010. *Universities in Translation*. 5 vols. Hong Kong University Press.

Delbridge, Arthur. 1991. *The Macquarie Dictionary*. 2nd edn. McMahons Point, NSW: Macquarie Library.

Derrida, Jacques. 1986. 'Declarations of Independence'. *New Political Science* 7.1: 7–15.

—. 1988. *Limited Inc*. Trans. Samuel Weber. Evanston, IL: Northwestern University Press.

—. 1997. *Politics of Friendship*. Trans. G. Collins. London: Verso.

—. 1998. *Monolingualism of the Other, or, the Prosthesis of Origin*. Stanford University Press.

—. 2001. *On Cosmopolitanism and Forgiveness*. London and New York: Routledge.

—. 2002. *Negotiations : Interventions and Interviews, 1971–2001*. Trans. and Ed. Elizabeth Rottenberg. Stanford University Press.

Derrida, Jacques, and Anne Dufourmantelle. 2000. *Of Hospitality*. Stanford University Press.

Derrida, Jacques, and Elizabeth Roudinesco. 2004. *For what Tomorrow ... A Dialogue*. Trans. Jeff Fort. Stanford University Press.

Derrida, Jacques, Maurizio Ferraris, Giacomo Donis, and David Webb. 2001. *A Taste for the Secret*. Cambridge: Polity Press.

Dhillon, Pradeep. 2003. 'Ethics in Language: The Case from World Englishes'. *World Englishes* 22.3: 217–226.

—. 2009. 'Colonial/Postcolonial Critique: The Challenge from World Englishes'. In *The Handbook of World Englishes*. Eds. Braj Kachru, Yamuna Kachru, and Cecil Nelson. Oxford: Blackwell. 529–544.

Dimock, Wai-chee. 2008. *Through Other Continents: American Literature across Deep Time*. Princeton University Press.

Dixon, R.M.W. 2008. 'Australian Aboriginal Words in Dictionaries: A History'. *International Journal of Lexicography* 21.2: 129–152.

Dobrin, Sidney I. 2007. 'The Occupation of Composition'. In *The Locations of Composition*. Eds. Christopher J. Keller and Christian R. Weisser. Albany, NY: State University of New York Press. 15–35.

—. 2011. *Postcomposition*. Carbondale, IL: Southern Illinois University Press.

Domosławski, Artur. 2012. *Ryszard Kapuściński: A Life*. Trans. and Ed. Antonia Lloyd-Jones. London: Verso.

Drichel, Simone. 2011. 'Slow Criticism: Responsibilities of Reading *Well*'. *Borderlands* 10.1: 1–8. www.borderlands.net.au/vol10no1_2011/drichel_editorial.htm.

During, Simon. 2012. 'Empire's Present'. *New Literary History* 43.2: 331–340.

Eagleton, Terry. 1998. 'Postcolonialism and "Postcolonialism"'. *Interventions* 1.1: 24–26.

Eakin, Paul John. Ed. 2004. *The Ethics of Life Writing*. London: Cornell University Press.

Ennew, Christine, and David Greenaway. 2012. *The Globalization of Higher Education*. Basingstoke: Palgrave Macmillan.

European Commission, Directorate-General for Translation. 2010. 'Contribution of Translation to the Multilingual Society in the EU'. 25 November 2010. http://ec.europa.eu/dgs/translation/publications/studies/multilingual_society_summary_en.pdf.

—. 2012a. *Translation and Multilingualism*. Luxembourg: Publications Office of the European Union.

—. 2012b. 'Quantifying Quality Costs and the Cost of Poor Quality in Translation'. http://bookshop.europa.eu/en/quantifying-quality-costs-and-the-cost-of-poor-quality-in-translation-pbHC3112463/.

Fairclough, Norman. 2006. *Language and Globalization*. New York: Routledge.

Fanon, Frantz. 1963 [1961]. *The Wretched of the Earth*. Trans. Constance Farrington. New York: Grove Press.

Finkelstein, David, and Alistair Mcleery. 2005. *An Introduction to Book History*. New York: Routledge.

Foley, J.A., et al. 1999. *English in New Cultural Contexts: Reflections from Singapore*. Oxford University Press.

Foshay, Raphael. 2011. *Valences of Interdisciplinarity: Theory, Practice, Pedagogy*. Edmonton: AU Press.

Freire, Paulo. 1993 [1970]. *Pedagogy of the Oppressed*. New York: Continuum.

Gao, Xuesong Andy. 2012. 'The Study of English in China as a Patriotic Enterprise'. *World Englishes* 31: 351–365.

Geertz, Clifford. 1973. *The Interpretation of Cultures: Selected Essays*. New York: Basic Books.

—. 2000. *Available Light: Anthropological Reflections on Philosophical Topics*. Princeton University Press.

Ghosh, Amitav, and Dipesh Chakrabarty. 2002. 'A Correspondence on Provincializing Europe'. *Radical History Review* 83: 146–172.

Gil, Jeffrey. 2010. 'The Double Danger of English as a Global Language'. *English Today* 26.0: 51.

Gilroy, Paul. 2002. *There Ain't no Black in the Union Jack: The Cultural Politics of Race and Nation*. 2nd edn. London: Routledge.

Gimenez, Telma. 2001. 'ETS and ELT: Teaching a World Language'. *ELT Journal* 55.3: 296–297.

Glissant, Édouard. 1989. *Caribbean Discourse: Selected Essays*. Trans. J. Michael Dash. Charlottesville, VA: University Press of Virginia.

Graddol, David. 1997. *The Future of English?: A Guide to Forecasting the Popularity of the English Language in the 21st Century*. London: British Council.

—. 2007. *Changing English*. Abingdon and New York: Routledge.

Graddol, David, and Ulrike Hanna Meinhof. 1999. *English in a Changing World*. Milton Keynes: Catchline on behalf of AILA.

Gramsci, Antonio. 1992. *Prison Notebooks*, vol. 1. Ed. Joseph A. Buttigieg. Trans. Joseph A. Buttigieg and Antonio Callari. New York: Columbia University Press.

Green, Jonathon. 1999. 'Language: Dictionary Wars'. *Critical Quarterly* 41: 127–131.

Greenbaum, Andrea. 2001. *Insurrections: Approaches to Resistance in Composition Studies*. Albany, NY: State University of New York Press.

Greene, Roland. 2006. 'Not Works but Networks: Colonial Worlds in Comparative Literature'. *Comparative Literature in an Age of Globalization*. Ed. Haun Saussy. Baltimore, MD: Johns Hopkins University Press. 212–223.

Grewal, David Singh. 2008. *Network Power: The Social Dynamics of Globalization*. New Haven, CT: Yale University Press.

Groves, Julie. 2010. 'Lexical Traps in Hong Kong English'. *English Today* 26.0: 44–50.

Guibernau, Montserrat. 2007. 'National Identity Versus Cosmopolitan Identity'. In *Cultural Politics in a Global Age: Uncertainty, Solidarity and Innovation*. Eds. David Held and Henrietta Moore with Kevin Young. Oxford: Oneworld. 148–156.

Gulick, Anne. 2011. 'Declarative Moments: Literature, Law and Transatlantic Postcolonialism, 1776–1996'. *Udini*. http://udini.proquest.com/view/declarative-moments-literature-law-goid:304636366/.

Gupta, Anthea Fraser. 1994. *The Step-Tongue: Children's English in Singapore*. Clevedon and Philadelphia, PA: Multilingual Matters.

Gupta, Suman. 2009. *Globalization and Literature*. Cambridge: Polity Press.

Ha, Kien Nghi, Lieven Dhulst, and Robert J.C. Young. 2010. 'Translation Studies Forum: Cultural Translation'. *Translation Studies* 3: 349–360.

Habermas, Jürgen, and Eduardo Mendieta. 2004. 'America and the World'. *Logos Journal*. http://www.logosjournal.com/habermas_america.htm.

Halasek, Kay. 1999. *A Pedagogy of Possibility: Bakhtinian Perspectives on Composition Studies*. Carbondale, IL: Southern Illinois University Press.

Hallward, Peter. 2001. *Absolutely Postcolonial: Writing between Singular and Specific*. Manchester University Press.

Han, Fook Kwang, et al. 2011. *Lee Kuan Yew: Hard Truths to Keep Singapore Going*. Singapore: Straits Times Press.

Hannerz, Ulf. 1996. *Transnational Connections: Culture, People, Places*. New York: Routledge.

Hardt, Michael, and Antonio Negri. 2000. *Empire*. Cambridge, MA: Harvard University Press.

Harissi, Maria, Emi Otsuji, and Alastair Pennycook. 2012. 'The Performative Fixing and Unfixing of Subjectivities'. *Applied Linguistics* 33: 524–543.

Harris, Roxy, and Ben Rampton. 2003. *The Language, Ethnicity and Race Reader*. London: Routledge.

Harris, Roy, and International Association for the Integrational Study of Language and Communication. 2002. *The Language Myth in Western Culture*. Richmond: Curzon.

Harris, Roy. 1981. *The Language Myth*. Basingstoke: Palgrave Macmillan.

—. 1989. 'The Worst English in the World?' *University of Hong Kong: Supplement to the Gazette* 36: 37–46.

Harris, Wilson. 1999. *Selected Essays of Wilson Harris: The Unfinished Genesis of the Imagination*. Ed. A.J.M. Bundy. London: Routledge.

Heater, Derek Benjamin. 2002. *World Citizenship: Cosmopolitan Thinking and its Opponents*. London and New York: Continuum.

Held, David. 2004. *A Globalizing World?: Culture, Economics, Politics*. 2nd edn. London and New York: Routledge in association with the Open University.

—. 2010. *Cosmopolitanism: Ideals and Realities*. Cambridge and Malden, MA: Polity Press.

Henry, Eric. 2010. 'Interpretations of "Chinglish": Native Speakers, Language Learners and the Enregisterment of a Stigmatized Code'. *Language in Society* 39.5: 669–688.

Hewings, Ann, and Caroline Tagg. 2012. *The Politics of English: Conflict, Competition, Co-Existence*. New York: Routledge.

Hiddleston, Jane. 2010. *Poststructuralism and Postcoloniality: The Anxiety of Theory*. Liverpool University Press.

Higgins, Christina. 2009. *English as a Local Language: Post-Colonial Identities and Multilingual Practices*.

Ho, Debbie G.E. 2006. '"I'm not west. I'm not east. So how leh?"'. *English Today* 3.0: 17–24.

Ho, E.L.Y. 2010. 'Language Policy, "Asia's World City" and Anglophone Hong Kong Writing'. *Interventions* 12: 428–441.

Hoffmann, Thomas, and Lucia Siebers. Eds. 2009. *World Englishes – Problems, Properties and Prospects*. Amsterdam and Philadelphia, PA: John Benjamins.

Holquist, Michael. 2003. 'What is the Ontological Status of Bilingualism?' *Bilingual Games: Some Literary Investigations*. Ed. Doris Sommer. New York: Palgrave Macmillan. 21–34.

Horner, Bruce. 2000. *Terms of Work for Composition: A Materialist Critique*. Albany, NY: State University of New York Press.

—. 2006. 'Cross-Language Relations in Composition'. *College English* 68: 569–574.

Huddart, David. 2008. *Postcolonial Theory and Autobiography*. London: Routledge.

Huggan, Graham. 2001. *The Postcolonial Exotic: Marketing the Margins*. London and New York: Routledge.

—. 2008. *Interdisciplinary Measures*. Liverpool University Press.

Hutton, Christopher. 2002. 'The Language Myth and the Race Myth: Evil Twins of Modern Identity Politics?' In *The Language Myth in Western Culture*. Ed. Roy Harris. London: Routledge. 118–138.

Jakobson, Roman, Linda R. Waugh, and Monique Monville-Burston. 1990. *On Language*. Cambridge, MA: Harvard University Press.

Jarratt, Susan C. 2004. 'Beside Ourselves: Rhetoric and Representation in Postcolonial Feminist Writing'. In *Crossing Borderlands: Composition and Postcolonial Studies*. Eds. Andrea A. Lunsford and Lahoucine Ouzgane. University of Pittsburgh Press. 110–128.

Jenkins, Jennifer. 2007. *English as a Lingua Franca: Attitude and Identity*. Oxford University Press.

—. 2009. *World Englishes: A Resource Book for Students*. 2nd edn. London and New York: Routledge.

Jiang, Yajun. 2003. 'English as a Chinese Language'. *English Today* 19.0: 3–8.

Johnson, Samuel. 2004. *Samuel Johnson's Dictionary: Selections from the 1755 Work that Defined the English Language*. Ed. Jack Lynch. London: Atlantic.

—. 2009. *Selected Writings*. Ed. Peter Martin. Cambridge, MA: Harvard University Press.

Joseph, John E. 2004. *Language and Identity: National, Ethnic, Religious*. New York: Palgrave Macmillan.

Kachru, Braj B. 2008. 'Symposium on Intelligibility and Cross-Cultural Communication in World Englishes [Special Section]'. *World Englishes* 27.3: 293–334.

Kachru, Braj B. 1988. 'Toward Expanding the English Canon: Raja Rao's 1938 Credo for Creativity'. *World Literature Today* 24: 582–586.

—. 1985. 'Standards, Codification and Sociolinguistic Realism: The English Language in the Outer Circle'. In *World Englishes: Critical Concepts in Linguistics*, vol. 3. Eds. Braj B. Kachru and Kingsley Bolton. London and New York: Routledge. 241–269.

—. 1986. *The Alchemy of English: The Spread, Functions, and Models of Non-Native Englishes*. Oxford and New York: Pergamon Press.

—. 1992. *The Other Tongue: English Across Cultures*. 2nd edn. Urbana, IL: University of Illinois Press.

—. 1996. 'World Englishes: Agony and Ecstasy'. *Journal of Aesthetic Education* 30: 135–155.

—. 1998. 'English as an Asian Language'. *Links and Letters* 5: 89–108.

—. 2005. *Asian Englishes*. Hong Kong University Press.

—. 2006. 'World Englishes and Culture Wars'. In *The Handbook of World Englishes*. Eds. Braj B. Kachru, Yamuna Kachru, and Cecil L. Nelson. Oxford: Blackwell. 446–471.

Kachru, Braj B., Yamuna Kachru, and Cecil L. Nelson. Eds. 2006. *The Handbook of World Englishes*. Malden, MA: Blackwell.

Kachru, Yamuna. 1998. 'Culture and Speech Acts: Evidence from Indian and Singaporean English'. *Studies in the Linguistic Sciences* 28.1: 79–98.

—. 2006. 'Mixers Lyricing in Hinglish: Blending and Fusion in Indian Pop Culture'. *World Englishes* 25: 223–233.

Kachru, Yamuna, and Cecil L. Nelson. 2006. *World Englishes in Asian Contexts*. Hong Kong University Press.

Kachru, Yamuna, and Larry E. Smith. 2008. *Cultures, Contexts and World Englishes*. New York: Routledge.

Kapuściński, Ryszard. 2007. *Travels with Herodotus*. New York: Vintage Books.

Kayman, Martin. 2004. 'The State of English as a Global Language: Communicating Culture'. *Textual Practice* 18: 1–22.

Keller, Christopher J., and Christian R. Weisser. 2007. *The Locations of Composition*. Albany, NY: State University of New York Press.

Kermas, Susan. 2012. 'Culture-specific Lexis and Knowledge Sharing in the Global Village'. In *English Dictionaries as Cultural Mines*. Ed. Roberta Facchinetti. Newcastle upon Tyne: Cambridge Scholars. 73–94.

Kirkpatrick, Andy. 2007. *World Englishes: Implications for International Communication and English Language Teaching*. Cambridge University Press.

—. 2008. 'English as the Official Working Language of the Association of Southeast Asian Nations (ASEAN): Features and Strategies'. *English Today* 24.2: 27–34.

—. 2010. *English as a Lingua Franca in Asean*. Hong Kong University Press.

—. 2011. *Internationalization Or Englishization: Medium of Instruction in Today's Universities*. Hong Kong: Centre for Governance and Citizenship, The Hong Kong Institute of Education.

—. 2012. *English as an International Language in Asia: Implications for Language Education*. Dordrecht: Springer.

Kjær, Anne, Anne Lise Kjr, and Silvia Adamo. 2011. *Linguistic Diversity and European Democracy*. Farnham and Burlington, VT: Ashgate Publishing Group.

Koeneke, Rodney. 2004. *Empires of the Mind: I.A. Richards and Basic English in China, 1929–1979*. Stanford University Press.

Kramer-Dahl, Anneliese. 2003. 'Reading the "Singlish Debate": Construction of a Crisis of Language Standards and Language Teaching in Singapore'. *Journal of Language, Identity, and Education* 2: 159–190.

Kunzru, Hari. 2005. *Transmission*. Oxford: ISIS.

Kymlicka, Will. 2001. *Politics in the Vernacular: Nationalism, Multiculturalism, and Citizenship*. Oxford University Press.

Laclau, Ernesto. 1996. *Emancipation(s)*. New York: Verso.

Laclau, Ernesto, and Chantal Mouffe. 1985. *Hegemony and Socialist Strategy: Towards a Radical Democratic Politics*. London and New York: Verso.

Lai, Mee-Ling. 2005. 'Language Attitudes of the First Postcolonial Generation in Hong Kong Secondary Schools'. *Language in Society* 34.3: 363–388.

Landau, Sidney I. 2000. Review. '*Encarta World English Dictionary* and *Microsoft Encarta World English Dictionary*'. *Dictionaries: Journal of the Dictionary Society of North America* 21: 112–124.

Lam, Wan Shun Eva. 2000. 'The Question of Culture in Global English-Language Teaching: A Postcolonial Perspective'. In *Tokens of Exchange: The Problem of Translation in Global Circulations*. Ed. Lydia H. Liu. Durham, NC: Duke University Press. 375–397.

Lederer, Richard. 2011. 'A Declaration of Linguistic Independence'. *USA Today Magazine* 13: 54–55.

Lee, Kuan Yew. 1998. *The Singapore Story: Memoirs of Lee Kuan Yew*. Singapore and New York: Prentice Hall.

—. 2000. *From Third World to First: Singapore and the Asian Economic Boom*. London: HarperCollins.

Lee, Kuan Yew, and Chee Lay Chua. 2005. *Keeping My Mandarin Alive: Lee Kuan Yew's Language Learning Experience*. Singapore: World Scientific Publishing and Global Publishing.

Leitner, Gerhard. 2004. *Australia's Many Voices: Australian English – The National Language*. Berlin: Mouton de Gruyter.

Lim, Lisa, Anne Pakir, and Lionel Wee. Eds. 2010. *English in Singapore: Modernity and Management*. Hong Kong University Press.

Lim, Shirley. 2001. 'English-Language Creative Writing in Hong Kong: Colonial Stereotype and Process'. *Pedagogy* 1: 178–184.

Lin, Angel M.-Y., and Evelyn Y.-F. Man. 2011. 'The Context and Development of Language Policy and Knowledge Production in Universities in Hong Kong'. In *Critical Qualitative Research in Second Language Studies: Agency and Advocacy*. Ed. K.A. Davis. Greenwich, CN: Information Age Publishing. 99–113.

Lippi-Green, Rosina. 1997. *English with an Accent: Language, Ideology and Discrimination in the United States*. London and New York: Routledge.

Lo Bianco, Joseph, Jane Orton, and Gao Yihong. 2009. *China and English: Globalisation and the Dilemmas of Identity*. Critical Language and Literacy Studies. Bristol and Buffalo, NY: Multilingual Matters.

Lok, Ian Mai-chi. 2006. 'Cultural Understanding in English Studies: An Exploration of Postcolonial and World Englishes Perspectives'. Ph.D. thesis. University of Hong Kong.

—. 2012. 'World Englishes and Postcolonialism: Reading Kachru and Said'. *World Englishes* 31: 419–433.

Lu, Min-Zhan. 2004. 'Compositing Postcolonial Studies'. In *Crossing Borderlands*. Eds. Andrea A. Lunsford and Lahoucine Ouzgane. Pittsburgh: University of Pittsburgh Press. 9–32.

Lunsford, Andrea, and Lahoucine Ouzgane. Eds. 2004. *Crossing Borderlands: Composition and Postcolonial Studies*. University of Pittsburgh Press.

McArthur, Tom. 1998. *Living Words: Language, Lexicography, and the Knowledge Revolution*. Exeter University Press.

—. 2002. *The Oxford Guide to World English*. Oxford University Press.

—. 2003. 'English as an Asian Language'. *English Today* 19.0: 19.

—. 2004. 'Is it World or International or Global English, and Does it Matter?' *English Today* 20.0: 3–15.

—. 2005. 'Chinese, English, Spanish – and the Rest'. *English Today* 21.0: 55.

MacCabe, Colin. 1999. *The Eloquence of the Vulgar: Language, Cinema and the Politics of Culture*. London: BFI Publishing.

McCrum, Robert. 2010. *Globish: How the English Language Became the World's Language*. New York: W. W. Norton.

McCrum, Robert, William Cran, and Robert MacNeil. 1986. *The Story of English*. New York: Penguin Books.

McLennan, Gregor. 2003. 'Sociology, Eurocentrism and Postcolonial Theory'. *European Journal of Social Theory* 6: 69–86.

McNamara, Tim. 2011. 'Multilingualism in Education: A Poststructuralist Critique'. Special issue: *Toward a Multilingual Approach in the Study of Multilingualism in School Context*. *Modern Language Journal* 95.3: 430–441.

—. 2012. 'Poststructuralism and its Challenges for Applied Linguistics'. *Applied Linguistics* 33: 473–482.

McWhorter, John. 2009. 'The Cosmopolitan Tongue: The Universality of English'. *World Affairs* 172: 61–68.

Mair, Christian. Ed. 2003. *The Politics of English as a World Language: New Horizons in Postcolonial Cultural Studies*. 7 vols. Amsterdam and New York: Rodopi.

Makoni, Sinfree, and Alastair Pennycook. 2007. Eds. *Disinventing and Reconstituting Languages*. Buffalo, NY: Multilingual Matters.

Malone, Kemp. 1925. 'A Linguistic Patriot'. *American Speech* 1: 26–31.

Matsuda, Paul Kei. 2012. 'Teaching Composition in the Multilingual World: Second Language Writing in Composition Studies'. In *Exploring Composition Studies: Sites, Issues, and Perspectives*. Eds. Kelly Ritter and Paul Kei Matsuda. Logan, UT: Utah State University Press. 36–51.

Maurais, Jacques, and Michael A. Morris. 2003. 'Introduction'. In *Languages in a Globalizing World*. Eds. Jacques Maurais and Michael A. Morris. Cambridge University Press. 1–10.

Melchers, Gunnel, and Philip Shaw. 2011. *World Englishes*. 2nd edn. London: Hodder Education.

Mesthrie, Rajend, and Rakesh Mohan Bhatt. 2008. *World Englishes*. Cambridge University Press.

Miedema, John. 2009. *Slow Reading*. Duluth, MN: Litwin Books.

Miller, Toby. 2012. *Blow Up the Humanities*. Philadelphia, PA: Temple University Press.

Modiano, Marko. 1999. 'International English in the Global Village'. *English Today* 15.0: 22–28.

—. 2004. 'English Only Europe? Challenging Language Policy'. *Applied Linguistics* 25: 119–123.

—. 2009. 'Inclusive/Exclusive? English as a Lingua Franca in the European Union'. *World Englishes* 28: 208–223.

Moore, Bruce. 2001. 'Australian English: Australian Identity'. *Who's Centric Now? The Present State of Post-Colonial Englishes*. Ed. Bruce Moore. Melbourne: Oxford University Press. 44–58.

Moore, Henrietta L., David Held, and Kevin Young. 2007. *Cultural Politics in a Global Age: Uncertainty, Solidarity and Innovation*. Oxford: Oneworld.

Moretti, Franco. 2005. *Graphs, Maps, Trees: Abstract Models for Literary History*. London: Verso.

Morozov, Evgeny. 2011. *The Net Delusion: The Dark Side of Internet Freedom*. New York: Public Affairs.

Morris, E.E. 1898. *Austral English: A Dictionary of Australasian Words, Phrases and Usages*. London: Macmillan and Company.

Morris, Meaghan. 2010. 'On English as a Chinese Language: Implementing Globalization'. Ed. Brett deBary. *Universities in Translation*. Hong Kong University Press. 177–196.

Morsink, Johannes. 1999. *The Universal Declaration of Human Rights: Origins, Drafting, and Intent*. Philadelphia, PA: University of Pennsylvania Press.

—. 2009. *Inherent Human Rights: Philosophical Roots of the Universal Declaration*. Philadelphia, PA: University of Pennsylvania Press.

Moyer, Alene. 2013. *Foreign Accent: The Phenomenon of Non-Native Speech*. Cambridge University Press.

Mufwene, Salikoko S. 2010. 'The *ET* Column: Globalization and the Spread of English: What does it Mean to be Anglophone?' *English Today* 26.0: 57.

Mugglestone, Lynda. 2002. *Lexicography and the OED: Pioneers in the Untrodden Forest*. Oxford and New York: Oxford University Press.

—. 2005. *Lost for Words: The Hidden History of the Oxford English Dictionary*. Cambridge, MA: Yale University Press.

Murata, Kumiko, and Jennifer Jenkins. 2009. *Global Englishes in Asian Contexts: Current and Future Debates*. Basingstoke and New York: Palgrave Macmillan.

Murray, Les. 1981. 'Centering the Language'. Cited in Jason Clapham, 'On the Mitchells'. www.lesmurray.org/mitchellsengrev.htm.

—. 1994. 'Kylies and Ratbags'. *Times Literary Supplement* 4781: 8.

Nakayama, Thomas K., and Rona Tamiko Halualani. 2010. *Handbook of Critical Intercultural Communication*. Chichester and Malden, MA: Wiley-Blackwell.

Nelson, Cecil. 1991. 'New Englishes, New Discourses: New Speech Acts'. *World Englishes* 10.3: 317–323.

Neo, Jack. 2002. 小孩不笨 *I Not Stupid*. Dir. Jack Neo. Cast: Shawn Lee, Ashley Leong, and Joshua Ang. Singapore: Mediacorp Raintree Pictures. Feature film.

Nerrière, Jean-Paul, and David Hon. 2009. *Globish the World Over: A Book Written in Globish*. Lexington, KY: International Globish Institute.

Ng, Aik Kwang, and Ian Smith. 2004. 'Why is there a Paradox in Promoting Creativity in the Asian Classroom?' In *Creativity: When East Meets West*. Eds. Sing Lau, Ana H.H. Hui, and Grace Y.C. Ng. Singapore: World Scientific. 87–112.

Ngũgĩ wa Thiong'o. 1972. *Homecoming: Essays on African and Caribbean Literature, Culture and Politics*. London: Heinemann.

—. 1981. *Decolonising the Mind: The Politics of Language in African Literature*. Oxford: James Currey.

—. 1997 [1981]. *Writers in Politics: A Re-engagement with Issues of Literature and Society*. Oxford: James Currey.

Nolan, Philip. 2012. 'Internationalization and the Idea of a University: The Meaning of Liberal Education in the Era of Globalization'. In *The Globalization of Higher Education*. Eds. Christine Ennew and David Greenaway. Basingstoke: Palgrave Macmillan. 105–116.

Nuttall, Paul. 2008. 'The Common Wealth: Our Alternative Future'. 10 March. www.smeggys.co.uk/news_uk_ip_party.php?match=uki&news_topic=34700&page=112.

Oakeshott, Michael. 1981 [1962]. *Rationalism in Politics and Other Essays*. London and New York: Methuen.

Obama, Barack. 2008. 'Burdens of Global Citizenship'. Speech in front of the Tiergarten's Victory Column in Berlin, 24 July 2008. http://abcnews.go.com/Politics/Vote2008/story?id=5442292.

Ogden, C.K. 1968. *Basic English: International Second Language*. New York: Harcourt, Brace & World.

Ogden, C.K., and W. Terrence Gordon. 1994a. *Counter-Offensive: An Exposure of Certain Misrepresentations of Basic English*. London: Routledge/Thoemmes Press.

—. 1994b. *From Bentham to Basic English*. London: Routledge/Thoemmes Press.

Ogilvie, Sarah. 2008. 'Rethinking Burchfield and World Englishes'. *International Journal of Lexicography* 21: 23–59.

—. 2012. *Words of the World*. Cambridge and New York: Cambridge University Press.

Okrent, Arika. 2009. *In the Land of Invented Languages: A Celebration of Linguistic Creativity, Madness, and Genius*. New York: Spiegel and Grau.

Olson, Gary. 2004. 'Encountering the Other: Postcolonial Theory and Composition Scholarship'. In *Crossing Borderlands*. Eds. Andrea A. Lunsford and Lahoucine Ouzgane. University of Pittsburgh Press. 84–94.

Omoniyi, Tope, and Mukul Saxena. 2010. *Contending with Globalization in World Englishes*. Bristol: Multilingual Matters.

Ostler, Nicholas. 2005. *Empires of the Word: A Language History of the World*. London: HarperCollins.

—. 2010. *The Last Lingua Franca: English Until the Return of Babel*. London: Allen Lane.

Oxford English Dictionary. 1884–1928. Eds. J.A.H. Murray, et al. 10 vols. Oxford: Clarendon Press.

—. 1972–1986. *A Supplement to the Oxford English Dictionary*. Ed. R.W. Burchfield. 4 vols. Oxford: Clarendon Press.

Pan, Lin, and Philip Seargeant. 2012. 'Is English a Threat to Chinese Language and Culture?' *English Today* 28.0: 60.

Pandey, Gyanendra. 2006. *Routine Violence: Nations, Fragments, Histories.* Stanford University Press.

Pang, Terrence T.T. 2003. 'Hong Kong English: A Stillborn Variety?' *English Today* 74.19: 12–18.

Parker, David. 2007. *The Self in Moral Space: Life Narrative and the Good*. New York: Cornell University Press.

Parry, Benita. 2012. 'What is Left in Postcolonial Studies?' *New Literary History* 43: 341–358.

Patel, Fahim. 2011. 'World Population Divided over Citizenship'. 18 November 2011. *The News Tribe*. www.thenewstribe.com/2011/11/18/world-population-divide-over-citizenship-gallup-survey-reveals/.

Pei, Mario. 1973 [1967]. *The Many Hues of English*. New York: Knopf.

Pennington, Martha Carswell. 1998. *Language in Hong Kong at Century's End*. Hong Kong University Press.

Pennycook, Alastair. 1994. *The Cultural Politics of English as an International Language*. London and New York: Longman.

—. 1998. *English and the Discourses of Colonialism*. New York: Routledge.

—. 2007a. *Global Englishes and Transcultural Flows*. New York: Routledge.

—. 2007b. '"The Rotation Gets Thick, the Constraints Get Thin": Creativity, Recontextualization, and Difference'. *Applied Linguistics* 28.4: 579–596.

—. 2008. 'English as a Language Always in Translation'. *European Journal of English Studies* 12: 33–47.

—. 2010. 'Rethinking Origins and Localization in Global Englishes'. In *Critical Language and Literacy Studies: Contending with Globalization in World Englishes*. Eds. Mukul Saxena and Tope Omoniyi. Clevedon: Multilingual Matter. 196–210.

Peters, Pam. 2009. 'Australian English as a Regional Epicenter'. In *World Englishes – Problems, Properties and Prospects*. Eds. Thomas Hoffmann and Lucia Siebers. Amsterdam and Philadelphia, PA: John Benjamins. 107–124.

Peters, Pam, Peter Collins, and Adam Smith. 2009. *Comparative Studies in Australian and New Zealand English Grammar and Beyond*. Amsterdam: John Benjamins.

Phillipson, Robert. 1992. *Linguistic Imperialism*. Oxford University Press.

—. 2003. *English-Only Europe?: Challenging Language Policy*. London: Routledge.

—. 2009. *Linguistic Imperialism Continued*. Hyderabad: Orient Blackswan Private Ltd.

Phipps, Alison. 2012. 'Voicing Solidarity: Linguistic Hospitality and Poststructuralism in the Real World'. *Applied Linguistics* 33: 582–602.

Poon, Franky Kai-Cheung. 2006. 'Hong Kong English, China English and World English'. *English Today* 86.22: 23–28.

Powell, Douglas Reichert, and John Paul Tassoni. 2009. *Composing Other Spaces*. Cresskill, NJ: Hampton Press.

Pratt, Mary Louise. 2010. 'Translation Studies Forum: Cultural Translation'. *Translation Studies* 3: 94–110.

Prendergast, David. 1998. 'Views on Englishes: A Talk with Braj Kachru, Salikoko Mufwene, Rajendra Singh, Loreto Todd and Peter Trudgill'. *Links and Letters* 5.

Qiang, Niu, and Martin Wolff. 2003. 'China and Chinese, or Chingland and Chinglish?' *English Today* 19.0: 9–11.

—. 2005. 'Is EFL a Modern Trojan Horse?' *English Today* 21.4: 55–60.

—. 2007. 'Linguistic Failures'. *English Today* 23.0: 61–64.

Qu, Weiguo. 2012. '"Practical" English and the Crisis of English Studies'. *English Today* 28.0: 15.

Quayson, Ato. 2012. 'The Sighs of History: Postcolonial Debris and the Question of (Literary) History'. *New Literary History* 43: 359–370.

Quirk, Randolph, with supplements by A.C. Gimson and Jeremy Warburg. 1968. *The Use of English*. London: Longman.

—. 1985. 'The English Language in a Global Context'. In *English in the World*. Eds. Randolph Quirk and H.G. Widdowson. Cambridge University Press. 1–6.

Quirk, Randolph, and Gabriele Stein. 1990. *English in Use*. Harlow: Longman.

Radhakrishnan, R. 1996. *Diasporic Mediations: Between Home and Location*. Minneapolis, MN: University of Minnesota Press.

—. 2003. *Theory in an Uneven World*. Malden, MA: Blackwell.

—. 2008. *History, the Human, and the World Between*. Durham, NC: Duke University Press.

Rampton, M.B.H. 1995. 'Displacing the "Native Speaker": Expertise, Affiliation and Inheritance'. *ELT Journal* 44: 97–101.

Rancière, Jacques. 2001. *The Ignorant Schoolmaster: Five Lessons in Intellectual Emancipation*. Trans. K. Ross. Stanford University Press.

Rhoads, Robert A., and Katalin Szelényi. 2011. *Global Citizenship and the University: Advancing Social Life and Relations in an Interdependent World*. Stanford University Press.

Richards, I.A. 1943. *Basic English and its Uses*. New York: W. W. Norton.

—. 1968. *So Much Nearer: Essays Toward a World English*. New York: Harcourt, Brace & World.

Robinson, Douglas. 1997. *Translation and Empire: Postcolonial Theories Explained*. Manchester: St. Jerome.

Royle, Nicholas. 2000. 'What is Deconstruction?' In *Deconstructions: A User's Guide*. Ed. Nicholas Royle. Basingstoke: Palgrave Macmillan. 1–13.

Rubdy, Rani. 2008. 'Enacting English Language Ownership in the Outer Circle: A Study of Singaporean Indians' Orientations to English Norms'. *World Englishes* 27: 40.

Runco, Mark. 2004. 'Personal Creativity and Culture'. In *Creativity: When East Meets West*. Eds. Sing Lau, Ana H.H. Hui, and Grace Y.C. Ng. Singapore: World Scientific. 9–23.

Rushdie, Salman. 1992. *Imaginary Homelands: Essays and Criticism, 1981–1991*. New York: Penguin Books.

Ryle, John. 2001. 'The Shadow of the Sun (Review)'. *Times Literary Supplement* 5130: 3.

Said, Edward W. 1979 [1978]. *Orientalism: Western Conceptions of the Orient*. New York: Vintage Books.

—. 1994 [1993]. *Culture and Imperialism*. London: Vintage.

—. 2004. *Humanism and Democratic Criticism*. New York: Columbia University Press.

Said, Edward W., Homi K. Bhabha, and W.J. Thomas Mitchell. 2005. *Edward Said: Continuing the Conversation*. University of Chicago Press.

Sakai, Naoki. 1997. *Translation and Subjectivity: On Japan and Cultural Nationalism*. Minneapolis, MN: University of Minnesota Press.

Sakai, Naoki, and Jon Solomon. 2006. *Translation, Biopolitics, Colonial Difference*. Hong Kong University Press.

Sakai, Naoki, and Yukiko Hanawa. 2001. *Specters of the West and the Politics of Translation*. Ithaca, NY: Cornell University.

Santos, Terrence. 1992. 'Ideology in Composition: L1 and ESL'. *Journal of Second Language Writing* 1.1: 1–15.

Sapir, Edward, and David Goodman Mandelbaum. 1962 [1949]. *Culture, Language and Personality*. Berkeley, CA: University of California Press.

Saraceni, Mario. 2010. *The Relocation of English: Shifting Paradigms in a Global Era*. Basingstoke and New York: Palgrave Macmillan.

Schneider, Edgar. 2003. 'The Dynamics of New Englishes: From Identity Construction to Dialect Birth'. *Language* 79: 233–281.

—. 2007. *Postcolonial English: Varieties Around the World*. Cambridge University Press.

—. 2012. Review. 'Paul Geraghty, France Mugler and Jan Tent. 2006. *Macquarie Dictionary of English for the Fiji Islands*; Patrick J. Cummings and Hans-Georg Wolf. 2011. *A Dictionary of Hong Kong English. Words from the Fragrant Harbor*'. *English World-Wide* 33.3: 358–362.

Schulze-Engler, Frank, and Sissy Helff. 2008. *Transcultural English Studies: Theories, Fictions, Realities*. Amsterdam: Rodopi.

Schwarz, Henry, and Sangeeta Ray. 2005. *A Companion to Postcolonial Studies: An Historical Introduction*. Oxford: Blackwell.

Seargeant, Philip. 2008. 'Language, Ideology and "English within a Globalized Context"'. *World Englishes* 27: 217–232.

—. 2009. *The Idea of English in Japan: Ideology and the Evolution of a Global Language*. Bristol and Buffalo, NY: Multilingual Matters.

—. 2010. 'Naming and Defining in World Englishes'. *World Englishes* 29: 97.

—. 2011. *English in Japan in the Era of Globalization*. New York: Palgrave Macmillan.

—. 2012. 'Disciplinarity and the Study of World Englishes'. *World Englishes* 31: 113.

Seargeant, Philip, and Joan Swann. 2012. *English in the World: History, Diversity, Change*. New York: Routledge.

Sell, Roger D. 2012. 'Cultural Memory and the Communicational Criticism of Literature'. *Journal for Communication Studies* 5.10: 201–225.

Shamsie, Kamila. 2009. *Burnt Shadows*. London: Bloomsbury.

Sharifian, Farzad. 2009. *English as an International Language*. Bristol and Buffalo, NY: Multilingual Matters.

Sheng, Anfeng. 2009. 'Minoritization as a Global Measure in the Age of Global Postcoloniality: An Interview with Homi Bhabha'. *Ariel: A Review of International English Literature* 40: 161–180.

Shome, Raka. 2002. 'Culture, Communication, and the Challenge of Globalization'. *Critical Studies in Media Communication* 19: 172–189.

—. 2006. 'Interdisciplinary Research and Globalization'. *Communication Review* 9: 1–36.

—. 2009. 'Post-Colonial Reflections on the "Internationalization" of Cultural Studies'. Special issue: *Transnationalism and Cultural Studies*. *Cultural Studies* 23.5: 694.

Shome, Raka, and Radha S. Hegde. 2002. 'Postcolonial Approaches to Communication:

Charting the Terrain, Engaging the Intersections'. *Communication Theory* 12: 249–270.

Skutnabb-Kangas, Tove. 2000. *Linguistic Genocide in Education or Worldwide Diversity and Human Rights?* Mahwah, NJ: L. Erlbaum Associates.

—. 2009. *Social Justice through Multilingual Education*. Bristol and Buffalo, NY: Multilingual Matters.

Skutnabb-Kangas, Tove, and Robert Phillipson, Robert. Eds. 1994. *Linguistic Human Rights: Overcoming Linguistic Discrimination*. Berlin: Mouton de Gruyter.

Smith, Larry E., and Michael L. Forman. 1997. *World Englishes 2000*. Honolulu: University of Hawaii and the East-West Center.

Sommer, Doris. 2003. *Bilingual Games: Some Literary Investigations*. Basingstoke and New York: Palgrave Macmillan.

Soukhanov, Anne H. 2001. *Microsoft Encarta College Dictionary*. New York: St. Martin's Press.

Spencer, Robert. 2009. '"Listening for the Echo": Representation and Resistance in Postcolonial Studies'. *Journal of Postcolonial Writing* 45: 71–81.

Spivak, Gayatri Chakravorty. 1999. *A Critique of Postcolonial Reason: Toward a History of the Vanishing Present*. Cambridge, MA: Harvard University Press.

—. 2003. *Death of a Discipline*. The Wellek Library Lectures. New York: Columbia University Press.

—. 2012. *An Aesthetic Education in the Era of Globalization*. Cambridge, MA: Harvard University Press.

Stam, Robert. 2012. 'Whence and Whither Postcolonial Theory?' *New Literary History* 43: 371–390.

Stanlaw, James. 2004. *Japanese English: Language and Culture Contact*. Hong Kong University Press.

Stavans, Ilan. 2003. *Spanglish: The Making of a New American Language*. New York: Rayo.

Steintrager, James. 2010. 'Hermeneutic Heresy: Rey Chow on Translation in Theory and the "Fable" of Culture'. *Postcolonial Studies* 13: 289–302.

Stroud, Christopher, and Lionel Wee. 2010. *Language Policy and Planning in Singaporean Late Modernity*. Hong Kong University Press.

—. 2011. *Style, Identity and Literacy: English in Singapore*. Bristol: Multilingual Matters.

Syrotinski, Michael. 2007. *Deconstruction and the Postcolonial: At the Limits of Theory*. Liverpool University Press.

Talib, Ismail S. 2002. *The Language of Postcolonial Literatures: An Introduction*. London and New York: Routledge.

Tam, Kwok-kan. Ed. 2009. *Englishization in Asia: Language and Cultural Issues*. Hong Kong: Open University of Hong Kong Press.

Tam, Kwok-kan, and Timothy Weiss. Eds. 2004. *English and Globalization: Perspectives from Hong Kong and Mainland China*. Hong Kong: The Chinese University Press.

Tam, Kwok-kan, Wimal Dissanayake, and Yip Terry Siu-han. 2002. *Sights of Contestation: Localism, Globalism and Cultural Production in Asia and the Pacific*. Hong Kong: The Chinese University Press.

Tan, Charlene. 2006. 'Change and Continuity: Chinese Language Policy in Singapore'. *Language Policy* 5: 41–62.

Taussig, Michael. 1992. *The Nervous System*. London and New York: Routledge.

Taylor, Charles. 1989. *Sources of the Self: The Making of the Modern Identity*. Cambridge University Press.

Taylor, Mark C. 2001. *The Moment of Complexity: Emerging Network Culture*. University of Chicago Press.

Teo, Andrea, and Kenneth Liang. 1997–2007. *Phua Chu Kang*. Cast: Gurmit Singh, Pierre Png, and Irene Ang. MediaCorp Television Corporation of Singapore. Television comedy series.

Thumboo, Edwin. Ed. 2001. *The Three Circles of English: Language Specialists Talk about the English Language*. Singapore: UniPress.

Tong, Q.S. 1999. 'The Bathos of a Universalism: I. A. Richards and his Basic English'. In *Tokens of Exchange: The Problem of Translation in Global Circulation*. Ed. Lydia Liu. Durham, NC: Duke University Press. 331–354.

Trimbur, John. 2008. 'The Dartmouth Conference and the Geohistory of the Native Speaker'. *College English* 71: 142–169.

Trivedi, Harish. 2007. 'Translating Culture vs. Cultural Translation'. In *In Translation: Reflections, Refractions, Transformations*. Eds. Paul St. Pierre and Prafulla C. Kar. Amsterdam: John Benjamins. 277–288.

Urry, John. 2003. *Global Complexity*. Cambridge: Polity Press.

Van Hooft, Stan. 2009. *Cosmopolitanism*. Durham, NC: Acumen.

Vasu, Norman, and Joanna Phua. 2008. 'A Common Tongue to Foster Singapore Spirit'. *Straits Times*. 14 August 2008: 34.

Velayutham, Selvaraj. 2007. *Responding to Globalization: Nation, Culture and Identity in Singapore*. Singapore: Institute of Southeast Asian Studies.

Venuti, Lawrence. 1998. *The Scandals of Translation: Towards an Ethics of Difference*. London: Routledge.

Viswanathan, Gauri. 1989. *Masks of Conquest: Literary Study and British Rule in India*. New York: Columbia University Press.

Volkan Kacso, Kinga. 2010. 'The Sociolinguistic Reality of Writers from the Expanding Circle: A New English Literature'. Ph.D. thesis. Purdue University.

Watts, Richard J. 2011. *Language Myths and the History of English*. Oxford University Press.

Watts, Richard J., and Peter Trudgill. 2002. *Alternative Histories of English*. London: Routledge.

Weber, Samuel. 2007. 'Reading Over a Globalized World'. In *Encountering Derrida: Legacies and Futures of Deconstruction*. Eds. Allison Weiner and Simon Wortham. London: Continuum. 58–67.

Webster, Noah. 1789. *Dissertations on the English Language. With notes, historical and critical: to which is added, by way of appendix, an essay on a reformed mode of spelling, with Dr. Franklin's arguments on that subject*. Boston: Printed for the author by Isaiah Thomas and Co.

Wechselblatt, Martin. 1996. 'The Pathos of Example: Professionalism and Colonization in Johnson's "Preface" to the Dictionary'. *Yale Journal of Criticism* 9: 381–403.

Wei, Rining, and Jinzhi Su. 2012. 'The Statistics of English in China'. *English Today* 28.0: 10.

Weiner, E.S.C. 1980. 'The Federation of English'. In *The State of the Language*. Eds. Leonard Michaels and Christopher Ricks. Berkeley, CA: University of California Press. 492–502.

Wells, Ronald. 1973. *Dictionaries and the Authoritarian Tradition: Study in English Usage and Lexicography*. Berlin: Mouton de Gruyter.

Whitman, Walt. 1904. *An American Primer … with Facsimiles of the Original Manuscript. Edited by H. Traubel*. Ed. Horace Logo Traubel. London: G.P. Putnam's Sons.

Wierzbicka, Anna. 2006. *English: Meaning and Culture*. New York: Oxford University Press.

—. 2010. *Experience, Evidence, and Sense: The Hidden Cultural Legacy of English*. New York: Oxford University Press.

Williams, Raymond. 1976. *Keywords: A Vocabulary of Culture and Society*. New York: Oxford University Press.

Willinsky, John. 1994. *Empire of Words: the Reign of the OED*. Princeton University Press.

Xie, Ming. 2011. *Conditions of Comparison: Reflections on Comparative Intercultural Inquiry*. New York: Continuum.

Xu Xi. 2004. *Overleaf Hong Kong: Stories & Essays of the Chinese, Overseas*. Hong Kong: Chameleon Press.

—. 2008. *Evanescent Isles: From My City-Village*. Hong Kong University Press.

Xu Xi, and Mike Ingham. 2003. *City Voices: Hong Kong Writing in English, 1945 to the Present*. Hong Kong University Press.

Young, Robert J.C. 1996. *Torn Halves: Political Conflict in Literary and Cultural Theory*. Manchester University Press.

—. 2001. *Postcolonialism: An Historical Introduction*. Oxford: Blackwell.

—. 2009. 'What is the Postcolonial?' *Ariel: A Review of International English Literature* 40: 13–24.

—. 2012. 'Postcolonial Remains'. *New Literary History* 43: 19–42.

Zhou, Xiaoyi, and Q.S. Tong. 2002. 'English Literary Studies and China's Modernity'. *World Englishes* 21: 337–348.

Index